Some Account of the Life of the Rev. Charles Wesley, A.M. Late Student of Christ-Church, Oxford. Collected From his Private Journal. By John Whitehead, M.D

SOME

ACCOUNT

OF THE

LIFE

OF THE

Rev. CHARLES WESLEY, A. M.

LATE STUDENT OF

CHRIST-CHURCH, OXFORD.

Collected from his PRIVATE JOURNAL.

By *JOHN WHITEHEAD*, M. D.

London:

PRINTED BY STEPHEN COUCHMAN,

AND SOLD BY DAN. TAYLOR, UNION-STREET,
BISHOPSGATE-STREET.

M DCC XCIII.

[Price Three Shillings and Sixpence in Boards]

ADVERTISEMENT.

HAVING been requefted to publifh the Life of the Rev. CHARLES WESLEY, in a Pamphlet, feparate from the larger Work, I have complied with that requeft; and hope it will be a bleffing to many, who cannot afford to purchafe two octavo volumes.

JOHN WHITEHEAD.

LONDON,
July 11, 1793.

CONTENTS.

CONTENTS.

CHAPTER I.

THE

THE

L I F E

OF THE

Rev. CHARLES WESLEY.

CHAPTER I.

Of his Birth, and Education until his Ordination in 1735.

Mr. *Charles Wesley* was born December 18th, 1708, old ftyle, feveral weeks before his time, at Epworth in Lincolnfhire; being about five years younger than his brother *John Wesley*, and about fixteen younger than *Samuel*.

He appeared dead rather than alive when he was born He did not cry, nor open his eyes, and was kept wrapt up in foft wool until the time when he fhould have been born accoiding to the ufual courfe of nature, and then he opened his eyes and cried.

He received the firft rudiments of learning at home, under the pious care of his mother, as all the other children did In 1716 he was fent to *Weftminfter* fchool, and placed under the care of his eldeft brother *Samuel Wefley*, an high church man, who educated him in his own principles.

A

He

He was exceedingly fprightly and active; very apt to learn, but arch and unlucky, though not ill-natured.

When he had been fome years at fchool, Mr. *R. Wefley*, a gentleman of large fortune in *Ireland*, wrote to his father, and afked if he had any fon named *Charles*; if fo, he would make him his heir. Accordingly a gentleman in *London* brought money for his education feveral years. But one year another gentleman called, probably Mr. *Wefley* himfelf, talked largely with him, and afked if he was willing to go with him to *Ireland*. Mr. *Charles* defired to write to his father, who anfwered immediately, and referred it to his own choice. He chofe to ftay in *England*. Mr. *W.* then found and adopted another *Charles Wefley*, who was the late *Earl* of *M--n--g--n*. A fair efcape, fays Mr. *John Wefley*, from whofe fhort account of his brother I have taken this anecdote.

From this time Mr. *Charles Wefley* depended chiefly on his brother *Samuel* till 1721, when he was admitted a fcholar of St *Peter's* College, *Weft-minfter* *. He was now a King's fcholar, and as he advanced in age and learning, he acted dramas, and at length became Captain of the fchool. In 1726 he was elected to *Chrift-Church, Oxford* †, at which time his brother was Fellow of *Lincoln College*. Mr. *John Wefley* gives the following account of him after he came to *Oxford*. " He purfued his ftudies diligently, and led a regular harmlefs life but if I fpoke to him about religion, he would warmly an-

---

* *Welch's* Lift of Scholars of St. *Peter's* College, *Weftminfter*, as they were elected to *Chrift-church* College, *Oxford*, and *Trinity* College, *Cambridge*, p 105.

† Ibid. p. 110.

fwer,

fwer, " What, would you have me to be a faint all
at once," and would hear no more. I was then
near three years my father's curate. During moft
of this time he continued much the fame ; but in
the year 1729 I obferved his letters grew much
more ferious, and when I returned to *Oxford* in
November that year, I found him in great earneft-
nefs to fave his foul."

Mr *Charles Wefley* gives the following account of
himfelf for the firft year or two after he went to
Oxford *. " My firft year at College I loft in di-
verfions the next I fet myfelf to ftudy. Diligence led me into ferious thinking. I went to the
weekly facrament, and perfuaded two or three
young ftudents to accompany me, and to obferve
the method of ftudy prefcribed by the ftatutes of
the univerfity. This gained me the harmlefs name of
Methodift In half a year (after this) my brother
left his curacy at *Epworth*, and came to our affiftance We then proceeded regularly in our ftudies,
and in doing what good we could to the bodies and
fouls of men."

It was in the year 1728, in the twentieth year
of his age, that he began to apply more clofely to
ftudy, and to be more ferious in his general deportment than ufual He foon gave proof of his fin-
cere defire to be truly religious, by expreffing a wifh
to write a diary, in which he intended to regifter
daily the ftate of his mind, and the actions of the day.
A diary of this kind, faithfully kept, is a delineation
of a man s moral and religious character, it is a moral picture of the man accurately drawn. No man

wifhes

wifhes to draw his own character in this way, in every little circumftance of life, and to review it often, but he who is defirous to think and act rightly, and to improve daily in knowledge and virtue. He knew that his brother, Mr *John Wefley*, had kept fuch a diary for feveral years, and was able to give him inftructions how to proceed He therefore wrote to him in January 1729, as follows " I would willingly write a diary of my actions, but do not know how to go about it. What particulars am I to take notice of? Am I to give my thoughts and words, as well as deeds, a place in it? I am to mark all the good and ill I do, and what befides? Muft I not take account of my progrefs in learning, as well as religion? What cypher can I make ufe of? If you would direct me to the fame, or like method to your own, I would gladly follow it, for I am fully convinced of the ufefulnefs of fuch an undertaking. I fhall be at a ftand till I hear from you.

" God has thought fit, it may be to increafe my warmnefs, to deny me at prefent your company and affiftance. It is through him ftrengthening me, I truft to maintain my ground till we meet And I hope, that, neither before nor after that time, I fhall relapfe into my former ftate of infenfibility. It is through your means, I firmly believe, that God will eftablifh what he has begun in me, and there is no one perfon I would fo willingly have to be the inftrument of good to me as you It is owing, in great meafure to fomebody's prayers (my mother's moft likely) that I am come to think as I do; for I cannot tell myfelf, how or when I awoke out

of

of my lethargy----only that it was not long after
you went away "

The enemies of the Chriftian Revelation, and
friends of Deifm, were fo much increafed about
this time, and were become fo bold and daring in
their attempts to propagate their principles in the
Univerfity, as to roufe the attention of the *Vice-
Chancellor*, who, with the confent of the Heads of
Houfes and Proctors, iffued the following *programma*,
or edict, which was fixed up in moft of the Halls of
the Univerfity.

" Whereas there is too much reafon to believe,
" that fome members of the Univerfity have of
" late been in danger of being corrupted by ill-
" defigning perfons, who have not only entertained
" wicked and blafphemous notions, contrary to the
" truth of the chriftian religion, but have endea-
" voured to inftil the fame ill principles into
" others and the more effectually to propagate
" their infidelity, have applied their poifon to the
" unguarded inexperience of lefs informed minds,
" where they thought it might operate with better
" fuccefs, carefully concealing their impious te-
" nets from thofe whofe riper judgment, and more
" wary conduct might difcover their falfe reafon-
" ing, and difappoint the intended progrefs of their
" infidelity And whereas therefore, it is more
" efpecially neceffary at this time, to guard the
" youth of this place againft thefe wicked advo-
" cates for pretended human reafon againft divine
" revelation, and to enable them the better to de-
" fend their religion, and to expofe the pride and
" impiety of thofe who endeavour to undermine
" it, Mr. Vice-Chancellor, with the confent of

" the

" the Heads of Houfes and Proctors, has thought
" fit to recommend it, as a matter of the utmoft
" confequence, to the feveral tutors of each Col-
" lege and Hall in the Univerfity, that they dif-
" charge their duty by a double diligence, in in-
" forming their refpective pupils in their chriftian
" duty, as alfo in explaining to them the articles
" of religion which they profefs, and are often
" called upon to fubfcribe, and in recommending
" to them the frequent and careful reading of the
" fcriptures, and fuch other books as may ferve
" more effectually to promote chriftianity, found
" principles, and orthodox faith. And further,
" Mr. Vice-Chancellor, with the fame confent,
" does hereby forbid the faid youth the reading of
" fuch books as may tend to the weakening of their
" faith, the fubverting of the authority of the
" fcripture, and the introducing of deifm, pro-
" fanenefs and irreligion in their ftead."---The
Dean of *Chrift-church* was fo much a friend to infidelity, that he would not fuffer this *programma*
to be put up in the Hall of his College.

It is always pleafing to a pious mind, to trace
the ways of providence, not only as they relate to
individuals, but as they affect large bodies of men,
collectively confidered. In the cafe before us there
is fomething worthy of obfervation. At the very
time when the friends of infidelity were making fo ftrong an effort to propagate their principles in this celebrated feminary of learning, God
was preparing two or three young men, to plant a
religious fociety in the fame place, which fhould
grow up with vigour, and fpread its branches
through

through feveral countries, in oppofition to the bane-
ful influence of infidelity and profanenefs.

In the courfe of the following fummer Mr.
Charles Wefley became more and more ferious, and
began to be fingularly diligent, both in the means
of grace and in his ftudies. His zeal for God began already to kindle, and manifeft itfelf in exci-
tions to do good beyond the common round of religious duties. He endeavoured to awaken an attention to religion in the minds of fome of the
ftudents, and was foon fuccefsful in one or two inftances. This appears from the following letter, which
he wrote to his brother *John Wefley* in May 1729.
" Providence has at prefent put it into my power
to do fome good. I have a modeft, humble, well
difpofed youth lives next me, and have been, thank
God, fomewhat inftrumental in keeping him fo.
He was got into vile hands, and is now broke loofe.
I affifted in fetting him free, and will do my utmoft
to hinder him from getting in with them again.
He was of opinion that paffive goodnefs was fufficient, and would fain have kept in with his acquaintance and God at the fame time. He durft
not receive the facrament, but at the ufual times, for
fear of being laughed at. By convincing him of
the duty of frequent communicating, I have prevailed on both of us to receive once a week

" I earneftly long for, and defire the bleffing
God is about to fend me in you. I am fenfible
this is my day of grace; and that upon my em-
ploying the time before our meeting and next
parting, will in great meafure depend my condition
for eternity."

From thefe extracts of two of Mr. *Charles Wefley's* letters to his brother, and from the account which he has given of himfelf in a letter to Dr. *Chandler*, the following particulars appear evident. 1. That he was awakened to a moft ferious and earneft defire of being truly religious and devoted to God, while his brother was at *Epworth*, as his father's curate. 2 That he obferved an exact *method* in his ftudies, and in his attendance on the duties of religion, receiving the facrament once a week. 3. That he perfuaded two or three young gentlemen to join him in thefe things, among whom I believe *Morgan* was one. 4 That the exact method and order which he obferved in fpending his time, and regulating his conduct, gained him the name of *Methodift*. Hence it appears that Mr *Charles Wefley* was the firft Methodift, and laid the foundation of that little fociety at *Oxford*, which afterwards made fo much noife in the world but it does not appear that any regular meetings were held, or that the members had extended their views beyond their own improvement in knowledge and virtue, until Mr. *John Wefley* left his curacy, and came to refide wholly at Oxford in November 1729. The beginning of this fociety was fmall, and it appeared contemptible to thofe around, but events have fhewn, that it was big with confequences of the utmoft importance to the happinefs of thoufands. So little do men know before-hand of the defigns of providence.

Man was made for focial intercourfe with man. A well regulated fociety of a few well chofen perfons, improves the underftanding, invigorates the powers of the mind, ftrengthens our refolutions,

and

and animates us to perſeverance in the execution of our deſigns. Theſe were the happy effects of the union of the two brothers in November this year, when Mr *John Weſley* left *Epworth*, and came to reſide at *Oxford*. They now formed a regular ſociety, and quickened the diligence and zeal of each other in the execution of their pious purpoſes. About this time Mr *Charles* began to take pupils. On this occaſion his father wrote to him as follows, in a letter dated January 1730, when *Charles* had juſt paſſed the 21ſt year of his age " I had your laſt, and you may eaſily gueſs whether I were not well pleaſed with it, both on your account and my own You have a double advantage by your pupils, which will ſoon bring you more, if you will improve it, as I firmly hope you will, by taking the utmoſt care to form their minds to piety as well as learning As for yourſelf, between *Logic, Grammar,* and *Mathematics,* be idle if you can. I give my bleſſing to the Biſhop for having tied you a little faſter, by obliging you to rub up your *Arabic.* and a fixed and conſtant method will make the whole both pleaſing and delightful to you. But for all that, you muſt find time every day for walking, which you know you may do with advantage to your pupils, and a little more robuſt exerciſe, now and then, will do you no harm You are now launched fairly *Charles,* hold up your head, and ſwim like a man, and when you cuff the wave beneath you, ſay to it, much as another hero did,

CAROLUM *vebis, et* CAROLI *fortunam* *.

But always keep your eye fixed above the pole-ſtar,

---

* Thou carrieſt *Charles,* and *Charles'* fortune.

and fo God fend you a good voyage through the
troublefome fea of life, which is the hearty prayer
of your loving father ''

Mr *Charles Wefley* and his brother *John* had been
always united in affection, they were now united
in their purfuit of learning, their views of religion,
and their endeavours to do good. Mr. *Morgan*
was to them as another brother, and united together, they were as a *three-fold cord*, which *is not
eafily broken.* Though few in number, of little reputation in the world, and unfupported by any
powerful allies, yet they boldly lifted up their
ftandard againft infidelity and profanenefs, the
common enemies of religion and virtue. They did
not indeed, at prefent, make any great inroads into
the enemy's territory, but they bravely kept their
ground, and defended their little fort with fuccefs,
againft every attempt of the enemy to diflodge them.
When death robbed them of *Morgan*, the two brothers remained unfhaken in their purpofe. They
were the bond of union between the members of
their little fociety at *Oxford*, and if one or more of
thefe deferted them, through fear, or fhame, or
being weary of reftraint, they ftood firm as a rock,
perfevering in their refolution to ferve God and do
good to men, without the leaft fhadow of wavering,
through evil report and good report, as if alike infenfible to either   Happily, they were not hurried
on by a rafh intemperate zeal in their proceedings;
which is the common failing of young men.   They
were cautious and wary, ufing every prudential
means in their power, to prevent the good that was
in them from being evil fpoken of *Charles* had much
more fire, and opennefs of temper than his brother,

ther, but he was not lefs cautious in this refpect.
If any doubts arofe in his mind, or if any practice,
which he thought proper and commendable, feemed
likely to give great offence to others, he afked the
advice of thofe who were older and wifer than
himfelf, how he ought to proceed.   This appears
from a letter which he wrote to his father in June
1731, in which he fays, " On Whitfunday the
whole College received the facrament, except the
fervitors (for we are too well bred to communicate
with them, though in the body and blood of *Chrift*)
to whom it was adminiftered the next day, on
which I was prefent at church, but with the Canons
left the facrament to thofe for whom alone it was
prepared   What I would beg to be refolved in
is, whether or no my being affured I fhould give
infinite fcandal by ftaying, could fufficiently juftify
me in turning my back of God's ordinance.   It is
a queftion my future conduct is much concerned
in, and I fhall therefore earneftly wait for your de-
cifion "

   Mr. *Charles Wefley* proceeded Mafter of Arts in
the ufual courfe, and thought only of fpending all
his days at *Oxford* as a tutor, for he " exceedingly
dreaded entering into Holy Orders *."   In 1735,
Mr *John Wefley* yielded to the preffing folicitations
of Mr. *Oglethorpe*, Dr. *Burton*, and fome others, to
go to *Georgia* as a miffionary, to preach to the *Indians*, and he prevailed on his brother *Charles* to accompany him   Their brother *Samuel* confented
that Mr. *John Wefley* fhould go, but vehemently
oppofed the defign of *Charles* to accompany him.

* His letter to Dr. *Chandler*.

But

But his oppofition had no effect, for Mr. *Charles* engaged himfelf as fecretary to Mr *Oglethorpe*, and alfo as fecretary to *Indian* affairs, and in this character he went to *Georgia*.   A little before they left England, Dr. *Burton* fuggefted that it might be well if Mr. *Charles Wefley* was ordained before he left this country   His brother *John* over-ruled his inclination in this thing alfo, and he was ordained Deacon by Dr. *Potter*, Bifhop of *Oxford*, and the Sunday following, Prieft, by Dr. *Gibfon*, Bifhop of *London* *.

* His letter to Dr. *Chandler*.

CHAPTER II.

Of Mr CHARLES WESLEY'S *Voyage to* Georgia, *his Situation there, and return to* England *in* 1736.

THEY failed from *Gravefend* the 22d of October 1735, but meeting with contrary winds, they did not leave *Cowes* till the 10th of December.   Mr. *Charles Wefley* preached feveral times, while they were detained here, and great crouds attended his miniftry.   His brother *Samuel*, who was violently againft his going abroad, obferves, that he hoped *Charles* was convinced by this inftance, that he needed not to have gone to *Georgia* to convert finners. After a ftormy paffage they arrived in *Savannah* river Feb 5th, 1736, and Mr. *John Wefley* was appointed to take charge of *Savannah*, Mr. *Charles* of *Frederica*, waiting for an opportunity of preaching

to

to the *Indians*. Mr *Charles Wesley* did not enter on
his ministry till March 9th, when he first set foot
on *Simon's* Island, and his spirit immediately revived. No sooner did I enter on my ministry, says
he, than God gave me a new heart, so true is that
saying of Bishop *Hall*, " The calling of God never
leaves a man unchanged ; neither did God ever
employ any in his service whom he did not enable
for the work "--- The first person that saluted him
on landing, was his friend Mr. *Ingham* · " Never,
says he, did I more rejoice to see him, especially
when he told me the treatment he had met with for
vindicating the Lord's day " This specimen of
the ignorance and unteachable temper of the people
among whom he had to labour was unpromising,
but he little expected the trials and dangers which
lay before him Like a faithful and diligent pastor,
he immediately entered on his office, not with joy
at the prospect of a good income, but with fear and
trembling, at the views which he had of the importance and difficulty of the ministerial office. In
the afternoon he began to converse with his parishioners, without which he well knew, that general instructions often lose their effect. But he observes on this occasion, " With what trembling
should I call them mine." He felt as every minister of the gospel ought to feel when he takes upon
him to guide others in the ways of God. In the
evening he read prayers in the open air, at which
Mr *Oglethorpe* was present The lesson was remarkably adapted to his situation, and he felt the
full force of it, both in the way of direction and
encouragement. " Continue instant in prayer, and
" watch in the same with thanksgiving, withal
" praying

" praying alfo for us, that God would open unto
" us a door of utterance to fpeak the myftery of
" Chrift, that I may make it manifeft as I ought to
" fpeak. Walk in wifdom toward thofe that are
" without, redeeming the time---Say to *Archippus*,
" take heed to the miniftry which thou haft re-
" ceived of the Lord that thou fulfil it."---After
the labours of the day, he returned and flept in the
boat.

The colony was at this time very fcantily pro-
vided with accommodations   There was no place
erected where the people could affemble for public
worfhip; for on March 10th, between five and fix
in the morning, Mr *C. Wefley* read fhort prayers to
a few perfons, before Mr *Oglethorpe's* tent, in a
hard fhower of rain---He afterwards talked with
Mrs. *W* who had come in the fhip with him and
his brother, and endeavoured to guard her againft
the cares of the world, and to perfuade her to give
herfelf up to God, but in vain   In the evening
he endeavoured to reconcile her and Mrs. *H* who
were greatly at variance, but to no purpofe.

Some of the women now began to be jealous of
each other, and to raife animofities and divifions in
the colony, which gave a great deal of trouble to
Mr. *Oglethorpe*.   Mr. *Wefley's* ferious and religious
deportment, his conftant prefence with them, and
his frequent reproof of their licentious behaviour,
foon made him an object of hatred, and plans
were formed either to ruin him in the opinion of
Mr. *Oglethorpe*, or to take him off by violence. We
fhall fee thefe plans open by degrees.

March 11th, at ten in the morning, he began the
full fervice to about a dozen women whom he had
                                          got

got together, intending to continue it, and only to read a few prayers to the men before they went to work. He also expounded the second leſſon with ſome degree of boldneſs, which he had done ſeveral times before, and it is probable that he did this extempore After prayers he met Mrs H's maid in a great paſſion and flood of tears, at the treatment ſhe had received from her miſtreſs She ſeemed determined to deſtroy herſelf, to eſcape her *Egyptian* bondage He prevailed with her to return, and went with her home. He aſked Mrs. H to forgive her, but ſhe refuſed with the utmoſt roughneſs, rage, and almoſt reviling. He next met with Mr. *Tackner*, who, he obſerves, made him full amends. he was in an excellent temper, reſolved to ſtrive, not with his wife, but with himſelf, in putting off the old man, and putting on the new ---In the evening he received the firſt harſh word from Mr. *Oglethorpe*, when he aſked for ſomething for a poor woman---The next day he received a rougher anſwer in a matter which deſerved ſtill greater encouragement. I know not, ſays he, how to account for his increaſing coldneſs. His encouragement, he obſerves, was the ſame in ſpeaking with Mrs. *W.* whom he found all ſtorm and tempeſt, ſo wilful, ſo untractable, ſo fierce, that he could not bear to ſtay near her. This evening Mr. *Oglethorpe* was with the men under arms, in expectation of an enemy, but in the ſame ill humour with Mr *Wesley* I ſtaid, ſays he, " as long as I could, however unſafe, within the wind of ſuch commotion, but at laſt the hurricane of his paſſion drove me away "

Mr.

Mr. *Wesley's* situation was now truly alarming, not only as it regarded his usefulness, but as it affected his safety. Many persons lost all decency in their behaviour towards him, and Mr. *Oglethorpe's* treatment of him, shewed that he had received impressions greatly to his disadvantage, at the same time he was totally ignorant of his accusers, and of what he was accused. But being conscious of his own innocence he trusted in God, and considered his sufferings as a part of the portion of those who will live godly in *Christ Jesus*, especially if they persuade others to walk by the same rule ----Sunday March 14th, he read prayers, and preached with boldness in singleness of intention, under a great tree, to about twenty people, among whom was Mr *Oglethorpe.* " In the Epistle, says he, I was plainly shewn what I ought to be, and what I ought to expect. " Giving no offence in any thing, that the ministry be not blamed, but in all things approving ourselves as the ministers of *Christ*, in much patience, in afflictions, in necessities, in distress, in stripes, in imprisonments, in tumults, in labours, in watchings," &c.

At night he found himself exceedingly faint; but had no better bed to lie down upon than the ground, on which he says, " I slept very comfortably before a great fire, and waked next morning perfectly well "

He spent March 16th wholly in writing letters for Mr. *Oglethorpe* He had now been six days at *Frederica*, and observes, " I would not spend six days more in the same manner for all *Georgia.*" But he had more than six days to spend in no better a situation, without being able to make any conditions.

Mr.

Mr. *Charles Wesley*, as well as his brother *John*, was so fully convinced at this time, that immersion was the ancient mode of baptizing, that he determined to adhere strictly to the rubric of the church of *England* in relation to it, and not to baptize any child by sprinkling, unless it was sickly and weak. This occasioned some contention among this people, who were governed chiefly by their passions, and a spirit of opposition. However, by perseverance and mild persuasion, he prevailed with some of of them to consent to it, and about this time, he adds with apparent pleasure, " I baptized Mr. *Colwell's* child by true immersion, before a large congregation "

March 18, Mr. *Oglethorpe* set out with the *Indians* to hunt the *buffalo* upon the main, and to see the utmost limits of what they claimed ---This day Mrs *W* discovered to Mr. *Wesley* " The whole mystery of iniquity " I suppose he means the plots and designs which were formed, chiefly against himself.

He went to his *myrtle* grove, and while he was repeating, " I will thank thee for thou hast heard me, and art become my salvation," a gun was fired from the other side of the bushes Providentially he had the moment before turned from that end of the walk where the shot entered, and heard it pass close by him. This was, apparently, a design upon his life

A circumstance now took place which soon brought on an explanation between Mr *Oglethorpe* and Mr *Wesley* Mr *Oglethorpe* had, more than once, given orders that no man should shoot on a Sunday , and *German* had been confined in the

B   guard-

guard-room for it. In the midst of sermon, on
Sunday the 21st, a gun was fired the constable
ran out, and found it was the Doctor, and told
him it was contrary to orders, and he must go with
him to the officer The Doctor's passion kindled ,
" What, said he, don't you know that I am not to
be looked upon as a common fellow ?" The constable not knowing what to do, went back, and
after consulting with *Hornsdorff*, returned with
two centinels, and took him to the guard-room.
His wife then charged and fired a gun, and ran
thither like a mad woman, and said she had shot,
and would be confined too She curst and swore in
the utmost transport of rage, threatening to kill the
first man that should come near her , but at last was
persuaded to go away. In the afternoon she fell
upon Mr *Wesley* in the street with the greatest bitterness and scurrility said he was the cause of her
husband's confinement, but she would be revenged,
&c &c. He replied, that he pitied her, but de-
fied all that she or the devil could do , and he
hoped she would soon be of a better mind " In
my evening hour of retirement, says he, I resigned
myself to God, in prayer for conformity to a suffering Saviour "

Before prayers this evening he took a walk with
Mr *Ingham*, who seemed surprized that he should
not think innocence a sufficient protection but
Mr *Wesley* had not acquainted him with the information he had received of designs formed against
him ----At night, he tells us, " I was forced to ex-
change my usual bed, the ground, for a chest, being
almost speechless with a violent cold."

Mr.

Mr *Oglethorpe* was now expected to return from his excursion with the *Indians*, and such was the violence of the party formed against Mr. *Wesley*, that the Doctor sent his wife to arm herself from the case of instruments, and forcibly to make her escape to speak to him first on his landing, and even to stab any person who should oppose her. " I was encouraged, says Mr *Wesley*, from the lesson, *God hath not given us the spirit of fear, but of power----Be not thou therefore ashamed of the testimony of our Lord*," &c.   March 24th, " I was enabled to pray earnestly for my enemies, particularly for Mr *Oglethorpe*, whom I now looked upon as the chief of them----Then gave myself up entirely to God's disposal, desiring that I might not now want power to pray, when I most of all needed it----Mr. *Ingham* then came and read the 37th psalm, a glorious exhortation to patience, and confidence in God ----When notice was given us of Mr *Oglethorpe's* landing, Mr. *H* Mr. *Ingham*, and I were sent for.   We found him in his tent, with the people round it, and Mr. and Mrs *H* within. After a short hearing the officers were reprimanded, and the prisoners dismissed.   At going out Mrs. *H.* modestly told me, she had something more to say against me, but she would take another opportunity,----I only answered, you know, Madam, it is impossible for me to fear you   When they were gone, Mr *Oglethorpe* said, he was convinced and glad that I had no hand in all this----I told him that I had something to impart of the last importance, when he was at leisure   He took no notice, but read his letters, and I walked away with Mr. *Ingham*, who was utterly astonished. The issue

is juſt what I expected--I was ſtruck with theſe words
in the Evening Leſſon " Thou therefore, my ſon,
be ſtrong in the grace that is in *Chriſt Jeſus* · remember that *Jeſus Chriſt* was raiſed from the dead,
according to my goſpel, wherein I ſuffer trouble as
an evil doer, even unto bonds, but the word of God
is not bound, therefore I endure all things for the
elect's ſake It is a faithful ſaying, for if we be
dead with him, we ſhall alſo live with him if we
ſuffer, we ſhall alſo reign with' him ---After reading theſe words, I could not forbear adding, I need
ſay nothing, God will ſhortly apply this---Glory
be to God for my confidence hitherto---O' what
am I, if left to myſelf, but I can do and ſuffer all
things through *Chriſt* ſtrengthening me."

He goes on, " Thurſday, March 25th, I heard
the ſecond drum beat for prayers, which I had deſired Mr. *Ingram* to read, being much weakened by
my fever, but conſidering that I ought to appear
at this time eſpecially, I roſe, and heard thoſe animating words, " It any man ſerve me, let him follow me, and where I am there ſhall my ſervant be.
If any man ſerve me, him will my Father honour,"
&c At half paſt ſeven, Mr *Oglethorpe* called me
out of my hut I looked up to God and went. He
charged me with mutiny and ſedition, with ſtirring up the people to leave the colony. Accordingly he ſaid, they had a meeting laſt night, and
ſent to him this morning, deſiring leave to go---
That their ſpeaker had informed againſt them, and
me the ſpring of all---That the men were ſuch as
conſtantly came to prayers, therefore I muſt have
inſtigated them---That he ſhould not ſcruple ſhoot-
ing half a dozen of them at once, but that he had,

out

out of kindnefs, firſt fpoken to me   My anfwer
was, I defire, Sir, that you would have no regard
to my friends, or the love you had for me, if any
thing of this charge be made out againſt me---I
know nothing of their meeting or defigns. Of
thofe you have mentioned, not one comes to prayers
or facrament---I never invited any one to leave the
colony---I defire to anfwer accufers face to face.
He faid my accufer was Mr. *Lawley*, whom he
would bring, if I would wait here---I added, Mr.
Lawley is a man who has declared, that he knows
no reafon for keeping fair with any one, but a defign to get all he can by him, but there was nothing
to be got by the poor Parfon. I afked whether he
was not affured that there were men enough in *Frederica*, who would fay or fwear any thing againſt
any man, if he were in difgrace---Whether if he
himfelf was removed, or fucceeded ill, the whole
ftream of the people would not be turned againſt
him, and even this *Lawley*, who was of all others
the moſt violent in condemning the prifoners, and
juftifving the officers? I obferved, this was the old
cry, a fay with the chriftians to the lions---I mentioned *R* and his wife fcandalizing my brother and
me, and vowing revenge againſt us both, threatening me yefterday even in his prefence   I afked what
fatisfaction or redrefs was due to my character---
What good I could do in my parifh, if cut off by
calumnies from ever feeing one half of it   I ended
with affuring him, that I had, and fhould make it
my bufinefs to promote peace among all ''

  '' When Mr. *Oglethorpe* returned with *Lawley*,
he obferved the place was too public---I offered to
take him to my ufual walk in the woods---In the

way,

way, it came into my mind to say to Mr Oglethorpe, shew only the least disinclination to find me
guilty, and you shall see what a turn it will give to
the accusation He took the hint, and insisted on Lawley to make good his charge He began
with the quarrel in general, but did not shew himself angry with me, or desirous to find me to
blame Lawley, who appeared full of guilt and
fear, upon this dropt his accusation, or rather
shrunk it into my forcing the people to prayers I
replied, the people themselves would acquit me of
that, and as to the quarrel of the officers, I appealed to the officers themselves for the truth of my
assertion, that I had no hand at all in it. I pro-
fessed my desire and resolution of promoting peace
and obedience----Here Mr Oglethorpe spoke of reconciling matters bid Lawley tell the people, that
he would not so much as ask who they were, if they
were but quiet for the future I hope, added he,
they will be so, and Mr Wesley here, hopes so too.
Yes, says Lawley, I really believe it of Mr Wesley.
I had always a great respect for him I turned and
said to Mr Oglethorpe, did I not tell you it would
be so? He replied to Lawley, yes, you had always
a very great respect for Mr. Wesley, you told me
he was a stirrer up of sedition, and at the bottom of all
this disturbance. With this gentle reproof he dismissed him, and I thanked Mr Oglethorpe for
having first spoken to me of the things of which I
was accused, begging he would always do so, which
he promised I walked with him to Mrs H's
door, she came out aghast to see me with him.
He there left me, and I was delivered out of the
mouth of the lion."

" I went

" I went to my hut, where I found Mr. *Ingham*.
he faid, this was but the beginning of forrows---
" Not as I will, but as thou wilt " About noon,
in the midft of a ftorm of thunder and lightning, I
read the 28th pfalm, and found it glorioufly fuited
to my circumftances I never felt the fcriptures as
now ---I now find them all written for my inftruction
or comfort---At the fame time I felt great joy in the
expectation of our Saviour's thus coming to judgment , when the fecrets of all hearts fhall be revealed, and God fhall make my innocency as clear
as the light, and my juft dealing as the noon day "

" At three in the afternoon I walked with Mr.
Ingham, and read him the hiftory of this amazing
day We rejoiced together in the protection of
God, and through comfort of the fcriptures The
Evening Leffon was full of encouragement " This
know, that in the laft days perilous times fhall
come , for men fhall be falfe accufers, incontinent,
fierce, defpifers of thofe that are good, traitors,
heady, high-minded ; but they fhall proceed no
further, for their folly fhall be made manifeft to all
men, &c ---All fcripture is given by infpiration
of God, and is profitable," &c. Bleffed be God
that I begin to find them fo---Meeting with Mr
Hird, I perfuaded him to ufe all his intereft with
the people, to lay afide their thoughts of leaving the
colony He told me, that he had affured Mr
Oglethorpe that this was always my language to him
and the reft, and that I had no hand in the late
difturbance , but was anfwered fhort, " you fhall
not tell me that, I know better "---After fpending
an hour at the camp, in finging fuch pfalms as

B 4   fuited

suited the occasion, I went to bed in the hut, which
was thoroughly wet with to-day's rain "

March 26. " My soul is always in my hand,
therefore will I not forget thy law---This morning
early Mr Oglethorpe called me out to tell me of
Mrs Lawley's miscarriage, by being denied access
to the Doctor for bleeding   He seemed very angry,
and to charge me with it, saying he should be the
tyrant if he passed by such intolerable injuries   I
answered, that I knew nothing of the matter, and it
was hard that it should be imputed to me   That
from the first Hermsdorff told the Doctor, he might
visit any patients that he pleased, but the Doctor
would not visit any---I denied that I had the least
hand in the business, as Hermsaorff himself had declared, and yet I must be charged with all the
mischief   How else can it be, said he, that there is
no love, no meeknefs, no true religion among the
people, but instead of this, meer formal prayers
I said, as to that I can answer for them, that they
have no more of the form of godliness than the
power   for I have seldom more than six at the
public service   " But what would an unbeliever
say to your raising these disorders ?"   I answered,
if I had raised them, he might say there is nothing
in religion, but what would that signify to those
who had experienced it ? they would not say so
He said the people were full of dread and confu-
sion---that it was much more easy to govern a thousand than sixty persons---that he durst not leave
them before they were settled   I asked him whether
he would have me altogether forbear to converse
with my parishioners ? To this I could get no answer   I went on to observe, that the reason why I
                                                    did

did not interpose for or against the Doctor, was his
having at the beginning charged me with his confinement ---I said, I have talked lefs with my parishioners thefe five days paft, than I had done in
any one afternoon before I have fhunned appearing in public, left my advice fhould be afked, or,
left if I heard others talking, my filence fhould be
deciphered into advice ---But one argument of my
innocence I can give, which will convince even you
of it I know my life is in your hands, and you
know, that were you to frown upon me, and give
the leaft intimation that it would be agreeable to you,
the generality of this wretched people would fay or
fwear any thing---To this he agreed, and owned the
cafe was fo with them all You fee, faid I, that
my fafety depends on your fingle opinion of me
muft I not therefore be mad, if, in fuch a fituation,
I fhould provoke you by difturbing the public
peace? Innocence, I know, is not the leaft protection, but my fure truft is in God Here company interrupted us, and I left him---I was no longer careful for the event, after reading thofe words in the
morning leffon, " Thou fhalt not follow me now,
but thou fhalt follow me afterwards " Amen
When thou pleafeft, thy time is beft "

While we pity the fituation, we cannot but admire the genuine piety, the patience and prudent
conduct of this good man, in the midft of fuch fevere and unexpected trials Though yet in the
ftorm, he writes to his brother with a degree of
calmnefs and moderation which fhews the greatnefs
of his mind.

FREDERICA,

" FREDERICA, *March* 27*th*.

" Dear Brother,

" I received your letter and box. My laſt to
you was opened, the contents being publicly proclaimed by thoſe who were ſo ungenerous as to inter-
cept it I have not yet complained to Mr *Oglethorpe*
--- Though I truſt I ſhall never either write or ſpeak
what I will not juſtify both to God and man, yet I
would not have the ſecrets of my ſoul revealed to
every one. For their ſakes, therefore, as well as
for my own, I ſhall write no more, and deſire you
will not Nor will you have occaſion, as you viſit
us ſo ſoon. I hope your coming may be of uſe to
many

Mr *Oglethorpe* gave me an exceeding neceſſary
piece of advice for you---" Beware of hypocrites, in
particular of *Log-houſe* converts " They conſider
you as favoured by Mr *Oglethorpe*, and will therefore put on the form of religion, to pleaſe---not
God, but you. To this I ſhall only add, Give no
temporal encouragement whatſoever to any ſeeming
converts, elſe they will follow you for the ſake of
the loaves Convince them thus, that it can never
be worth their while to be hypocrites. Stay till
you are in diſgrace, in perſecution, by the heathen,
by your own country-men, till you are accounted
the offscouring of all things (as you muſt infallibly
be, if God is true) and then ſee who will follow
you---I.

" God, you believe, has much work to do in
America I believe ſo too, and begin to enter into
the deſigns which he has over *me* I ſee why he
brought me hither, and hope ere long to fly with
Jg natius,

Ignatius, " It is now that I BEGIN to be a difciple of *Chrift* " God direct you to pray for me. Adieu."

On the evening of the day when Mr *Charles Wefley* wrote this letter, a thought came into his mind to fend Mr *Ingham* for his brother Mr. *Ingham* was at firft much averfe to leave him in his trials, but at length was perfuaded to go to *Savannah*, and Mr *John Wefley* fet out from thence on the 4th of April.* I fhall now purfue Mr. *Charles'* narrative

" Sunday, March 28 I went to the ftorehoufe, our tabernacle at prefent, to hearken what the Lord God would fay concerning both myfelf and the congregation. I was ftruck with the firft leffon, *Jofeph* and *Potiphar's* wife. The fecond was ftill more animating " If the world hate you, ye know it hated me before it hated you, if ye were of the world," &c. After prayers, poor Mr *Davifon* ftaid behind to take his leave of Mr. *Ingham*. He burft into tears, and faid, one good man is leaving us already, I forefee nothing but defolation. Muft my poor children be brought up like thefe favages? We endeavoured to comfort him, by fhewing him his calling ---At ten o'clock Mr *Ingham* preached an alarming fermon on the day of judgment---In my walk at noon I was full of heavinefs, I complained to God that I had no friend but him, and even in him could find no comfort---Immediately I received power to pray, then opening my Bible, I read as follows " Hearken unto me ye that feek the Lord, look unto the rock from whence you

were hewn fear not the reproach of men, neither
be ye afraid of their reviling---Awake, awake, flee
away, who art thou, that thou should'ft be afraid
of a man that fhall die, and haft feared continually
every day, becaufe of the fury of the oppreffor?
and where is the fury of the oppreffor?'" After
reading this, it is no wonder that I found myfelf
renewed in confidence---While Mr. *Ingham* waited
for the boat, I took a turn with Mr *Horton*. he
fully convinced me of the true character of Mrs *H.*
In the higheft degree ungrateful, &c &c I then
hafted to the water-fide, where I found Mr. *Ingham*
juft put off. O! happy happy friend! *abiit, erupit
evafit* † but woe is me that I am ftill conftrained
to dwell in *Mefbech* I languifhed to bear him
company, followed him with my eye till out of fight,
and then funk into deeper dejection of fpirit than I
had known before "

"March 29. I was revived with thofe words of
our Lord " Thefe things have I fpoken unto you,
that you fhould not be offended They fhall put
you out of their fynagogues, yea, the time cometh,
that whofoever killeth you fhall think that he doeth
God fervice," &c.----Knowing when I left *England,*
that I was to live with Mr *Oglethorpe*, I brought
nothing with me but my clothes and books This
morning afking a fervant for fomething I wanted, I
think a tea-kettle, he told me that Mr *Oglethorpe*
had given orders that no one fhould ufe his things.
I anfwered, that order, I fuppofed, did not extend
to me yes, Sir, faid he, you were excepted by

---

* He is gone, he has broke loofe, he has efcaped.

name.

name. Thanks be to God, that it is not yet made capital to give me a morsel of bread."

March 30 "Having lain hitherto on the ground, in a corner of Mr. *Reed's* hut, and hearing some boards were to be difposed of, I attempted in vain to get some of them to lie upon---they were given to all befides---the minifter of *Frederica* only muft be αφρητωρ αθιμιςτο,, ανιοτιος* Yet are we not hereunto called αστατιι, κακσπαθιιτ†. Even the Son of Man had not where to lay his head---I find the fcriptures an inexhauftable fund of comfort--- "Is my hand fhortened at all that I cannot fave, or have I no power to deliver---Behold the Lord God will help me, who is he that fhall condemn me ?

March 31 " I begin now to be abufed and flighted into an opinion of my own confiderablenefs I could not be more trampled upon, were I a fallen Minifter of State The people have found out that I am in difgrace, and all the cry is, *curramus pracipites, et dum jacet in ripa, calcemus Cafaris hoftem* ‡ My few well wifhers are afraid to fpeak to me, fome have turned out of the way to avoid me, others have defired that I would not take it ill if they feemed not to know me when we fhould meet The fervant that ufed to wafh my linen, fent it back unwafhed It was great caufe of triumph that I was forbid the ufe of Mr. *Ogle-thorpe's* things, which in effect debarred me of moft

* Treated as an enemy to fociety, as an unjaft perfon, and be deftitute of an habitation

† To have no certain dwelling place, to fuffer afflictions 1 Cor iv 11 2 Tim iv o

‡ Let us run quick, and while he is down let us trample on the enemy of Cafar

of

of the conveniences, if not the neceffaries of life---
I fometimes pitied them, and fometimes diverted
myfelf with the odd expreffions of their contempt
but I found the benefit of having undergone a much
lower degree of obloquy at Oxford "

April 1. In the midft of morning fervice, a poor
fcout boat man was brought in, who was almoft
killed by the burfting of a cannon   I found him
fenfelefs and dying, and all I could do, was to pray
for him, and try by his example to wake his two
companions   He languifhed till the next day, and
then died.----Hitherto I have been born up by a
fpirit not my own   but exhaufted nature finks at
laft.   It is amazing fhe has held out fo long   My
outward hardfhips and inward conflicts, the bitternefs of reproach from the only man I wifhed to
pleafe, down at laft have worn my boafted courage.
Accordingly this afternoon, I was forced by a
friendly fever to take my bed.   My ficknefs, I
knew, could not be of long continuance, as I was in
want of every help and convenience, it muft either
foon leave me, or releafe me from further fufferings
In the evening Mr. Hird and Mr. Rchinfon called to
fee me, and offered me all the affiftance in their
power.   I thanked them, but defired they would
not prejudice themfelves by taking this notice of
me.   At that inftant we were alarmed with a cry
of the Spaniards being come, we heard many guns
fired, and faw the people fly in great confternation
to the fort.   I felt not the leaft difturbance or fur-
prife; bid the women not fear, for God was with
us   In a few minutes, news was brought, that it
was only a contrivance of Mr Oglethorpe's to try
the people.   My charitable vifitants then left me,
and

and foon returned with fome gruel, which threw me
into a fweat The next morning, April 2, they
ventured to call again---at night, when my fever
was fomewhat abated, I was led out to bury the
Scout boat man, and envied him his quiet grave.
April 3 I found nature endeavoured to throw off
the difeafe by exceffive fweating, I therefore drank
whatever the women brought me---April 4. My
flux returned, but notwithftanding this, I was
obliged to go abroad, and preach and adminifter
the facrament.   My fermon, "On keep innocency
and take heed to the thing that is right, for this
fhall bring a man peace at the laft," was decyphered
into a fatire againft Mrs H --At night I got an old
bedftead to fleep upon, being that on which the
Scout boat man had died ---April 6 I found myfelf fo faint and weak, that it was with the utmoft
difficulty I got through the prayers.   Mr. Drwifon,
my good Samaritan, would often call or fend his
wife to attend me, and to their care, under God, I
owe my life   To day Mr Oglethorpe gave away
my bedftead from under me, and refufed to fpare
one of the carpenters to mend me up another "

April 10 Mr Reed waked me with the news
that my brother and Mr. Delamotte were on their
way to Frederica I found the encouragement I
fought, in the Scripture for the day, Pfalm lii.
"Why boafteft thou thyfelf, thou tyrant, that thou
canft do mifchief, whereas the goodnefs of God endureth yet daily.   Thy tongue imagineth wickednefs, and with lies thou cutteft like a fharp razor,"
&c ---At fix my brother and Mr Delamotte landed,
when my ftrength was fo exhaufted, that I could
not have read prayers once more.---He helped me
                                                   into

into the woods, for there was no talking among a people of spies and ruffians, nor even in the woods, unless in an unknown tongue----And yet Mr *Oglethorpe* received my brother with abundant kindness ---I began my account of all that had passed, and continued it till prayers. It would be needless to mention all the Scriptures, which, for so many days have been adapted to my circumstances. But I cannot pass by the lesson for this evening, Heb. xi. I was ashamed of having well nigh sunk under my sufferings, when I beheld the conflicts of those triumphant sufferers of whom the world was not worthy. April 11. What words could more support our confidence, than the following? out of the Psalms for the day "Be merciful unto me O God, for man goeth about to devour me. He is daily fighting and troubling me ---Mine enemies be daily in hand to swallow me up, for they be many that fight against me---I will put my trust in God, and will not fear what flesh can do unto me They daily mistake my words," &c the next Psalm was equally animating---"Be merciful unto me, O God, for my soul trusteth in thee, and under the shadow of thy wings shall be my refuge, till this tyranny be overpast I will call unto the most high God, even unto the God that shall perform the cause that I have in hand--My soul is among lions, and I lie even among the children of men that are set on fire, whose teeth are spears and arrows, and their tongue a sharp sword," &c ---I just recovered strength enough to consecrate at the Sacrament, my brother performed the rest We then went out of the reach of informers, and I proceeded in my account, being fully persuaded of the truth of Mrs *W's* information

formation againſt Mr. *Oglethorpe*, Mrs. *H* and herſelf At noon my brother repeated to me his laſt
conference with Mrs. *W* in confirmation of all ſhe
had ever told me.

" April 16. My brother prevailed with me to
break a reſolution which honour and indignation
had induced me to form, of ſtarving rather than
aſk for neceſſaries Accordingly I went to Mr.
Oglethorpe, and aſked for ſome little things I wanted He ſent for me back and ſaid, pray Sir ſit
down, I have ſomething to ſay to you , I hear you
have ſpread ſeveral reports about "

" The next day my brother and Mr. *Delamotte*
ſet out in an open boat for *Savannah*. I preached
in the afternoon, on, " He that now goeth on his
way weeping and beareth good ſeed, ſhall doubtleſs
come again with joy, and bring his ſheaves with
him " Eaſter-eve, April 24, I was ſent for at 10
by Mr *Oglethorpe* " Mr. *Weſley*, you know what
has paſſed between us I took ſome pains to ſatisfy
your brother about the reports concerning me, but
in vain , he here renews his ſuſpicion in writing.
I did deſire to convince him, becauſe I had an eſteem
for him , and he is juſt as conſiderable to me as my
eſteem makes him I could clear up all, but it
matters not, you will ſoon ſee the reaſon of my actions. I am now going to death, you will ſee me
no more. Take this ring, and carry it from me to
Mr. *V* if there be a friend to be depended on he is
one His intereſt is next to Sir *Robert*'s , whatever
you aſk, within his power, he will do for you, your
brother and family. I have expected death for ſome
days Theſe letters ſhew that the *Spaniards* have
long been ſeducing our Allies, and intend to cut us

C   off

off at a blow. I fall by my friends, on whom I depended to fend their promifed fuccours But death
is nothing to me, I will purfue all my defigns, and
to Him I recommend them and you." He then
gave me a diamond ring, I took it, and faid, " If,
poftremum fato quod te alloquor, hoc ift,[*] hear, what
you will quickly know to be a truth as foon as you
are entered on a feparate ftate, this ring I fhall never make any ufe of for myfelf I have no worldly
hopes, I have renounced the world---Life is bitternefs to me---I came hither to lay it down---You
have been deceived as well as I---I proteft my innocence of the crimes I am charged with, and think
myfelf now at liberty to tell you what I thought never to have uttered." It is probable that he un-
folded to Mr. *Oglethorpe* the whole plot, as Mrs *H*.
had difcovered it to him

" When I had finifhed this relation he feemed
entirely changed, full of his old love and confidence
in me. After fome expreffions of kindnefs, I afked
him, are you now fatisfied? He replied, " Yes in-
tirely." Why then Sir, I defire nothing more on
earth, and care not how foon I follow you He
added, how much he defired the converfion of the
heathen, and believed my brother intended for it
But I believe, faid I, it will never be under your
patronage, for then men would account for it, without taking God into the account He replied, I
believe fo too---Then embraced and kiffed me with
the moft cordial affection. I attended him to the
Scout boat, where he waited fome minutes for his
fword They brought a mourning fword the firft

---

[*] This be the laft time I am allowed to fpeak to you

o   and

and a fecond time, at laft they gave him his own,
which had been his father's---With this fword, faid
he, I was never yet unfuccefful When the boat
put off, I ran into the woods to fee my laft of him.
Seeing me and two others run after him, he ftopt
the boat and afked if we wanted any thing ? Capt.
Mackintoſh, whom he left commander, defired his
laft orders I then faid, God is with you, go forth,
Chriſto duce, et aufpice Chriſto.   You have, faid he,
fome verfes of mine, you there fee my thoughts of
fuccefs. The boat then carried him out of fight---
I interceded for him, that God would fave him
from death, and wafh away all his fins "

" April 29 About half paft 8, I went down to
the bluff, to fee a boat that was coming up.   At
9 it arrived, with Mr *Oglethorpe*   I bleffed God
for ftill holding his foul in life.   In the evening
we took a walk together, and he informed me more
particularly of our paft danger   Three large fhips
and four fmaller, had been feen for three weeks together at the mouth of the river, but the wind
continuing againft them, they were hindered from
making a defcent until they could ftay no longer. I
gave him back his ring, and faid, I need not, indeed
I cannot, Sir, tell you how joyfully and thankfully I
return this---When I gave it you, faid he, I never
expected to receive it again, but thought it would
be of fervice to your brother and you.   I had many
omens of my death---but God has been pleafed to
preferve a life which was never valuable to me, and
yet in the continuance of it, I thank God, I can rejoice.   He appeared full of tendernefs to me, and
paffed on to obferve the ftrangenefs of his deliverance, when betrayed on all fides, without human

support, and utterly helpless He condemned himself for his late anger, which he imputed to want of
time for confideration. I longed Sir, said I, to fee
you once more, that I might tell you fome things
before we finally parted   But then I confidered,
that if you died, you would know them all in a moment.   I know not, faid he, whether fepaiate fpirits regaid our little conceins   if they do, it is as
men regard the follies of their childhood , or, as I
my late paffionatenefs---April 30, I had fome further talk with him , he oidered me every thing he
could think I wanted , and piomifed to have an
houfe built for me immediately.   He was juft the
fame to me, he formerly had been."

From a caicful examination of the whole of this
affair, it appeais to me that Mr *Wefley's* conduct is
not only fiee from blame, but that his integrity and
prudence deferve the higheft commendation   Confcious of his innocence, and loaded with contempt
and reproach under the moft irritating and pio-
voking circumftances, his patience, and confidence
in God, in expectation of deliverance, ftand forth in
a confpicuous light, and form the moft prominent
features of his character   Mis *H* and Mis. *I*.
were women of very loofe morals, they had come
from *Ligland* in the fhip with Mr *Oglithorpe*, and
while at fea, Mis *H* feemed to be under fome religious impieffions, but foon loft them on fhore
The character of Mrs *H* was well known in *England*, Mr *Charles Wefley* was informed by Mr. *Hird*,
that Mr *Oglethorpe* declared he would rather give
an hundred pounds than take her in the fhip.
Though Mr. *Wefley* knew this, and the whole of
her character, yet he never upbraided her with it,
                                                        but

but patiently endured her revilings His innocence
appears on the very face of their proceedings, and
hence Mr *Oglethorpe*, when undeceived, attributed
his conduct to a want of time for confideration ---
The second day after his coming among them, Mrs.
H began to abuse him, and seven days after, their
whole plot was difcovered to him, which makes it
almoft certain that their defigns were formed before
he came among them, under an apprehenfion that he
would be too great a check on their licentious behaviour After fuch an inftance as this, of the principles and practices of this people, ought we to wonder
at any reports they might raife concerning either of
the two brothers?

Mr *Charles Wefley* being now more at eafe from
his perfecutors, gradually regained his ftrength,
and on the 11th of May he was fufficiently recovered to expound the Leffon.---On the 12th, the
morning Leffon was, *Elifha* furrounded with the hoft
of *Dothan*. "It is our privilege as chriftians, Mr.
" *Wefley* obferves, to apply thofe words to our-
" felves,' "there be more that be for us, than
" thofe that be againft us"   God fpoke to us yet
plainer in the Second Leffon ---" Behold I fend
" you forth as fheep in the midft of wolves, be ye
" therefore wife as Serpents and harmlefs as Doves
" ---But beware of men, for they will deliver you
" up, and ye fhall be brought before Governors
" and Kings for my name's fake, and ye fhall be
" hated of all men, but he that endureth to the
" end fhall be faved----The difciple is not above
" his Mafter, fear ye not therefore, for there is
" nothing covered which fhall not be revealed, and
" hid which fhall not be made known."   In ex-

plaining

plaining this, he adds, " I dwelt on that bleffed
" topic of confolation to the innocent, that how-
" ever he may fuffer here, he will fhortly be cleared
" at God's righteous bar, where the accufer and
" the accufed fhall meet face to face, and the
" guilty perfon acquit him whom he unjuftly
" charged, and take back the wickednefs to him-
" felf. Poor Mrs W. who was juft over againft
" me, could not ftand it, but firft turned her back,
" and then retired behind the congregation."---
No one would have rejoiced more in her repentance
and converfion to God, than Mr Wefley

May 13, Mr. Oglethorpe being gone to the Southward, Mr. Charles Wefley fet out for Savannah,
whither the Indian traders were coming down to
meet him, in order to take out their licences.   On
the 16th, he reached Thunderbolt at fix in the evening, and from thence walked to Savannah, * which
is about five miles   His brother, Mr Ingham, and
Mr Delamotte were furprized at his unexpected
vifit, but it being late, each retired to his corner
of the room, and " Without the help of a bed,
" fays Mr Charles, we flept foundly till the morn-
" ing "---On the 19th, Mr John Wefley fet out
for Frederica, and Mr Charles took charge of Savannah in his abfence. " The hardeft duty, fays he,
" impofed on me, was, expounding the Leffon
" morning and evening to one hundred hearers
" I was furprifed at my own confidence, and ac-
" knowledged it was not my own "---The day was
ufually divided between vifiting his parifhoners,

* This accords with Mr John Wefley's Journal. See his Works, Vol. 26.
p 130

confidering

confidering the Leſſon, and converſing with Mr.
Ingham, Delamotte, &c.   On the 22nd he firſt met
the traders, at Mr. *Cauſton's*, and continued to meet
ſome or other of them every day for ſeveral weeks.

May 31. Mr. *Oglethorpe* being returned from
the Southward, and come to *Savannah*, he this day
held a court   " We went, ſays Mr. *Weſley*, and
" heard his ſpeech to the people," in the cloſe of
which he ſaid, " If any one here has been abuſed,
" or oppreſſed by any man, in or out of office, he
" has free and full liberty of complaining. let him
" deliver in his complaints in writing at my houſe;
" I will read them all over by myſelf, and do every
" particular man juſtice."---At eight in the evening I waited upon him, and found the three Magiſtrates with him, who ſeemed much alarmed by his
ſpeech---" *they hoped he would not diſcourage govern-*
" *ment* "---" He diſmiſſed them "---We have here
a curious ſpecimen of the notions which the Magiſtrates of *Savannah* had of government   They ſeem
to have thought it their privilege, as Governors, to
oppreſs any individual without reſtraint, as it ſuited
their convenience or inclination   I am ſorry to ſay,
that we too often ſee this notion of government
manifeſt itſelf in the conduct of little petty Governors, both in matters *eccleſiaſtical* and civil.

In the beginning of July, I find Mr *Oglethorpe*,
Mr *John* and Mr *Charles Weſley*, all at *Savannah*
but there is no intimation how long they had been
there, or on what occaſion they were together.
On the 21ſt, ſays Mr *Charles*, " I heard by my
" brother, that I was to ſet ſail for *England* in a
" few days." This was not merely on account of
his health, which was now a little recovered.   He

was to carry difpatches from Mr *Oglethorpe*, to the Truftees of *Georgia*, to the Board of Trade, and probably to Government.   The next day, July 22, he got all the licences figned by Mr *Oglethorpe*, and counter figned them himfelf, and fo, fays he, " I " entirely wafhed my hands of the Traders   This feems to have been a bufinefs which he cordially difliked, and thinking the prefent a favourable opportunity of efcaping from his difagrecable fituation, he wrote a letter to Mr *Oglethorpe* on the 25th, refigning his office of Secretary   In the evening Mr. *Oglethorpe* took him afide, and afked whether the fum of all he had faid in the letter, was not contained in the following line, which he fhewed him,

" *Magis apta Tuis, tua dona relinquo.*"

" Sir, to yourfelf your flighted gifts I leave
    Lefs fit for me to take, than you to give "

Sir, faid Mr *Wefley*, I do not wifh to lofe your efteem, but I cannot lofe my foul to preferve it He anfwered, " I am fatisfied of your regard for " me, and your argument drawn from the heart " is unanfwerable   yet I would defire you not to " let the Truftees know your refolution of re- " figning.   There are many hungry fellows ready " to catch at the office, and in my abfence I can- " not put in one of my own choofing   Perhaps " they may fend me a bad man, and how far " fuch a one may influence the Traders, and " obftruct the reception of the Gofpel among the " heathen, you know---I fhall be in *England* be- " fore you hear of it, and then you may either put " in a Deputy or refign "

July

July 26. Mr *C. Wesley* set out for *Charles-Town* on his way to *England* Thus far his brother accompanied him, and here they arrived on the 31st of July. * He now found his desires renewed to recover the image of God, and at the Sacrament was encouraged, in an unusual manner, to hope for pardon, and to strive against sin.

In every place where he came, Mr. *Wesley* was attentive to the things which passed round about him We cannot therefore wonder that the wretched situation of the *Negroes* should attract his notice. " I had observed much, and heard more, says he, " of the cruelty of masters towards their Negroes; " but now I received an authentic account of some " horrid instances thereof I saw myself, that the " giving a slave to a child of its own age, to ty- " rannize over, to abuse and beat out of sport, was " a common practice nor is it strange, that being " thus trained up in cruelty, they should afterwards " arrive at such a perfection in it "

Mr *Wesley* mentions several methods of torturing the poor slaves that were common, and even talked of with indifference by some who practised them — For instance, Mr *Star* informed Mr *L.* with whom Mr *Wesley* was intimate, that he had ordered a slave, first to be nailed up by the ears, and then to be whipt in the severest manner, and to finish the whole, to have scalding water thrown all over his body, after which the poor creature could not move himself for four months.

* This account agrees with Mr *John Wesley's* Journal See his Works Vol 26 p. 140.

" Another

" Another, much applauded punifhment, fays
" Mr. *C Wefley* is, drawing the teeth of their flaves
" ---It is univerfally known, that Colonel *Linch*
" cut off the legs of a poor Negro, and that he kills
" feveral of them every year by his barbarities "

" It were endlefs to recount all the fhocking in-
" ftances of diabolical cruelty, which thefe men,
" as they call themfelves, daily practife upon their
" fellow-creatures, and that upon the moft trivial
" occafions---I fhall only mention one more, related
" to me by an eye-witnefs   Mr *Hill* a Dancing-
" mafter in *Charles-Town*, whipt a female flave fo
" long, that fhe fell down at his feet, in appear-
" ance dead   when by the help of a Phyfician fhe
" was fo far recovered as to fhew fome figns of
" life, he repeated the whipping with equal rigour,
" and concluded the punifhment with dropping
" fcalding wax upon her flefh-----Her crime was,
" over filling a tea-cup ---Thefe horrid cruelties
" are the lefs to be wondered at, becaufe the law
" itfelf, in effect, countenances and allows them
" to kill their flaves, by the ridiculous penalty ap-
" pointed for it ---The penalty is about feven
" pounds fterling, one half of which is ufually re-
" mitted if the criminal inform againft himfelf '

Thefe inftances, to which ten thoufand others
might be added, of deliberate mercilefs cruelty, exercifed by one part of mankind over another, often
without any caufe that can be called a provocation,
fhew us to what a wretched ftate of depravity and
infenfibility, human nature may be reduced by
vicious habits.   How much lefs would have been
the fufferings of thefe miferable Negroes, if they
had fallen into the power of their *more merciful* enemies,

mies, the lions, bears, and tygers of *Africa*! Yet
these wild beasts are hunted and destroyed as enemies to the human species what then do the cruel
Slave-holders and Masters deserve? who have more
cruelty, and ten times the art of exercising it, even
upon their own species. But what is more wonderful than all the rest, if possible, is, that in this
free and enlightened country, which boasts of the
mild and equitable principles of christianity, there
is a large body of men who defend the Slave-trade,
the source of all these miseries, and from which it
can never be wholly separated And they defend
it too, on the principle of advantage Now what
is it which these men, in fact, say to us in their
defence of the Slave-trade? Do they not tell us,
that they would reduce all other men to a state of
Slavery for their own advantage, if they had the
power of doing it?---But I say no more the *British*
Nation has at length awaked from its deep sleep;
it has opened its eyes, and viewed the enormity of
the crimes attendant on the Slave-trade, it has
called on the Legislature to put a stop to them by
abolishing it, and, for the honour of our country,
the *British* House of Commons has condemned the
trade as cruel and unjust, and has determined to
abolish it. Every friend to humanity waits with
impatience to see this resolution fully and effectually executed Had the two Mr *Wesleys* been
now living, they would have rejoiced greatly, and
have praised God, for the present prospect of a total
abolition of the Slave-trade.

While Mr *Wesley* stayed at *Charles-Town*, his
bloody flux and fever hung upon him, and rather
increased. Notwithstanding this, he was determined

mined to go in the firſt ſhip that ſailed for *England*.
His friends endeavoured to diſſuade him from it,
both becauſe the ſhip was very leaky, and the Captain a mere beaſt of a man, being almoſt continually drunk   But he was deaf to their advice
" The public buſineſs, ſays he, that hurried me to
" *England*, being of that importance, as their Secre-
" tary, I could not anſwer to the Truſtees for
" *Georgia*, the loſs of a day "   Accordingly he engaged his paſſage on board the *London* Galley, which
left *Charles-Town* on the 16th of Auguſt   But they
ſoon found, that the Captain while on ſhore, had
neglected every thing to which he ought to have
attended.   The veſſel was too leaky to bear the
voyage , and the Captain drinking nothing ſcarcely
but gin, had never troubled his head about taking
in a ſufficient quantity of water , ſo that on the
26th they were obliged to be reduced to ſhort allowance   Meeting afterwards with ſtormy weather,
the leak became alarming, and their difficulties increaſed ſo faſt upon them, that they were obliged
to ſteer for *Boſton* in *New England*, where they arrived, with much difficulty and danger, on the 24th
of September.

    Mr. *Wſley* was ſoon known at *Boſton*, and met
with a hoſpitable reception amongſt the Miniſters,
both of the town and neighbourhood   Having experienced much difficulty at *Frederica*, to prevent
his letters to his brother from being read by others,
he learned *Byrom*'s Short-hand, and now for the
firſt time wrote to his brother in thoſe characters.
He tells him, " If you are as deſirous as I am of a
" correſpondence, you muſt ſet upon *Byrom*'s Short-
" hand immediately."   Mr *John Weſley* did ſo,
and their correſpondence was afterwards carried on
chiefly in it.   This

This letter was evidently written in a hurry, probably in the midst of company   A part of it is in Latin, which, as it shews the facility with which he wrote in this language, and also discovers something of the turn of his mind, I shall transcribe it below. * The substance of it I shall give in *English*.

Boston, Oct. 5,

" I am wearied with this hospitable people, they
" so vex and teſe me with their civilities.   They
" do not suffer me to be alone   The Clergy, who
" come from the country on a visit, drag me along
" with them when they return.   I am constrained
" to take a view of this *New England*, more
" pleasant even than the old.   I cannot help
" exclaiming, O ! happy country, that cherishes
" neither *flies*, † nor *crocodiles*, ‡ nor *informers* §

* " Tædet me populi hujasce φιλοξ. », ita me urbanitate sua diverſant et persequuntur.   Non patiuntur me esse solum E rure veniunt invisentes Clerici, me revertentes in rus trahunt   Cogor hanc Angliam contemplari, etiam ant ſ ſ amœniorem, et nequeo non exclamare, O fortunata regio, nec muscas alens, nec crocodilos, nec delatores ! Sub fine hujus hebdomadis navem certiſsime conscendimus, duplicato ſumptu paratam empturi   Carolinenſium nemo, viatica ſuppeditavit, et hic iisdem nil niſi cum pretio   Peſsime me habet quod cogor moram hare emere, magnumque pretium digreſsionis ſolvere "
Morbus meus, aere hoc ſaluberrimo ſemel fugatus, iterum rediit Suadent amici omnes ut medicum conſulem, ſed " Funera non poſsum tam pretioſa pati

† When Mr *Wesley* was at *Frederica*, the Sand-flies were one night ſo exceedingly troubleſome, that he was obliged to riſe at one o'clock, and ſmoke them out of his hut   He tells us that the whole town was employed in the ſame wa

‡ He means that ſpecies of the Crocodile called the Alligator   When at Sa-annah, he and Mr *Delamotte* uſed to bathe in the *Savannah* river between four and five o'clock in the morning, before the Alligators were ſtirring, but they heard them ſnoring all round them   One morning Mr *Delamotte* was in great danger, an Alligator roſe juſt behind him, and purſued him to the land, whither he eſcaped with difficulty

§ He puts informers in good company , they are always troubleſome, and ſometimes deſtructive creatures   They ſeldom or never confine themſelves to ſimple facts , ſuſpicion ſupplies much matter, and invention more After what he had ſuffered, it is no wonder he ſpeaks of them in ſo feeling a manner

About

" About the end of this week we shall certainly go
" on board the ship, having to pay a second time
" for our passage . even here, nothing is to be had
" without money. It vexes me to be obliged to
" purchase this delay, and to pay a great price for
" my departure "

" My disorder, once removed by this most salu-
" brious air, has again returned, All my friends
" advise me to consult a Physician, but I cannot
" afford so expensive a funeral."

Mr. *Wesley* did not go on board as he expected,
the ship being detained some time longer. During
his stay here, his disorder returned with violence,
and reduced him to a state of very great weakness.
On the 15th of October he wrote to his brother,
and continues his letter in a kind of Journal to the
25th, when he went on board the ship, and sailed
for *England*. His account of himself is as follows.

" I should be glad for your sake to give a satis-
" factory account of myself, but that you must
" never expect from me----It is fine talking while
" we have youth and health on our side , but sick-
" ness would spoil your boasting as well as mine.
" I am now glad of a warm bed , but must soon
" betake myself to my board again '

" Though I am apt to think that I shall at length
" arrive in *England* to deliver what I am intrusted
" with, yet do I not expect, or wish for a long life.
" How strong must the principle of self-preserva-
" tion be, which can make such a wretch as I am
" willing to live at all '---or rather unwilling to
" die , for I know no greater pleasure in life, than
" in considering that it cannot last for ever."

------ " The

———— " The temptations paſt
" N> more ſhall vex me, every grief I feel
" Shortens the deſtin'd number, every pulſe
" Beats a ſharp moment of the pain away,
" And the laſt ſtroke will come. By ſwift degrees
'- Time ſweeps me off, and I ſhall ſoon arrive
" At life's ſweet period O¹ Celeſtial point
" That ends this mortal ſtory "————

" To-day compleats my three weeks unneceſſary
" ſtay at *Boſton* To-morrow the ſhip falls down———
" I am juſt now much woiſe than ever, but
" nothing leſs than death ſhall hinder me from
" embaiking."

October 18 The ſhip that carries *me*, *muſt* meet
with endleſs delays it is well if it ſails this week.
———I have lived ſo long in honours and indulgences,
that I have almoſt forgotten whereunto I am called,
being ſtrongly urged to ſet up my reſt here. But
I will lean no longer upon men, nor again put
myſelf into the power of any of my own mercileſs
ſpecies, by either expecting their kindneſs or deſiring their eſteem.———Mr. *Appy*, like an errant
gentleman as he is, has drawn me into monſtrous
expences for ſhip ſtores, &c So that, what with
my three week's ſtay at *Charles-Town*, my month's
ſtay here, and my double paſſage,———fiom *Courtier* I
am turned *Philoſopher* *

October 21. " I am worried on all ſides by the
" ſolicitations of my friends to defer my winter
" voyage till I have recovered a little ſtrength.————

---

* Among the ancients a philoſopher and a beggar were almoſt ſynoni-
mous terms In modern times, the philoſopher holds a reſpectable rank in
ſociety We commonly aſſociate the ideas of a poet and a garret, but then
we mean a poet by profeſſion, one who procures a livelihood by writing
verſes.

Mr.

" Mr ---- I am apt to think would allow me to
" wait a fortnight for the next fhip, but then if I
" recover, my ftay will be thought unnecessary.
" I muft die to prove myfelf fick, and I can do no
" more at fea I am therefore determined to be
" carried on board to-morrow, and leave the event
" to God "

October 25 " The fhip fell down as was ex-
" pected, but a contrary wind prevented me from
" following till now ---At prefent I am fomething
" better on board the *Hannah*, Captain *Corney*,
" in the ftate-room, which they have forced upon
" me. I have not ftrength for more. Adieu."

On the 27th, Mr. *Wefley* had fo far recovered
ftrength that he was able to read prayers The next
day the Captain informed him that a ftorm was approaching In the evening it came on with dreadful violence and raged all night On the 29th in
the morning they fhipped fo prodigious a fea, that
it wafhed away their fheep, half their hogs, and
drowned moft of their fowl. The fhip was heavy
laden, and the fea ftreamed in fo plentifully at the
fides, that it was as much as four men could do by
continual pumping, to keep her above water " I
" rofe, and lay down by turns, adds Mr. *Wefley*,
" but could remain in no pofture long I ftrove
" vehemently to pray, but in vain, I ftill perfifted
" in ftriving, but without effect. I prayed for
" power to pray, * for faith in *Jefus Chrift*, con-
" tinually repeating his name, till I felt the virtue
" of it at laft, and knew that I abode under the
" fhadow of the ALMIGHTY "

* He means with confidence and comfort.

At

At three in the afternoon the storm was at the height, at four, the ship made so much water, that the Captain finding it otherwise impossible to save her from sinking, cut down the mizen-mast. "In "this dreadful moment, says Mr *Wesley*, I bless "God I found the comfort of hope, and such joy "in finding I could hope, as the world can neither "give nor take away.   I had that *conviction* of the "power of God present with me, overbalancing "my strongest passion, fear, and raising me above "what I am by nature, as surpassed *all rational* "*evidence*, and gave me a taste of the divine "goodness."

On the 30th the storm abated, and "On Sun- "day the 31st, he observes, my first business was, "may it be the business of all my days, to offer "up the sacrifice of praise and thankfgiving --- "We all joined in thanks for our deliverance most "of the day"

They soon met with another storm, but not so violent as the former, and continuing their voyage with some intervening difficulties and dangers, till the third of December, the ship arrived oppo- site *Deal*, and the passengers came safe on shore "I kneeled down, says Mr *Wesley*, and blessed the "hand that had conducted me through such in- "extricable mazes, and desired I might give up "my country again, whenever God should require "it."

D   CHAPTER

CHAPTER III.

Of Mr. CHARLES WESLEY *from December 3d,* 1736, *until the end of June* 1738.

MR. *Charles Wesley,* had been abfent from *England* upwards of thirteen months, during this time he had paffed through a feries of trials and difficulties, which in all their circumftances are not very common   He had indeed been in the wildernefs, where the hand of God had been manifefted in his pre-fervation, and finally in his deliverance   Here God had proved him, and tried him, and fhewn him what was in his heart   In this ftate of fuffering, he was led to a more perfect knowledge of hu-man nature, than he could have obtained from books and meditation, through the whole courfe of his life. His knowledge was derived from ex-perience, which is the moft certain, and the moft ufeful in the conduct of life, and makes the deepeft impreffion on the mind.   In his diftrefs the Scrip-tures became more precious than he had ever found them before. He now faw a beauty in them, which the moft learned and refined criticifm can never difcover.   From the frequent and pointed appli-cation of them to his ftate and circumftances, they were the means of giving a degree of confolation

and

and hope, which human prudence and human help
can never beftow.   His fituation abroad may be
called a fchool, in which the difcipline indeed was
fevere, but the knowledge acquired by it, valuable,
as it prepared him to underftand, and difpofed him
by degrees to embrace, the fimple gofpel way of
falvation, which the pride of man hath always
rejected.

Both the Mr *Wefleys* had formed a large acquaintance in *London* among the ferious profeffors
of religion, by whom they were greatly efteemed.
When Mr *Charles* arrived in town, his friends received him with inexpreffible joy, as one reftored
from the dead , a report having been fpread, that
the fhip in which he came home, had been feen to
fink at fea ---He called upon one lady while fhe
fhe was reading an account of his death.----After
he had delivered his letters, he waited on their
friend Mr *Charles Rivington,* in St *Paul's* Church-
Yard.   Here he met with letters, and a journal
from his brother in *Georgia,* which informed him
of what had taken place, foon after he left it ---
Before he finally quitted *America,* Mr *Charles Wefley*
had written a letter to his brother *John,* in which
he had expreffed his fentiments of fome particular
perfons with freedom, but by way of caution, had
pointed out two individuals by two Greek words
This letter Mr *John Wefley* dropt, and it fell into
the hands of thofe who were enemies to both of
them   Mr *John Wefley* was fo incautious alfo, as
to tell who were meant by the two Greek words.
This was fure to raife great difturbance among a
people fo irritable, and fo revengeful, as the *Georgians*

were

were at this time Mr. *Charles*, had happily escaped
out of their reach, and the storm fell with double
violence on his brother * The journal which he
now received from Mr *Rivington*, informed him of
the particulars ---" I read it, says Mr *Charles*,
" without either surprise or impatience The drop-
" ping of my fatal letter, I hope will convince him,
" of what I never could, his own great carelessness.
" and the sufferings which it has brought upon him,
" *may shew him* his blindness. His simplicity in tel-
" ling, what, and who were meant by the *two Greek*
" words, was out-doing his own out-doings Surely
" all this will be sufficient to teach him a little of
" the wisdom of the Serpent, of which he seems as
" entirely void, as Mrs *H* is of the innocency of
" the dove "

Mr. *Charles Wesley* has given us in these remarks,
a striking instance of the artless undisguised conduct of his brother. He supposes indeed, that his
brother wanted foresight , that he did not perceive
the consequences which would follow from his open
avowal of the *whole* truth This however was far
from being the case Mr *John Wesley* had too
much penetration and knowledge of human nature,
not to foresee what would follow from his conduct
on this occasion The truth is, that Mr. *John Wesley*
had adopted a principle of unreserved openness in
his conversation with others, which, on particular
occasions he carried abundantly too far. His conduct in the present instance, may prove his sincerity,
and firm attachment to his principle, but prudence

* This was eight or nine months previous to the persecution he suffered
on account of Mrs. *Williamson*.

cannot

cannot juftify it, even on the moft rigid principles of morality.

It appears from Mr *Charles Wesley*'s journal, that moft of the Truftees for *Georgia* were Diffenters: they have given us however, an unequivocal proof that the Diffenters at this time poffeffed great liberality of fentiment , or they would not have approved of the nomination of the two Mr. *Wesleys*, men avowedly of very high Church principles, to go and preach the gospel in *Georgia ;* efpecially as their father had been fo public an oppofer of the Diffenting intereft ---December the 7th, one of these Truftees called on Mr. *Wesley*   He obferves, " We had much difcourfe of *Georgia,* and of my " brother's perfecution ⁻ among that ftiff-necked " people.   He feems a truly pious humble chrif- " tian , full of zeal for God, and love to man "---- It has been generally acknowledged that Mr. *Charles Wesley* was a more rigid *Church-man* than his brother. I was therefore pleafed to find this teftimony of his candid judgment of a Diffenter   Could he have faid more in favour of the moft pious *Church-man ?*

Mr *Oglethorpe* left *Georgia* and fet fail for *England* on the 26th of November, and arrived in *London* on the 7th of January 1737. Mr. *Charles Wesley* waited upon him the next day, and the moft cordial friendfhip fubfifted between them , which continued till death

About the middle of January, Count *Zinzendorff* arrived in *England*   I fuppofe it was the firft time that he vifited this country   One principal object

---

* Occafioned by Mr. *Charles Wesley*'s letter to his brother, juft now mentioned

of

of this visit, seems to have been, to procure a union
between the *Moravian* Church, and the Church of
England, in *Georgia*, and to get them acknowledged
by this country, as one Church   The Count had
been informed of the piety and zeal of the two
brothers, and on the 19th, a few days after his arrival, he sent for Mr *Charles Wesley*   He went, and
the Count saluted him with all possible affection,
and made him promise to call every day   Here he
was acquainted with the object of the Count's visit
to this country   From him he went to the Bishop
of *Oxford*, who received him with equal kindness,
and desired him to call as often as he could, without
ceremony or further invitation   They had much
talk of the state of religion among the *Moravians*;
of the object of the Count's visit, and the Bishop
acknowledged that the *Moravian* Bishops had the
true succession

On the 25th, he paid a visit to the celebrated Dr.
Hales,* near *Twickenham*, who was one of the Trustees

* *Hales (Stephen)* D D a celebrated divine and philosopher, was born
in 1677   In 1696 he was entered at *Bennet*-College, *Cambridge*, and admitted a Fellow in 1703   He soon discovered a genius for natural philo-
sophy   Botany was his first study, and he used to make excursions among
the hills with a view of prosecuting it   In the study of astronomy he was
equally assiduous   Having made himself acquainted with the *Newtonian*
System, he contrived a machine for shewing the phenomena of the heavenly
bodies, on much the same principles with that afterwards made by Mr
Rowley, which, from the name of his patron, was called an *Orrery*

In 1718, he was elected Fellow of the Royal Society, and the year following, read an account of some experiments he had lately made on the
effect of the Suns warmth in raising the sap in trees   These experiments
being highly approved by the Royal Society, he was encouraged to proceed,
which he did, and in 1727, published them enlarged and improved, under the
title of *Vegetable Statics*, and in 1733, he added another volume, under the
title of *Statical Essays*   In 1732, he was appointed one of the Trustees for
establishing a new Colony in *Georgia*   On the 5th of July 1733, the University of *Oxford* honoured him with a *diploma* for the Degree of Doctor in
Divinity)

tees for *Georgia*.   The next day they took a walk
to see Mr *Pope*'s house and gardens, " Justly, he
" observes, called a burlesque on human greatness "
He adds, " I was sensibly affected with the plain
" Latin sentence on the Obelisk, in memory of his
" mother ----*Ah Editha, Matrum optima, Mulierum*
" *amantissima, vale !* * How far superior to the most
" laboured Elegy which he, or *Prior* himself could
" have composed "

As *Georgia* was supposed to be under the Jurisdiction of the Bishop of *London*, Mr *Wesley* took an
early opportunity of waiting on his Lordship with
the Count's proposition.   But the Bishop refused to
meddle in that business   He waited again on the
Bishop of *Oxford*, and informed him the Bishop
of *London* declined having any thing to do with
Georgia, alleging that it belonged to the Arch-

Divinity; a mark of distinction the more honourable, as it is not usual for
one University to confer academical honours on those who were educated at
another   In 1739, he printed a volume in octavo, entitled Philosophical
Experiments on Sea-water, Corn, Flesh, and other substances.   In 1742, he
read before the Royal Society an account of an instrument he had invented
called a *Ventilator*, for conveying fresh air into mines, hospitals, prisons, and
the close parts of ships, which was used with great success, not only for these
purposes, but also for preserving corn sweet in Granaries, &c   Many of his
papers are printed in the Philosophical Transactions, and some he published,
for more general usefulness, in the Gentleman's Magazine

Dr *Hales* was several years honoured with the friendship of his Royal
Highness, *Frederick* Prince of *Wales*, who frequently visited him, and took
a delight in surprising him in the midst of his curious researches into the
various parts of Nature   The Prince dying in 1750, Dr *Hales* was appointed Almoner to her Royal Highness, the Princess Dowager, without
his solicitation or knowlege   In the Church he held the perpetual Curacy
of *Teddington*, near *Twickenham*, and the Living of *Farringdon* in *Hampshire*
He objected to any other preferment, for when his late Majesty nominated
him to a Canonry of *Windsor*, he engaged the Princess to prevail with his
Majesty to recall his nomination   He was remarkable for benevolence,
cheerfulness and temperance   He died at *Teddington* in 1761, in the 84th
year of his age

* Ah *Editha*, the best of Mothers, the most loving of women, farewel !

---

bishop to unite the *Moravians* with the *English*
Church. He replied that it was the Bishop of
London's proper office. " He bid me, adds Mr.
" *Wesley*, assure the Count, we should acknowledge
" the *Moravians* as our brethren, and one Church
" with us "---The Count seemed resolved to carry
his people from *Georgia*, if they might not be permitted to preach to the *Indians* ---He was very desirous to take Mr. *Charles Wesley* with him into
Germany

Mr. *Wesley* spent this year in attending on the
Trustees and the Board of Trade, in visiting his
friends in *London, Oxford,* and different parts of the
country, and his brother and mother in the West
of *England.* He preached occasionally at the places
which he visited   and was every where zealous for
God, and remarkably useful to a great number of
persons by his religious conversation.

In August he was requested to carry up the Address from the University of *Oxford,* to his MAJESTY.
Accordingly, on the 26th, he waited on the KING
with the Address, at *Hampton*-Court, accompanied
with a few friends. They were graciously received,
and the Arch-Bishop told him, he was glad to see
him there. They kissed their Majesties' hands,
and were invited to dinner. Mr. *Wesley* left the
dinner and the company, and hasted back to Town
The next day he waited on his ROYAL HIGHNESS '
the PRINCE of WALES, and dined at St *James's*

Mr. *Wesley* did not experience that peace and
happiness in religion, nor that renewal of his heart
in holiness, which he earnestly laboured to attain.
He was not therefore satisfied with his present state.
On

On the 31ſt of Auguſt he conſulted Mr *Law*, the ſum of whoſe advice was, "Renounce yourſelf, and "be not impatient "----In the beginning of September he conſulted him again, and aſked ſeveral queſtions, to which Mr *Law* gave the following anſwers. "With what Comment ſhall I read the "Scriptures?" None. "What do you think of "one who dies unrenewed while endeavouring after "it?" It neither concerns you to aſk, * nor me to anſwer "Shall I write once more to ſuch a per- "ſon?" No "But I am perſuaded it will do him "good" Sir, I have told you my opinion "Shall "I write to you? Nothing I can either ſpeak or "write will do you any good "

To oblige Mr *Oglethorpe*, Mr *Weſley* ſtill held his office of Secretary, and had formed a reſolution to return to *Georgia* About the middle of October, he was informed at the Office, that he muſt ſail in three weeks This appointment however did not take place, and his mother vehemently proteſted againſt his going back to *America*, but this did not alter his reſolution

In the beginning of February 1738, *Peter Bohler* arrived in *England*, about the time Mr *John Weſley* returned from *Georgia*. *Bohler* ſoon became acquainted with the two brothers, and on the 20th of this month prevailed with Mr *Charles Weſley* to aſſiſt him in learning *Engliſh* Mr *Charles* was now at *Oxford*, and *Bohler* ſoon entered into ſome cloſe converſation with him, and with ſome Scholars who

---

* Mr *Weſley* found that he was not renewed, and thought he might die while endeavouring after it. The queſtion therefore was to him of ſerious importance.

were

were ferious.   He preffed upon them the neceffity
of converfion; he fhewed them that many who had
been awakened, had fallen afleep again for want of
attaining to it   He fpoke much of the neceffity of
prayer and faith, but none of them feemed to underftand him.

Mr. *Charles Wefley* was immediately after this,
taken ill of a pleurify   On the 24th, the pain became fo violent as to threaten fudden death. While
in this ftate, *Peter Bohler* came to his bed fide.   " I
" afked him, adds Mr *Wefley*, to pray for me.   He
" feemed unwilling at firft, but beginning faintly,
" he raifed his voice by degrees, and prayed for my
" recovery with ftrange confidence   Then he took
" me by the hand and calmly faid, You will not die
" now.   I thought within myfelf, I cannot hold
" out in this pain till morning---He faid, " Do you
" hope to be faved ?" I anfwered, yes   " For what
" reafon do you hope to be faved ?" Becaufe I have
ufed my beft endeavours to ferve God   He fhook
his head and faid no more   I thought him very
uncharitable, faying in my heart, " What! are not
" my endeavours a fufficient ground of hope?
" Would he rob me of my endeavours ? I have no-
" thing elfe to truft to "

Mr *Wefley* was now bled three times in about
the fpace of twenty-four hours, after which the
difeafe abated, and he foon began gradually to recover his ftrength   As he ftill retained his office,
and his intention of returning to *Georgia* with Mr.
Oglethorpe, he was called upon to embark before he
was perfectly recovered.   The Phyficians abfolutely
forbid him to attempt the voyage, if he regarded his
                                                        life.

life They likewise advised him, as friends, to stay
at Oxford, where, being Senior Master in his College,
he might accept of offices and preferment. His
brother urged the same advice, and in compliance
with it, he wrote to Mr Oglethorpe on the 3d of
April, resigning his office of Secretary Mr. Oglethorpe was unwilling to lose him, having now had
ample proof of his integrity and ability, and wrote
for answer, that if he would keep his place, it should
be supplied by a Deputy until he could follow.
But Mr Wesley now finally relinquished his intention
of going back to America

April 24th, he was able to take a ride to Blendon,
where he met with his brother and Mr. Broughton.
The next day, April 25th, Mrs. Delamotte, his
brother, Mr Broughton and himself being met in
their little Chapel, they fell into a dispute whether
conversion was gradual or instantaneous Mr. John
Wesley very positively contended for the latter, *
and his assertions appeared to Mr Charles shocking,
especially when he mentioned some late instances of
gross sinners being converted in a moment. Mrs
Delamotte left the room abruptly " I staid, adds
" Charles, and insisted that a man need not know
" when he first had faith." His brother's obsti-
" nacy, as he calls it, in maintaining the contrary
opinion, at length drove him out of the room Mr.
Broughton kept his ground, not being quite so much
offended as Mr Charles Wesley.

* I continually follow, in the life of Mr Charles Wesley his own private
journal, which was never published, nor intended for publication It is
pleasing to observe the agreement between this and Mr John Wesley's printed
journal where the same circumstances are mentioned by both. See his
Work, Vol. 26 page 261, at the bottom.

This

This warm debate happened early in the morning. After dinner Mr. *Broughton* and Mr *John Wesley* returned to *London*, and Mr. *Charles* began reading *Haliburton*'s life to the family, one instance, and but one, he observes, of instantaneous conversion.

The next day he finished reading *Haliburton*'s life. It produced in him great humiliation, self-abasement, and a sense of his want of that faith which brings *righteousness, peace, and joy in the Holy Ghost*. But these effects soon passed away as a morning cloud. A degree of conviction, however, that possibly he might be wrong, had taken hold of his mind, and continued to make him uneasy. This uneasiness was increased by a return of his disorder on the 28th, when he arrived in *London*. Here *Peter Bobler* visited him again, and prayed with him. Mr *Charles Wesley* now thought it was his duty to consider *Bobler*'s doctrine, and to examine himself whether he was in the faith, and if not, never to rest till he had attained it. Still, however, there was a secret wish within his heart that this new doctrine, as he then thought it, might not be true; and hence arose a joy when he imagined he had found an argument against it. He soon was furnished with an argument from his own experience, which he deemed unanswerable. Having received benefit by bleeding, he was at the sacrament on the first of May, and felt a degree of peace in receiving it. " Now, said he to himself, I have demonstration " against the *Moravian* doctrine, that a man cannot " have peace without assurance of his pardon. I " now have peace, yet cannot say of a surety that " my sins are forgiven." His triumph was very short.

short his peace immediately left him, and he sunk into greater doubts and diſtreſs than before. He now began to be convinced that he had not that faith which puts the true believer in poſſeſſion of the benefits and privileges of the goſpel. For ſome days following he had a faint deſire to attain it, and prayed for it. He then began to ſpeak of the ne‑ceſſity of this faith to his friends, his earneſtneſs to attain it increaſed, and he determined not to reſt till he had the happy experience of it in himſelf

Soon afterwards Mr. *Broughton* called upon him at the houſe of Mr. *Bray.* The ſubject was preſently introduced Mr. *Broughton* ſaid, " As for you Mr. " *Bray,* I hope you are ſtill in your ſenſes, and not " run mad after a faith that muſt be felt." He continued contradicting this doctrine of faith, till he rouſed Mr. *Wesley* to defend it, and to confeſs his want of faith " God help you, poor man, ſaid ' *Broughton,* if I could think that you have not " faith, I am ſure it would drive me to deſpair " Mr. *Wesley* then aſſured him, he was as certain that *he had not the faith of the goſpel,* as he was that he hoped for it, and for ſalvation

It is commonly ſaid, that *paſſion* and *prejudice* blind the mind We ſhould rather ſay, they give the underſtanding a falſe view of objects, by *changing the media* through which it ſees them. Mr. *Broughton* was a man of learning, had been a member of their little ſociety at *Oxford,* and was well diſpoſed to religion He viewed the notion of faith which the two brothers had now embraced, through the *me‑dium* of prejudice, and his underſtanding was con‑fuſed and his judgment perverted He ſeemed to think, that he could not place the abſurdity of their

notion

notion in a ftronger light, than by faying, this faith muft be felt   He thought a man muft be out of his fenfes before he can perfuade himfelf that he muft feel that he has faith.   As if it were poffible for a man to believe a propofition, whatever it may be, and not be confcious that he believes it   or to have doubts, and be totally unconfcious and ignorant of them, the impoffibility of which is evident

Mr *Charles Wefley* now faw, that the gofpel promifes to man a knowledge of God reconciled in *Chrift Jefus*, which he had not attained, that a perfon prepared to receive it as he was by knowing his want of it, muft attain it by clear views of *Chrift*, and a living faith in him, and he became more and more earneft in purfuit of it.   On the 12th of May he waked in the morning, hungering and thirfting after righteoufnefs, *even the righteoufnefs which is of God by faith.*   He read *Ifaiah*, and faw, that unto him were the promifes made.   He now fpent the whole of his time in difcourfing on faith, either with thofe who had it, or with thofe who fought it ; and in reading the Scriptures and prayer

On this day Mr. *Wefley* obferves, that he was much affected at the fight of old Mr. *Ainfworth*, a man of great learning, and near eighty years of age. " Like old *Simeon*, he was waiting to fee the Lord's " falvation, that he might die in peace   His tears, " his vehemency, and child-like fimplicity, fhewed " him upon the entrance of the kingdom of " heaven." Mr. *Ainfworth* * feems to have been

fully

* This is a moft pleafing anecdote of a man of fo much reading and ftudy as Mr *Robert Ainfworth*   It fhews the great goodnefs of his mind, which was not puffed up with extenfive knowledge, acquired by long induftry, nor with the labours of many years, fuccefsfully employed for the promotion of literature and the honour of his country. He was born in *Lancafhire*

fully convinced of the true doctrines of the gofpel,
and to have joined himfelf to this little company
who were endeavouring to know and ferve God as
the gofpel directs   Mr. *Wefley* mentions him afterwards, with great admiration of his fimplicity and
child-like difpofition.

May 17th, Mr. *Wefley* firft faw *Luther* on the
Galatians, which Mr. *Holland* had accidentally met
with   They immediately began to read him;
" And my friend, adds Mr *Wefley*, was fo affected
" in hearing him read, that he breathed fighs and
" groans unutterable   I marvelled that we were
" fo foon and entirely removed from him that
" called us into the grace of Chrift, unto another
" gofpel. Who would believe that our Church
" had been founded on this important article of
" juftification by faith alone? I am aftonifhed I
" fhould ever think this a new doctrine, efpecially
" while our Articles and Homilies ftand unrepealed,
" and the key of knowledge is not yet taken away.
" From this time I endeavoured to ground as many
" of our friends as came to fee me, in this fun-
" damental truth.----Salvation by faith alone----not
" an idle dead faith, but a faith which works by
" love, and is inceffantly productive of all good
" works and all holinefs "

May the 19th, a Mis. *Turner* called upon him,
who profeffed faith in Chrift. Mr *Wefley* afked her
feveral queftions, to which fhe returned the following anfwers.   Has God beftowed faith upon

cafhire in 1660, and was Mafter of a Boarding-School at *Bethnal*-Green,
from whence he removed to *Hackney* ----After acquiring a moderate fortune,
he retired and lived privately We are indebted to him for the beft *Latin*
and *Englifh* Dictionary extant, He died in 1743.

you ?

you ? " Yes he has." Why, have you peace with
God ? " Yes, perfect peace." And do you love
Chrift above all things.   " I do, above all things "
Then you are willing to die   " I am, and would
" be glad to die this moment, for I know that all
" my fins are blotted out, the hand-writing that
" was againft me, is taken out of the way, and
" nailed to the crofs   He has faved me by his
" death, he has wafhed me in his blood, I have
" peace in him, and rejoice with joy unfpeakable
" and full of glory "---Mr. *Wefley* adds, " Her
" anfwers were fo full to thefe and the moft fearch-
" ing queftions I could afk, that I had no doubt of
" her having received the atonement; and waited
" for it myfelf with more affured hope, feeling an
" anticipation of joy on her account "

Religious converfation, efpecially when it is a
fimple artlefs relation of genuine experience, is often
of fingular ufe   Chriftian experience implies a con-
fcioufnefs which a man has in himfelf, that he lives
in the poffeffion of certain fpiritual benefits and
privileges, which the gofpel promifes to thofe who
cordially embrace it, and in hope of others which
he has not yet attained.   Mr. *Wefley* experienced
great humiliation and felf-abafement, he was fully
confcious of his own helpleffnefs and total inability
to reconcile himfelf to God, or to make atonement
for the leaft of his fins, by the beft endeavours to
ferve him.   His whole hope, therefore, of pardon
and falvation was in Chrift, by attaining thofe benefits which the *Holy Jefus*, by the whole procefs of
redemption, had procured for him.   He had already been the means of awakening feveral perfons
to a fenfe of their finfulnefs and danger, by defcribing

scribing the state of his own mind, and shewing them the evidences on which his convictions of sin were founded. And he also was both instructed and encouraged by hearing the experience of those who had attained that knowledge of Christ, and of the power of his resurrection, which he was now earnestly seeking. The practice of thus conversing together on experience, is peculiar to Christians; Christianity being the only religion that was ever published to the world, which leads man to an intercourse and fellowship with God in spiritual things. It is pleasing to observe, that those who associated together, at the very commencement of this revival of religion, immediately fell into this most excellent method of building one another up in their most holy faith. Their daily conversation became a powerful means of keeping their minds watchful against sin, and diligent and zealous in pursuit of holiness, it tended to give consolation, to increase patience under affliction, and to strengthen their confidence of deliverance and victory in God's own time. I believe this method of religious improvement has been more universally and constantly attended to among the *Methodists*, than among any other class of people professing religion In this, I apprehend, they have very much resembled the Primitive Christians, as long as these retained their first zeal and simplicity, which probably was till towards the latter end of the second Century, and in some places much later. What a pity that any denomination of Christians, the *Methodists* in particular, should ever lose *this characteristic* of the followers of Christ.

E

When

When perfons began to relate their experience in
religion, at the period of which I am now fpeaking,
it appeared to many as a new thing in *England*.
The phrafes they made ufe of, had not as yet been
learned by heart, they were the genuine expreffions
of what had paffed in their own hearts, and therefore
fignified fomething fixed and determinate, which
all who experienced the fame things, or their want
of them, would eafily underftand, though to others
they would appear, as they do now, mere cant
phrafes, without any determinate ideas affixed to
them   Mr. *Wefley's* knowledge of himfelf, and
confcious want of peace with God, on a foundation
which cannot be fhaken, furnifhed him with a key
which opened their true meaning   He faw the gofpel contained ample provifion for all his wants, and
that its operation on the mind is admirably adapted
to the human faculties   He perceived, that, however learning might affift him in judging of his experience, and in regulating the means of retaining
and increafing it, yet experience is diftinct both
from learning and mere fpeculative opinion, and
may be, and often is, feparated from them   He
was therefore convinced, that all his learning could
neither give him an experimental knowledge of
Chrift, nor fupply the place of it, and he faw feveral
perfons, who had no pretenfions to learning, rejoicing in it, which made him willing to be taught,
in matters of experience, by the illiterate.   He now
loft the *pride* of *literature*, and fought the kingdom
of heaven as a little child   he counted all things,
as dung and drofs in comparifon of it, and all his
thoughts, his defires, his hopes and his fears, had
fome relation to it   But God did not leave him
                                                    long

long in this state On Whitsunday, May 21st, he
waked in hope and expectation of soon attaining
the object of his wishes, the knowledge of God
reconciled in Christ Jesus. At nine o'clock his
brother and some friends came to him, and sung a
hymn suited to the day. When they left him he
betook himself to prayer Soon afterwards a person
came and said, in a very solemn manner, believe in
the name of *Jesus* of *Nazareth* and thou shalt be
healed of all thine infirmities The words went
through his heart, and animated him with confidence He looked into the Scripture, and read,
" Now Lord, what is my hope ? truly my hope is
" even in thee." He then cast his eye on these
words, " He hath put a new song into my mouth,
" even thankfgiving unto our God, many shall see
" it and fear, and put their trust in the Lord "
Afterwards he opened upon Isaiah xl 1 " Com-
" fort ye, comfort ye my people, saith our God,
" speak comfortably to Jerusalem and cry unto her,
" that her warfare is accomplished, that her ini-
" quity is pardoned, for she hath received of the
" Lord's hand double for all her sins " In reading
these passages of Scripture, he was enabled to view
Christ as set forth to be a propitiation for *his sins*,
through faith in his blood, and received that peace
and rest in God, which he had so earnestly sought.

The next morning he waked with a sense of the
divine goodness and protection, and rejoiced in reading the 107th Psalm, so nobly descriptive, he observes, of what God had done for his soul This
day he had a very humbling view of his own
weakness, but was enabled to contemplate Christ
in his power to save to the uttermost, all those who

come

come unto God by him Many evil thoughts were fuggefted to his mind, but they immediately vanifhed
away   In the afternoon he was greatly ftrengthened
by thofe words in the 43d of Ifaiah, which he
faw were fpoken to encourage and comfort the true
Ifrael of God, in every age of his church   " But
" now thus faith the Lord that created thee, O
" Jacob, and he that formed thee O Ifrael, fear not ;
" for I have redeemed thee, I have called thee by
" thy name, thou art mine   When thou paffeft
" through the waters I will be with thee. and
" through the rivers, they fhall not overflow thee.
" when thou walkeft through the fire, thou fhalt
" not be burned, neither fhall the flame kindle
" upon thee   For I am the Lord thy God, the
" Holy One of Ifrael, thy Saviour "
    Mr Wefley had long been well acquainted with
the Scriptures, he had now an enlarged and diftinct
view of the doctrines of the gofpel, and experienced in himfelf the bleffings it promifeth to thofe
who cordially embrace them   A man thus qualified
to inftruct others, will find many occafions of prayer
and praife, which will fuggeft matter adapted to
particular perfons and circumftances   If he be a
man of tolerable good fenfe and fome vigour of
thought, and efpecially if he have had a liberal
education, he will never want words to exprefs the
ideas and feelings of his own mind.   Such a perfon
will therefore often find a prefcribed form of prayer
to be a reftraint upon the exercife of his own powers,
under circumftances which become powerful incen-
tives to an animated and vigorous exercife of them,
and by varying from the words and matter fuggefted
by the occafion, it will often throw a damp on the
                                                     ardour

ardour of his foul, and in fome degree obftruct the
profit of his devotion   We may obferve likewife,
that a form of prayer becomes familiar by frequent
repetition , and, according to a well-known principle in human nature, the more familiar an object,
or a form of words become, the lefs effect they have
on the mind, and the difficulty is increafed of fixing
the attention fufficiently to feel the full effect which
otherwife they would produce   Hence it is, that
we find the moft folemn forms of prayer, in frequent
ufe, are often repeated by rote, without the leaft
attention to the meaning and importance of the
words, unlefs a perfon be under fome affliction,
which difpofes him to feel their application to himfelf   *Extempore* prayer has therefore a great advantage over fet forms, in awakening and keeping
up the attention of an audience   Whether Mr *Wefley*
had reafoned thus on forms of prayer, I cannot fay ;
but he evidently found them, at this time, to be a
reftraint on the freedom of his devotional exercifes,
and now began to pray occafionally without a form,
with advantage and comfort to himfelf and others.
It was however a new practice with him, and he
feemed furprifed both at his boldnefs and readinefs
in performing it, and hence he fays, " Not unto
" me, O Lord, not unto me, but unto thy name
" be the glory."

Both the Mr *Wefleys* were greatly cenfured by
fome perfons, particularly by their brother *Samuel*,
when they began this practice   I cannot fee any
caufe for cenfure   The moft fenfible and moderate
men have allowed, that a form of prayer may be
ufeful to fome particular perfons in private , and
that it may be proper on fome occafions in public

E 3   worfhip.

worfhip. But the more zealous advocates for forms
of prayer are not fatisfied with this, they wifh to
bind them upon all perfons, as a univerfal rule of
prayer in public worfhip, from which we ought in
no inftance to depart   This appears to me un-
juftifiable on any ground whatever   To fay that
we fhall not afk a favour of God, nor return him
thanks, that we fhall hold no intercourfe with him
in our public affemblies, but in a fet of words dictated to us by others, is an affumption of power in
facred things, which is not warranted either by
Scripture or reafon   it feems altogether as improper as to confine our intercourfe with one another to *prefcribed forms* of converfation.   Were this
reftraint impofed upon us, we fhould immediately
feel the hardfhip, and fee the impropriety of it,
and the one appears to me as ill adapted to edification and comfort, as the other would be.

This day an old friend called upon him, under
great apprehenfions that he was running mad. His
fears were not a little increafed, when he heard him
fpeak of fome inftances of the power and goodnefs
of God   His friend told him that he expected to
fee rays of light round his head, and faid a
good deal more in the fame ftrain   Finding by
Mr. *Wefley's* converfation that he was paft recovery,
he begged him to fly from *London*, and took his leave
in defpair of doing him any good.

May the 23d, he wrote an hymn on his own converfion   Upon fhewing it to Mr. *Bray*, a thought
was fuggefted to his mind, that he had done wrong
and difpleafed God   His heart immediately funk
within him, but the fhock lafted only for a moment, " I clearly difcerned, fays he, it was a device
" of

" of the enemy to keep glory from God. It is
" moft ufual with him to preach humility when
" fpeaking would endanger his kingdom and do
" honour to Chrift. Leaft of all would he have
" us tell what God has done for our fouls, fo ten-
" derly does he guard us againft pride But God has
" fhewed me, that he can defend me from it while
" fpeaking for him   In his name therefore, and
" through his ftrength, I will perform my vows
" unto the Lord, of not hiding his righteoufnefs
" within my heart "

Mr *Wefley* had now fatisfactory evidence that he
was a pardoned finner, accepted of God in Chrift
Jefus, and quickened by his Spirit.   He enjoyed
conftant peace, was extremely watchful over the
motions of his own heart, and had a degree of
ftrength to refift temptation, and to do the will of
God, which he had not found before his juftification, but he felt no great emotion of mind or
tranfport of joy in any of the means of grace   He
now intended to receive the facrament, and was
fearful left he fhould be as flat and comfortlefs in
this ordinance as formerly   he received it without
any very fenfible effect on his mind more than ufual,
but with this difference from his former ftate, that
he found himfelf, after it was over, calm and fatisfied with the goodnefs of God to his foul, and free
from doubt, fear or fcruple, of his intereft in Chrift.
In this way he was early taught by experience, to
place little confidence in any of thofe fudden and
tranfient impreffions which are often made on the
mind in public or private acts of devotion   Nor
was he uneafy becaufe deftitute of that rapturous
joy which fome perfons have experienced   he was

E 4   thankful

thankful for the more calm and more permanent operations of divine grace on the mind, by which his heart was kept in peace, ftaid upon God, and watching unto prayer

May 28, He rofe in great heavinefs, which neither private nor joint prayer with others could remove. At laft he betook himfelf to interceffion for his relations, and was greatly enlarged therein, particularly for a moft profligate finner He fpent the morning with *James Hutton* in prayer, finging and rejoicing In the afternoon his brother came, and after prayer for fuccefs on their miniftry, Mr. *John Wefley* fet out intending to go to *Tiverton*, and Mr. *Charles* began writing his firft fermon after his conversion, " In the name of Chrift his prophet."

He had before this time been the means of leading feveral perfons to a knowledge of themfelves, and to a fenfe of their want of faith in Chrift he was now the inftrument in the hands of God of bringing one to an experimental *knowledge of falvation by the remiffion of fin,* fo that fhe rejoiced in God her Saviour A fevere exercife of faith and patience foon followed. June the 1ft, he found his mind fo exceedingly dull and heavy that he had fcarcely any power to pray. This ftate increafed upon him for feveral days, till at length he became infenfible of any comfort, or of any impreffion of good upon his mind in the means of grace. He was averfe to prayer, and though he had but juft recovered ftrength fufficient to go to Church, yet he almoft refolved not to go at all. when he did go, the prayers and facrament were a grievous burden to him, inftead of a fruitful field, he found the whole fervice a dreary barren wildernefs, deftitute

of

of comfort and profit. He felt what he calls, "A
" cowardly defire of death," to escape from his
prefent painful feelings. He began to examine himfelf, and to enquire wherein his prefent ftate differed
from the ftate he was in before he profeffed faith.
He foon found there was a difference in the following particulars he obferved the prefent darknefs
was not like the former, there was no guilt in it;
he was perfuaded God would remove it in his own
time; and he was confident of the love and mercy
of God to him in Chrift Jefus.----The former ftate
was night, the prefent only a cloudy day, at length
the cloud difperfed, and the Sun of righteoufnefs
again fhone with brightnefs on his foul

This was a moft inftructive exercife. It fhewed
him, 1. His own utter helpleffnefs in the work of
his falvation He found by experience that he
could not produce comfort, or any religious affection
in himfelf when he moft wanted them. The work
is God's, when he gives light and ftrength, man
may work, and he is required to work out his falvation with fear and trembling, but till God begin
the work, man cannot move a ftep in it 2 It
taught him to value the gifts of God which nothing
can purchafe, and to guard them as his treafure,
and not barter them for the goods of this life. 3.
He faw hereby, that if he could not produce comfort and religious affections in himfelf, he was ftill
lefs able to produce them in others, and therefore,
whenever they were experienced under his miniftry,
the work was God's, he was only the mean humble
inftrument in his hand. Thus God prepared
him for great ufefulnefs and guarded him againft
pride. When the trial was over, he faw the excellent

cellent fruits of it, and thanked God that it continued so long.

June the 7th, Dr. *Byrom* * called upon him Mr. *Wesley* had a hard struggle with his bashfulness before he could prevail on himself to speak freely to the Doctor on the things of God   At length he gave him a simple relation of his own experience · this brought on a full explanation of the doctrine of faith, which Dr. *Byrom* received with wonderful readiness

Mr. *Wesley* having recovered strength, began to move about among his friends   He went to *Blendon*, and to some other places in the country, and found, that the more he laboured in the work of the ministry, the more his joy and happiness in God was increased   He was remarkably diligent, zealous, and successful wherever he went, seldom staying a night or two in any place, but several persons were convinced of the truth and converted to God   In this journey he met with the Rev Mr *Piers*, and on the 9th of this month, in riding to *Bexley*, spake to him of his own experience, with great simplicity, but with confidence ---He found Mr. *Piers* ready to receive the faith----Greatest part of the day was spent

---

* *John Byrom*, an ingenious poet of *Manchester*, was born in 1691   His first poetical Essay appeared in the Spectator, No 603, beginning, "My "time, O ye Mules was happily spent," which, with two humourous letters on dreams, are to be found in the eighth Volume   He was admitted a Member of the Royal Society in 1724   Having originally entertained thoughts of practising Physic, he received the appellation of Doctor, by which he was always known, but reducing himself to narrow circumstances by a precipitate marriage, he supported himself by teaching a new method of writing Short Hand, of his own invention, until an estate devolved to him by the death of an elder brother   He was a man of a ready lively wit, of which he gave many humourous specimens, whenever a favourable opportunity tempted him to indulge his disposition   He died in 1763, and a collection of his Miscellaneous Poems was printed at *Manchester*, in two Volumes Octavo, 1773

in

in the fame manner, Mr. *Bray*, who was with Mr. *Wefley*, relating the dealings of God with his own foul, and fhewing what great things God had done for their friends in *London*. "Mr. *Piers* liftened with eager attention to all that was faid, made not the leaft objection, but confeffed that thefe were things which he had never experienced. They then walked, and fung, and prayed in the garden he was greatly affected, and teftified his full conviction of the truth, and defire of finding Chrift. "But, faid he, I muft " firft prepare myfelf by long exercife of prayer " and good works."

The day before Mr. *Wefley* and Mr. *Bray* arrived at *Blendon*, Mr. *Piers* had been led to read the Homily on juftification, by which he was convinced that in him, by nature, dwelt no good thing. This prepared him to receive what thefe meffengers of peace related, concerning their own experience. He now faw that all the thoughts of his heart were evil, and that continually, forafmuch as whatfoever is not of faith is fin.

June the 10th, He became earneft for prefent falvation; he prayed to God for comfort, and was encouraged by reading Luke v 23 "Whether is " it eafier to fay, thy fins be forgiven thee, or to " fay, rife up and walk? But that ye may know " that the Son of Man hath power on earth to for-" give fins, (he faid unto the fick of the palfy) I " fay unto thee arife, and take up thy bed, and go " unto thine houfe," &c. Mr. *Wefley* and Mr *Bray* now converfed with him on the power of Chrift to fave, and then prayed with him, they afterwards read the 65th Pfalm, and all of them were animated with hope in reading, "Thou that heareft
" prayer,

" prayer, unto thee fhall all flefh come. Bleffed is
" the man whom thou choofeft, and recciveft unto
" thyfelf, he fhall dwell in thy court, and fhall be
" fatisfied with the plenteoufnefs of thy houfe, even
" of thy holy temple Thou fhalt fhew us won-
" derful things in thy righteoufnefs, O God of our
" falvation ! Thou art the hope of all the ends of the
" earth," &c. In the continuance of thefe exercifes
alternately, of converfing, reading, and praying together, Mr. *Piers* received power to believe on the
Lord Jefus Chrift, and had peace and joy in believing.

The next day Mr. *Piers* preached on death , and
in hearing him, Mr *Wefley* obferves, " I found great
" joy in feeling myfelf willing, or rather defirous to
" die "---This however did not proceed from impatience, or a fear of the afflictions and fufferings of
life, but from a clear evidence of his acceptance in
the beloved After fermon they went to the houfe of
Mr. *Piers*, and joined in prayer for a poor woman
in deep defpair then going down to her, Mr.
Wefley afked whether fhe thought God was love,
and not anger, as Satan would perfuade her ? He
fhewed her the gofpel plan of falvation , a plan
founded in mercy and love to loft perifhing finners.
She received what he faid with all imaginable eagernefs. When they had continued fome time together
in prayer for her, fhe rofe up a new creature,
ftrongly and explicitly declaring her faith in the
blood of Chrift, and full perfuafion that fhe was accepted in him.

Mr *Wefley* remained weak in body, but grew
ftronger daily in faith, and more zealous for God
and the falvation of men, great power accompanying
his

his exhortations and prayers   On the evening
of this day, after family prayer, he expounded the
Leſſon, and one of the ſervants teſtified her faith in
Chriſt and peace with God.   A ſhort time afterwards the gardener was made a happy partaker of
the ſame bleſſings.   Mr *Piers* alſo began to ſee the
fruit of his miniſterial labours.   Being ſent for to
viſit a dying woman in deſpair, becauſe ſhe had
done ſo little good, and ſo much evil; he declared
to her the glad tidings of ſalvation by grace, and
ſhewed her, that if ſhe could ſincerely repent and
receive Chriſt by a living faith, God would pardon
her ſins and receive her graciouſly.   This opened
to her view a ſolid ground of comfort, ſhe gladly
quitted all confidence in herſelf, to truſt in Jeſus
Chriſt, and ſhe expreſſed her faith in him by a calm,
chearful, triumphant expectation of death.   Her
fears and agonies were at an end, being juſtified
by faith ſhe had peace with God, and only entered
farther into her reſt, by dying a few hours after.
The ſpectators of this awful joyful ſcene, were
melted into tears, while ſhe calmly paſſed into the
heavenly *Canaan*, and brought up a good report of
her faithful Paſtor, who under Chriſt ſaved her ſoul
from death.

The next day, June the 14th, Mr *Weſley* returned to *London*, and was informed that his brother,
Mr. *John Weſley* was gone to *Hernhuth*.   The news,
he obſerves, ſurprized, but did not diſquiet him.
He ſtaid only two days in *London*, and then returned
with *J. Delamotte* to *Blendon*, and from thence to
Bexley   Here his complaints returned upon him,
and he was obliged to keep his bed   " Deſires
" of death, ſays he, often roſe in me, which I la-
                                                    boured

boured to check, not daring to form any with concerning it." His pains abated, and on the 21ft,
I find him complaining, that feveral days had
elapfed and he had done nothing for God, fo earneftly did he defire to be inceffantly labouring in
the work of the miniftry

In this excurfion Mr. *Wefley* was very fuccefsful
in doing good, but he met with ftrong oppofition
to the doctrine of juftification by faith alone, from
William Delamotte, whom he calls his fcholar, and
from Mrs. *Delamotte*, who was ftill more violent
againft it than her fon, both were zealous defenders of the merit of good works Mr. *Delamotte*
fuppofed, that if men were juftified by faith alone,
without any regard to works, then finners obtaining
this juftification, and dying foon after, would be
equal in heaven with thofe who had laboured many
years in doing good and ferving God But, faid
he, " It would be unjuft in God to make finners
" equal with us, who have laboured many years."
The *Jews* of old reafoned in a fimilar manner concerning the reception of the *Gentiles* into the gofpel
church, on the fame conditions and to the fame privileges with themfelves Their difpofition towards
the *Gentiles* is beautifully defcribed, and gently re-
proved, in the parable of the prodigal fon The
cafes indeed are not perfectly fimilar, the one relating to our ftate in heaven, the other to the bleffings and privileges of the gofpel in this life Mr.
Delamotte's conclufion however, does not follow
from the doctrine of juftification by faith. As all
men have finned, fo all men muft be juftified, or
pardoned, and be admitted to a participation of
gofpel bleffings, as an act of mere grace or favour;
and

and the condition required of man, is, faith alone;
but it is fuch a faith as becomes a practical principle of obedience to every part of the gofpel, fo
far as a man underftands it   Thus far all men,
who hear the gofpel, are equal, they muft be pardoned and accepted by an act of grace or favour,
and the fame condition of receiving thefe bleffings
is required of every man, without any regard to his
works, which are all finful   Our ftate in heaven
will be regulated by a different rule   All who are
faved, will not be treated as equal   *Every man will
be rewarded according to his works,*" that is, according to his improvement in practical holinefs, on
gofpel principles   Heaven will undoubtedly be a
ftate of fociety, this appears evident, not only from
fome paffages of fcripture, but from the faculties
of man, which are formed for focial intercourfe, in
order to obtain the higheft degree of happinefs.
But in a ftate of fociety, the members occupy different ranks and degrees, there are certain honours
and rewards to be beftowed   in heaven thefe will
all be diftributed in proportion to our works, and
the conformity to *Chrift*, to which we may attain in
this life

 Mr. D.lamotte however, thought his conclufion
good, and was animated with zeal againft this new
faith, as it was then commonly called   He collected his ftrong reifons againft it, and filled two
fheets of paper with them   but in fearching the
fcripture for paffages to ftrengthen his arguments,
he met with *Titus* iii 5. "Not by works of righ-
" teoufnefs which we have done, but according to
" his mercy he hath faved us"   This paffage of
Scripture cut him to the heart, deftroyed all confidence

dence in the fpecious reafoning he had ufed on this
fubject, and convinced him he was wrong.   He
burned his papers, and began to feek in earneft that
faith which he had before oppofed.

Mrs *Delamotte* continued her oppofition.   In
reading a fermon, one evening in the family, Mr.
Wefley maintained the doctrine of faith   Mrs. *Delamotte* oppofed.   " Madam, faid Mr *Wefley*, we
" cannot but fpeak the things we have feen and
" heard   I received faith in that manner, and fo have
" more than thirty others in my prefence "   Her
paffion kindled ;   faid fhe could not bear this, and
haftily quitted the room.----Mr. *Wefley* here gives
us fome idea of his fuccefs in converfing and praying with the people.   A month had now elapfed
fince his juftification   A part of this time he had
been confined by ficknefs, and was not yet able to
preach   Notwithftanding this, more than thirty
perfons had been juftified in the little meetings at
which he had been prefent!   Mrs *Delamotte* was
afterwards convinced of the truth, and cordially
embraced it

June the 30th, Mr. *Wefley* received the following
letter from Mr. *William Delamotte.*

" Dear Sir,

" God hath heard your prayers.   Yefterday
" about twelve, he put his *fiat* to the defires of his
" diftreffed fervant , and glory be to him, I have
" enjoyed the fruits of his holy Spirit ever fince.
" The only uneafinefs I feel, is, want of thankful-
" nefs and love for fo unfpeakable a gift.   But I am
" confident of this alfo, that the fame gracious hand
                                        " which

" which hath communicated, will communicate
" even unto the end ---O my dear friend, I am free
" indeed! I agonized some time between darkness
" and light; but God was greater than my heart,
" and burst the cloud, and broke down the partition
" wall, and opened to me the door of faith."

CHAPTER VI.

SECTION IV.

Containing some Account of Mr CHARLES WESLEY'*s*
public MINISTRY, *until he became an* ITINERANT.

If we consider how necessary the gospel is, to the
present and future happiness of men, we shall rea-
dily acknowledge that a minister of it, occupies the
most important office in society, and hence it
becomes a matter of the utmost importance, that
this office be filled with men properly qualified for
it   Christianity is a *practical science*, the theory of
its principles being only preparatory to the practice
of those duties which it enjoins.   A preacher therefore should not only understand the doctrines of the
gospel, and be able to arrange them according to
the natural order in which they are intended to influence the mind, and direct the conduct of life;
but he ought to experience their influence on his

F   own

own heart, and be daily converfant in a practical
application of them to every duty which he owes to
God and man. Here, as in every other practical
art or fcience, principles and practice muft be conftantly united, they illuftrate and confirm each
other Fundamental principles muft firft be learned,
they muft be applied to the heart, fo as to awaken
the confcience to a fenfe of the evil of fin, &c and
have a fuitable influence on our actions   This firft
ftep in chriftian knowledge will prepare the mind
for the fecond, and fo on till we come to the
meafure of the ftature of the fulnefs of Chrift.   If a
minifter of the gofpel be unacquainted with this
practical application of the principles of the chriftian religion to his own heart and life, he is de-
ficient in one of the moft effential qualifications for
his office, whatever may be the degree of his
fpeculative knowledge.

   The obfervations of a Profeffor of Divinity in a
foreign univerfity, on the qualifications of a gofpel
minifter, appear to me fo juft and excellent, that
I fhall take the liberty to tranflate them, and prefent them to the reader

   " If, fays he, an *Evangelical* paftor be only a
" *voice*, a voice crying in the temple, and nothing
" more, as many feem to think, if he be nothing,
" but a man who has fufficient memory to retain a
" difcourfe, and boldnefs fufficient to repeat it be-
" fore a large congregation---If an evangelical
" paftor be only an orator, whofe bufinefs it is to
" pleafe his audience and procure applaufe---then
" we have nothing to do, but to make the voice of
" our pupils as pleafing and fonorous as poffible---
" to exercife their memory, and to give them a bold
                                              and

" and hardened countenance, not to fay impudent--
" to teach them a rhetoric adapted to the pulpit
" and our audiences, and by perpetual decla-
" mation, like the *Sophifts* of old, render them
" prompt and ready in fpeaking with plaufibility
" on any fubject, and to point out to them the
" fources from whence they may draw matter for
" declamation   But the Paftor whom we fhould
" form in our Academies, is fomething much
" greater and more divine than all this   He is a
" man of God, who is influenced by nothing but
" high and heavenly thoughts, of promoting the
" glory of God, of propagating the kingdom of
" Chrift, and deftroying the power of Satan, of
" obtaining daily a more perfect knowledge of that
" fublime fcience on which eternal happinefs de-
" pends, of more widely diffufing it, and more ef-
" ficacioufly perfuading others to embrace it; of
" reftoring fallen chriftianity, binding up the
" wounds of the Church, and healing her divifions.
" ---He is a man whofe bufinefs it is to perform
" and direct all the parts of divine worfhip before
" the whole Church, to offer to God, the defires,
" the prayers, the praifes and thankfgivings of the
" people affembled --- This Paftor is a man divinely
" called, an Embaffador of God fent to men, that
" he may bring as many fouls as poffible, from
" darknefs to light, from the world to Chrift, from
" the power of Satan to God, from the way of per-
" dition to the way of falvation   a man who, by
" public preaching and private inftruction, faith-
" fully explains the word of God, efpecially the
" doctrines of falvation contained in it, and by the
" fimplicity and clearnefs of explanation adapts

" them

" them to the capacity of every individual perfon.
" O tremendous employment !" &c. *

I have no intention, by thefe obfervations, to re-
flect on any denomination of men filling the facred
office; I have introduced them merely with a view
to fhew, what are the qualifications effentially neceffary in a Minifter of the Gofpel, confidering
them as diftinct from thofe peculiarities of opinion
and modes of worfhip by which true Chriftians are
diftinguifhed from one another, and to illuftrate
the character of Mr *Wefley* as a true Gofpel Minifter.
He poffeffed the requifites for his office in no fmall
degree. he had a clear view of the ftate of human
nature, and of the doctrines of the Gofpel, pointing
out God's method of reftoring finners to his favour
and image. Sin blinds the underftanding, hardens
the heart, makes the confcience infenfible of the
defilement of evil, and renders a man carelefs of his
fpiritual and eternal concerns. Like a wife mafter-
builder, he explained and enforced the doctrines of
repentance towards God, and of faith in the Lord
Jefus Chrift, as firft principles in chriftian experience, as the entrance into it, and the foundation on which it is built. His own experience
illuftrated and confirmed the fcriptural views he
had obtained of thefe doctrines. he fpake of them
in their proper order, and defcribed their effects
with clearnefs and firmnefs, not as the uncertain
conjectures of a fpeculative philofophy, but as the
certain practical truths of divine revelation. He
was now in the habit of giving a practical application to the higher principles of the gofpel, in the

* *Werenfelfius* in Differt. de Scopo Doctoris Theologi.

government of his heart and life, and was daily
growing in grace, and in the knowledge of our
Lord and Saviour Jesus Christ, in a way which
could not deceive him, where theory and practice
were thus combined. He was therefore, well prepared for the Ministry, not only by learning and
deep study, in which he had been conversant for
many years, but also by such exercises of the heart,
as led him to a thorough knowledge of human nature, and of the method of salvation laid down in
the gospel. If all the Ministers in *England*, of every
denomination, were thus qualified for their office,
and animated with the same zeal, to propagate the
truths of religion by every means in their power,
what an amazing change should we soon see in the
morals of the people! It is an awful consideration,
that Ministers, who are set for the defence of the
gospel, and the propagation of true christian piety,
should be the hinderances of it in any degree,
through a want of knowledge, experience, diligence
and zeal. It would be well if every Minister would
seriously examine himself on these heads, as Mr.
Wesley did, and keep in view the account which he
must soon give to the great Shepherd and Bishop of
souls.

Though Mr *Wesley* had been very diligent in his
Master's service, since the 21st of May, he had not
yet been able to preach   On Sunday, July 2nd, he
observes, " Being to preach this morning for the
" first time, I received strength for the work of
" the ministry.   The whole service at *Basingshaw*
" Church, was wonderfully animating, especially
" the gospel, concerning the miraculous draught of
" fishes. I preached salvation by faith, to a deeply

attentive

" attentive audience, and afterwards gave the cup.
" Obferving a woman full of reverence, I afked
" her if fhe had forgivenefs of fins? fhe anfwered
" with great fweetnefs and humility, yes, I know it
" now, that I have forgivenefs."

" I preached again at *London*-Wall, without fear
" or wearinefs.   As I was going into the church, a
" woman caught hold of my hand and bleffed me
" moft heartily, telling me fhe had received for-
" givenefs of fins while I was preaching in the
" morning"   In the evening they held a meeting
for prayer, when two other perfons found peace
with God

July 10th, Mr *Wefley*, was requefted by the Rev.
Mr *Sparks*, to go to *Newgate* he went and
preached to the ten malefactors under fentence of
death.   But he obferves it was with a heavy heart.
" My old prejudices, fays he, againft the poffibility
" of a death-bed repentance, ftill hung upon me,
" and I could hardly hope there was mercy for
" thofe whofe time was fo fhort"   But in the
midft of his languid difcourfe, as he calls it, his
mind acquired a fudden confidence in the mercy of
God, and he promifed them all pardon in the name
of Jefus Chrift, if they would even then, as at the
laft hour, repent and believe the gofpel   He adds,
" I did believe they would accept the proffered
" mercy, and could not help telling them, I had no
" doubt but God would give me every foul of
" them."   He preached to them again the next
day with earreftnefs, from the fecond Leffon, when
two or three began to be deeply affected

This day Mr. *Wefley* received a letter from Mr.
William Delamotte, giving an account of his mother.
" I cannot

' I cannot keep peace, fays he, the mercies of
" God come fo abundantly on our unworthy family,
" that I am not able to declare them.   Yet as they
' are his bleffings through your miniftry, I muft
" inform you of them, as they will ftrengthen your
" hands, and prove helpers of your joy ---Great
" then, I believe, was the ftruggle in my mother,
" between nature and grace but God who know-
" eth the very heart and reins, hath fearched her
" out.   Her fpirit is become as that of a little
" child.   She is converted, and Chrift hath fpoken
" peace to her foul   This change was begun in
" her the morning you left us (the 8th) though fhe
" concealed it from you.   The next morning when
" fhe waked the following words of Scripture were
" prefent to her mind. "Either what woman, having
" ten pieces of filver, if fhe lofe one of them, doth
" not light a candle and fweep the houfe diligently
" till fhe find it "   She rofe immediately, took up
" Bifhop *Taylor*, and opened on a place which fo
" ftrongly affected this living faith, that fhe was fully
" convinced.   But the enemy preached humility to
" her, that fhe could not deferve fo great a gift God,
" however, ftill purfued, and fhe could not long for-
" bear to communicate the emotion of her foul to me.
" We played, read, and converfed for an hour The
" Lord made ufe of a mean inftrument to convince
" her of her ignorance of the word of God. Through-
" out that day fhe was more and more enlightened
" by the truth, till at length fhe broke out, " Where
" have I been? I know nothing, I fee nothing;
" my mind is all darknefs, how have I oppofed
" the Scripture!" She was tempted to think, fhe
" was labouring after fomething that was not to be

F 4   attained;

" attained · but Christ did not suffer her to fall · she
" flew to him in prayer and singing, and continued
" agonizing all the evening. The next morning,
" when reading in her closet, she received recon-
" ciliation and peace She could not contain the joy
" attending it   nor forbear imparting to her friends
" and neighbours, that she had found the piece which
" she had lost. Satan in vain attempted to shake her,
" she felt in herself,

> " Faith's assurance, Hope's increase,
> All the confidence of Love."

Mr. *Sparks* asked him if he would preach at St
Hellen's. He agreed to supply Mr *Broughton's*
place, who was at *Oxford*, "Aiming our friends,
" says Mr *Wesley* against the faith " He adds, " I
" preached faith in Christ to a vast congregation,
" with great boldness, adding much extempore "
In his discourses, Mr. *Wesley* proposed the doctrines
of the gospel with clearness, and illustrated them
with great strength of evidence from the Scriptures,
in which he was remarkably ready, and delivering
them in a warm animated manner, he generally
carried conviction to the minds of those who gave
him a fair and candid hearing   After this Sermon,
Mrs *Hind*, with whom Mr *Broughton* lodged, sent
for Mr *Wesley*, and acknowledged her agreement with
the doctrine he had preached, she wished him to
come and talk with Mr *Broughton*, who, she thought,
must himself agree to it

The next day, July 12th, he preached at *Newgate*
to the condemned felons. He visited one of them
in his cell, sick of a fever, a poor Black, who had
robbed his master. " I told him, says Mr. *Wesley*,
" of

‘ of one who came down from heaven to fave loft
" finners, and him in particular.   I defcribed the
" fufferings of the Son of God , his forrows, agony,
" and death   He liftened with all the figns of
" eager aftonifhment.   The tears trickled down
" his cheeks, while he cried,   " What was it
" for me ! Did the Son of God fuffer all this for fo
" poor a creature as me !" I left him waiting for
" the falvation of God "

July 13th, "I read prayers and preached at
" Newgate, and adminiftered the facrament to our
" friends and five of the felons.   I was much af-
" fected and affifted in prayer for them with com-
" fort and confidence ----July 14th, I received the
" facrament from the Ordinary, and fpake ftrongly
" to the poor Malefactors, and to the fick Negro
" in the condemned hole   was moved by his for-
" row and earneft defire of Chrift Jefus.   The next
" day, July 15th, I preached there again, with an
" enlarged heart , and rejoiced with my poor Black,
" who now believes that the Son of God loves him,
" and gave himfelf for him "

" July 17th, I preached at Newgate on death,
" which the malefactors muft fuffer, the day after
" to-morrow   Mr Sparks affifted in giving the
" facrament, and another Clergyman was prefent
‘ Newington afked me to go in the coach with
" him ----At one o'clock, I was with the Black in
" his cell, when more of the malefactors came to
" us.   I found great help and power in prayer for
" them.   One of them rofe all in a fweat (probably
" with the agitation of his mind) and profeffed
" faith in Chrift. I found myfelf overwhelmed with
" the love of Chrift to finners.   The Negro was
                              " quite

" quite happy, and another criminal in an excel-
" lent temper. I talked with one more, concerning
" faith in Chrift he was greatly moved The
" Lord, I truft, will help his unbelief alfo "---
The Clergymen now left them, and Mr. *Wefley* with
feveral others, joined in fervent prayer and thankfgiving at Mr *Bray's* At fix in the evening, he
returned to the prifoners, with Mr. *Bray.* They
talked chiefly with *Hudfon* and *Newington* They
prayed with them, and both feemed deeply affected
Newington declared, that he had fome time before,
felt inexpreffible joy and love in prayer, but was
much troubled at its being fo foon withdrawn.

Mr *Wefley* goes on " July 18th, the Ordinary
" read prayers and preached, I adminiftered the
" facrament to the *Black* and eight more, having
" firft inftructed them in the nature of it ---One
" of them told me, in the cells, that whenever
" he offered to pray, or had a ferious thought,
" fomething came and hindered him, and that it
" was almoft continually with him. After we had
" prayed for him, he rofe amazingly comforted ;
" full of joy and love, fo that we could not doubt,
" but he had received the atonement " In the
evening, he and Mr *Bray*, were locked in the cells,
" We wreftled fays he, in mighty prayer all the
" criminals were prefent, and chearful The
" foldier in particular, found his comfort and
" joy increafe every moment Another, from the
" time he communicated, has been in perfect
" peace Joy was vifible in all their faces.---
" We fang,

                              " Behold

> " Behold the Saviour of mankind,
>   Nail'd to the ſhameful Tree,
> How vaſt the loʋe that him inclin'd,
>   To bleed and die for Thee."

" It was one of the moſt triumphant hours I have
" eʋer known. Yet, on July 19th, I roſe very
" heavy and backward to viſit them for the laſt
" time At ſix in the morning, I prayed and
" ſung with them all together. The Ordinary
" would read prayers, and he preached moſt
" miſerably " Mr *Sparks* and Mr *Broughton*
were preſent, the latter of whom adminiſtered the
ſacrament, and then prayed, Mr. *Weſley* prayed
after him. At half paſt nine o'clock, their irons
were knocked off, and their hands tied, and they
prepared for the ſolemn journey and the fatal hour.
The Clergymen went in a coach, and about eleven
the criminals arrived at *Tyburn*.   Mr *Weſley*, Mr.
Sparks, and Mr *Broughton* got upon the cart with
them the Ordinary endeavoured to follow, but
the poor priſoners begged that he would not, and
the mob kept him down   They were all cheerful;
full of comfort, peace, and triumph, firmly per-
ſuaded that Chriſt had died for them, had taken
away their ſins, and waited to receive them into
paradiſe ---None ſhewed any natural terror of death·
no fear, or crying, or tear   " I never ſaw, ſays
" Mr *Weſley*, ſuch calm triumph, ſuch incredible
" indifference to dying   We ſang ſeveral hymns,
" particularly,

> A guilty, weak and helpleſs worm,
>   Into thy hands I fall,
> Be Thou my Life, my Righteouſneſs,
>   My Jeſus and my All.

" I took

" I took leave of each in particular Mr. *Broughton*
" bid them not to be surprifed when the cart fhould
" draw away. They chcerfully replied, they fhould
" not We left them, going to meet their Lord
" They were turned off exactly at twelve o'clock,
" not one ftruggled for life. I fpoke a few fuitable
" words to the crowd, and returned full of peace
" and confidence of our friends happinefs "

The whole of this awful fcene, mufl have appeared very extraordinary.   The newnefs and fin-
gularity of it, would add greatly to its effects, not
only on the minds of the Clergymen concerned in
it, but on the populace, at the place of execution.
Some, well-meaning perfons, have greatly objected
to the publication of fuch convulfions as thefe, even
fuppofing them pofitible and real, apprehending,
that they may give encouragement to vice among
the lower orders of the people. The poffibility of
fuch converfions, can hardly be difputed, by thofe
who underftand, and believe the New Teftament.
we mufl judge of their reality, by fuch evidence,
as the circumftances of the perfons will admit The
objection againft their publication when they
really happen, for fear they fhould encourage vice,
appears to me without any folid foundation.   It is
pretty certain, the perfons who commit crimes that
bring them to the gallows, have no thoughts either
of heaven or hell, which have any influence on their
actions.   They are fo far from paying any regard to
the publication of thefe converfions, that they mock
and laugh at them Converfion, is the turning of
a finner from his fins to the living God it is a
change, 1. In a man's *judgment* of himfelf, fo that
he condemns his former courfe of life, and the principles

ciples from which he acted even in his best works:
2 In his *will*, he now chooses God and the ways
of God, in preference to vice, under any of its en-
ticing forms . 3. In his affections; he hates the
things he formerly loved, and loves the things
which lead to God and heaven.   To say, that the
publication of such conversions, which in every step
of their progress, condemn sin, can encourage the
practice of it, appears to me little less than a contradiction.   Is it possible, that any person, who has
the least serious thought of heaven, would volun-
tarily choose to go thither by the way of *Tyburn* or
Newgate? Can we for a moment suppose, that a
person who thinks of finally going to heaven, will
plunge himself deeper into sin in order to get there?
that he will bring himself so close to the brink of
hell as *Tyburn* or *Newgate*, (where there is a bare
possibility, but little probability, that he will not
fall into the pit of destruction) in hopes of conversion and heaven? such a conduct would be a
proof of insanity.   It seems to me, as certain a
principle as any from which we can reason, that
the conversion of notorious sinners from vice to
virtue, is a public condemnation of vice, and must
discourage it, in proportion as these conversions are
made known, and firmly believed to be genuine
and real

July 20th, Mr *Wesley* was at the morning prayers
at *Islington*, and had had some serious conversation
with Mr. *Stonehouse*, the Vicar.   The next day, Mr.
Robson confessed that he believed there was such a
faith as Mr *Wesley* and his friends spake of, but
thought it impossible for him to attain it . he
thought also, that it must necessarily bring on a
perfecution,

perfecution, which feems to have had a very un-
favourable influence on his mind, though convinced
in his judgment, of the truth.   In the evening Mr
Chapman, who had embraced the doctrine of juftification by faith, came from Mr. *Broughton*, and
feemed quite eftranged from his friends. He thought
their prefent proceedings would raife a perfecution,
and he inliftcd that there was no neceffity for ex-
pofing themfelves to fuch difficulties and dangers,
in the prefent circumftances of things.   This kind
of *worldly* prudence in propagating the doctrines of
the gofpel, is fure to produce lukewarmnefs and a
cowardly mind, if it do not arife from them   It has
occafioned greater evils to the church of Chrift,
than all the perfecutions that ever happened   It
is this principle of worldly prudence, that has induced fome Minifters to adulterate the moft important doctrines of grace, with the prevailing philofophy of the age in which they have lived, to
make them pleafing and palatable to the more polite and learned part of their congregations   By
this means the Preacher has gained reputation, but
his miniftry has loft its authority and power, to change
the heart and reform the life   the natural powers
of man have been raifed to a fufficiency for every
duty required of him, and the gofpel has been funk
into a mere collection of moral precepts, enforced
by the certain profpect of future rewards and punifh-
ments   In this way the true doctrine of faith, and
of a divine fupernatural influence, accompanying the
means of grace, have been gradually loft fight of,
and at length denied, and the gofpel thus mutilated
has never been found of fufficient efficacy to accomplifh the purpofes for which it was promulgated
                                                    to

to the world. It is remarkable, that in every great
revival of religion, thefe doctrines have been par-
ticulaiy infifted upon, and have generally occafioned
fome oppofition, both from the wife and ignorant
among mankind.   And when the profeffors of religion of any denomination, wifhing to avoid perfecution and become more refpectable in the eyes of
men, have either concealed the truth, or debafed it
by philofophical explanations, the offence of the
crofs indeed ceafed, but the glory of the gofpel departed from them. they became lukewarm, and
gradually dwindled away, unlefs held together by
fome temporal confideration, having a name to live,
but were dead

I cannot, on the contrary, commend the rafh intemperate zeal of fome young converts in religion,
who have often, both in ancient and modern times,
invited perfecution by their own imprudence , either
by ill-timed reproofs, or an improper introduction
of their religious fentiments in difcourfe.   Nor can
I approve of the rude vulgarity, which has fome
times been ufed both in converfation and in the
pulpit, under a pretence of fpeaking the plain truths
of the gofpel.   There is a *medium* between thefe
extremes , and I would fay, to myfelf, and to the
reader, *medio tutiffimus ibis*, the middle path is the
fafeft, though perhaps the moft difficult to keep on
fome trying occafions.

Had Mr *Wefley* and his brother liftened to the
Syren fong of eafe and reputation, they would never
have been the happy inftruments of fo much good
as we have feen produced by their means   On this
occafion Mr *Wefley* faid to Mr *Chapman*, "I be-
" lieve every doctrine of God, muft have thefe two
                                  " marks,

" marks, 1. It will meet with opposition from men
" and devils, 2 It will finally triumph and pre-
" vail. I expressed my readiness to part with him,
" and all my friends and relations for the truth's
" fake   I avowed my liberty and happiness, fince
" Whitfunday, made a bridge for a flying enemy,
" and we parted tolerable friends "

July 24th, He preached on juftification by faith,
at Mr. *Stonehoufe* s, who could not yet conceive how
God can juftify the ungodly, upon repentance and
faith in Chrift, without any previous holinefs   He
feemed to think that a man muft be fanctified before he can know that he is juftified.   It is probable Mr. *Stonehoufe* did not confider, that, to juftify, in the language of St *Paul*, is to pardon a re-
penting believing finner, as an act of grace, not for
the fake of any previous holinefs in him, but in and
by Jefus Chrift, with whom he is then united by a
living faith, and entitled to fuch gofpel bleffings as
may lead him on to true holinefs of heart and life --
This day Mr. *Wefley* agreed with Mr. *Stonehoufe*, to
take charge of his Parifh, under him as Curate
after which, he read prayers at *Iflington* almoft every
day, and had frequent opportunities of converfing
with Mr *Stonehoufe*, and of explaining the nature of
juftification, and of juftifying faith

July 26th, Mr *Wefley* was at *Blendon*. Here Mrs.
Delamotte called upon him to rejoice with her in
the experience of the divine goodnefs   She then
confeffed, that all her defire had been to affront,
or make him angry   fhe had watched every word
he fpake, had perfecuted the truth, and all who
profeffed it, &c ---A fine inftance of the evidence
and power of gofpel truth, to fubdue a mind blinded
by the moft obftinate prejudice.   Mr.

Mr *Wesley* was now inceffantly employed in his blessed Master's fervice, either in reading prayers and preaching in the Churches, or holding meetings in private houfes, for prayer and expounding the Scriptures, and the number of perfons convinced of fin, and converted to God, by his miniftry, was aftonifhing ----Auguft 3, he obferves, " I corrected " Mr *Whitfield*'s Journal for the prefs, my advice " to fupprefs it, being over-ruled " In the end of this month he went to *Oxford*, where he faw and converfed with Mr. *Gambold*, Mr *Kinchin*, and feveral others of his old friends, who furprifed him by their readinefs to receive the doctrine of faith.

The number of perfons who attended their evening meetings in *London*, were now much increafed. September the 10th, he tells us, that, after preaching at Sir *George Wheeler*'s Chapel in the morning, and at St *Botolph*'s in the afternoon, he prayed and expounded at *Sims's* to above three hundred attentive hearers Saturday, Sept 16th, in the evening, Mr *John Wesley* returned from *Hernhuth*, when he and Mr *Charles Wesley* took fweet counfel together, and compared their experience in the things of God On the 22nd, in expounding the firft chapter of the Epiftle to the *Ephefians*, at *Bray*'s, a difpute arofe, concerning abfolute predeftination. This is the firft time I find any mention of this mifchievous difpute. Mr *Wesley* fays, " I en_ " tered my proteft againft that doctrine "

Mr *Wesley*, by the daily exercife of preaching, expounding, exhorting, and praying with the people, had now acquired fome degree of boldnefs in public fpeaking, the great and leading doctrines of the gofpel were become familiar to his mind, and ex-

G

preffion

preffion flowed natural and eafy in converfing on
them   He preached at *Iflington*, October 15th, and
added to his notes, a good deal *extempore*. On Friday
the 20th, feeing few people prefent, at St. *Antholin's*,
he thought of preaching *extempore*.   " I was afraid,
" fays he, yet ventured, trufting in the promife,
" Lo ! I am with you always.   I fpoke on juf-
" tification, from the third chapter of the Epiftle
" to the *Romans*, for three quarters of an hour,
" without hefitation.   Glory be to God, who
" keepeth his promife for ever "

This day, he and his brother Mr *John Wefley*
waited on Dr *Gibfon*, * the Bifhop of *London*, to anfwer the complaints which he had heard alleged

---

* Dr *Edmund Gibfon*, Bifhop of *London*, was born in *Weftmoreland* in
1669   He applied himfelf early and vigoroufly to learning, and difplayed
his knowledge in feveral writings, which recommended him to the patronage
of Archbifhop *Tennifon*, who made him his domeftic Chaplain   Being now
a Member of Convocation, he engaged in a controverfy, in which he defended his Patron's rights, as Prefident, in eleven Pamphlets   He afterwards enlarged them on a more comprehenfive plan, containing a view of
the legal duties and rights of the *Englifh* Clergy, which was publifhed under the title of *Codex Juris Feclefiaftici Anglicani*, in folio   Archbifhop *Tennifon* dying in 1715, and Dr *Wake*, Bifhop of *Lincoln*, being made Archbifhop of *Canterbury*, Dr *Gibfon* fucceeded him as Bifhop of *Lincoln*, and
in 1720, was promoted to the Bifhoprick of *London*   He governed his
Diorefe with the moft exact care, but was extremely jealous of the leaft
privileges belonging to the Church   He approved of the toleration of
Proteftant Diffenters, but oppofed all attempts, to procure a repeal of
the Corporation and Teft Acts   His oppofition to thofe licentious affemblies, called *Mafquerades*, gave great umbrage at Court, and prevented further preferment   His paftoral letters are juftly efteemed mafterly productions   Befide the *Codex* above-mentioned, he publifhed, 1 An edition
of *Drummond's Polemo-Middiana*, and *James V* of *Scotland's Cantilena Ruf
tica*, with notes   2 The *Cronicon Saxonicum*, with a Latin tranflation, and
notes   3 *Reliquiæ Spelmanniana*   4. An edition of *Quintilian de Arte
Oratoria*, with notes   5 An Englifh tranflation of *Camden's Britannia*, with
additions, 2 vols folio   6 A number of fmall pieces collected together and
printed in 3 vols folio —He died in September, 1748   He was a fteady
friend to the eftablifhed Church, but a great enemy to perfecution a great
Economift, but liberal and beneficent   Dr *Crow*, who had once been his
Chaplain, left him two thoufand five hundred pounds, the whole of which,
the Bifhop gave to Dr *Crow's* own relations who were very poor   He cor-
refponded with Dr *Watts*, and expreffed a friendly concern for the interefts
of religion, among Diffenters as well as in his own Church.

againft

against them, respecting their preaching an absolute
assurance of salvation.   Some of the Bishop's words
were, " If by assurance you mean, an inward per-
" suasion, whereby a man is conscious in himself,
" after examining his life by the law of God, and
" weighing his own sincerity, that he is in a state
" of salvation, and acceptable to God, I do not see
" how any good christian can be without such an
" assurance."   They answered, " We do con-
" tend for this, but we have been charged with
" Antinomianism, because we preach justification
" by faith alone.   Can any one preach otherwise,
" who agrees with our Church and the Scriptures ?"'
Indeed by preaching it strongly, and not sufficiently
inculcating good works as following justification,
and being the proper evidences of it, some have
been made Antinomians in theory rather than practice, particularly in the time of King *Charles.*
" But, said the Bishop, there is a very heavy charge
" brought against us, Bishops, in consequence of
" your having re-baptized an adult, and alleged
" the Archbishop's authority for doing it."   Mr.
John Wesley answered, that he had expressly declared
the contrary, and acquitted the Archbishop from
having any hand in the matter, but added, " If a
" person dissatisfied with Lay-Baptism, should de-
" sire Episcopal, I should think it my duty to ad-
" minister it, after having acquainted the Bishop,
" according to the Canon."   " Well, said the
" Bishop, I am against it myself, when any one has
" had Baptism among the Dissenters "--The Bishop
here shews that he possessed a candid and liberal
mind ----Mr. *Charles Wesley* adds, " My Brother
" enquired whether his reading in a religious So-

" ciety made it à Conventicle? His Lordship
" warily referred us to the Laws but, on urging
" the question, "Are religious Societies Conven-
" ticles?" He answered, "No, I think not how-
" ever you can read the Acts and Laws as well as I,
" I determine nothing." We hoped his Lordship
" would not, henceforward, receive an accusation
" against a Presbyter, but at the mouth of two or
" three witnesses He said, "No, by no means,
" and you may have free access to me at all times.
" We thanked him and took our leave "

Tuesday, November 14th, Mr. *Charles Wesley* had
another Conference with the Bishop of *London*, without his Brother " I have used your Lordship's
" permission, said he, to wait upon you A woman
" desires me to baptize her, not being satisfied with
" her baptism by a Dissenter " She says, sure and
unsure, is not the same. He immediately took fire,
and interrupted me. " I wholly disapprove of it.
" it is irregular." My Lord, said Mr. *Wesley*, I
did not expect your approbation, I only came in
obedience, to give you notice of my intention. " It
" is irregular, I never receive any such informa-
" tion, but from the Minister " My Lord, your
rubric does not so much as require the Minister to
give you notice, but any discreet person I have
the Minister's leave. " Who gave you authority to
" Baptize?" Your Lordship, * and I shall exercise
it in any part of the known world " Are you a
" licensed Curate?" I have the leave of the proper
Minister. " But do you not know, that no man
" can exercise parochial duty in *London*, without

* See above, page 108.

" my leave? It is only *sub silentio.*" But you know, many do take that permission for authority, and you yourself allow it. " It is one thing to " connive, and another to approve; I have power " to inhibit you." Does your Lordship exert that power? Do you now inhibit me? "O why will " you push matters to an extreme? I do not in- " hibit you." Why then, my Lord, according to your own conceffion, you permit, or authorise me. " I have power to punish and to forbear." To punish that feems to imply, that I have done fome- thing worthy of punishment, I should be glad to know, that I may anfwer. Does your Lordship charge me with any crime? " No, no, I charge " you with no crime." Do you then difpenfe with my giving you notice of any Baptisms in future? " I neither difpenfe, nor not difpenfe "---" He cenfured *Lawrence* on Lay-Baptifm, and blamed my Brother's Sermon as inclining to *Antinomianifm.* I charged Archbishop *Tillotfon* with denying the faith, he allowed it, and owned they ran into one extreme to avoid another. He concluded the confe- rence, with " Well Sir, you knew my judgment be- fore, and " you know it now, good morrow to you."

November 22nd, Mr. *Wefley* fet out in the coach, to vifit his friends at *Oxford.* We may obferve, that he was in the firft part of his Miniftry, very much alone, having preached the Gofpel, fully, and boldly, in many of the Churches, in *Newgate,* and at *Iflington;* while his Brother was in *Germany,* and Mr *Whitefield* in *America.* He had met with little oppofition, except from fome private friends, and at *Iflington;* where the polite part of his congregation, had fometimes fhewn a want of regard to decency

in their behaviour, and many had frequently gone
out of the Church.   He now clearly faw, that a
faithful difcharge of his duty, would expofe
him to many hardfhips and dangers, and though he
generally had great confidence in God, yet he had
alfo his feafons of dejection, when he was ready to
fink under the preffure of his difficulties, which
made him fully fenfible of his weaknefs, and, that
he muft be fupported in his work by a power not
his own.   On the 25th, at *Oxford*, he experienced
great depreffion of mind ; " I felt, fays he, a pining
" defire to die, forefeeing the infinite dangers and
" troubles of life."   But as he was daily engaged
in the exercife of fome part or other of his minifterial office, *the times of refreshing, from the prefence
of the Lord*, frequently returned upon him, his
ftrength was renewed, and he was again enabled to
go on his way rejoicing.

Mr. *Whitefield* was at this time, at *Oxford*, and
was earneft with Mr. *Wesley* to accept a College
Living.   This gives pretty clear evidence that no
plan of Itinerant preaching was yet fixed on, nor indeed thought of. had any fuch plan been in agitation
among them, it is very certain Mr. *Whitefield* would
not have urged this advice on Mr *Charles Wesley*,
whom he loved as a Brother, and whofe labours he
highly efteemed.

Decembei the 11th, Mr *Wesley* left *Oxford*, and
coming to *Wickham* in the evening, took up his
lodgings with a Mr. *Hollis*, to whom, I fuppofe,
he had been recommended.   " He entertained me,
" adds Mr. *Wesley*, with his *French* Prophets, who
" in his account, are equal, if not fuperior, to the
" Prophets of the Old Teftament.   While we were
                                        " undreffing,

" vndreffing, he fell into violent agitations, and
" gabbled like a *Turkey*-Cock I was frightened,
" and began exorcifing him, with, Thou deaf and
" dumb devil, &c He foon recovered from his
" fit of infpiration.----I prayed and went to bed,
" not half liking my bed-fellow; nor did I fleep
" very found with Satan fo near me." He efcaped,
however, without harm, and came fafe to *London*
the next day, where he heard a glorious account of
the fuccefs of the Gofpel at *Iflington*, fome of the
fierceft oppofers being converted

January 5th, 1739, Mr *Wefley* gives us another
convincing proof, that no plan of becoming *Itine-*
rants, was yet formed. He fays, " My Brother,
" Mr. *Seward, Hall, Whitefield, Ingham, Kinchin*,
" and *Hutchins*, all fet upon me to fettle at *Oxford* "
----But he could not agree to their propofal, without being more fully fatisfied that it was the order
of Providence. This advice, however, and a fimilar
inftance above-mentioned, plainly fhew, that their
views at prefent extended no further than to preach
the Gofpel in the Churches, wherever they had opportunity.

About this time fome perfons being greatly affected under the public prayers and preaching, fell
into violent convulfive motions, accompanied with
loud and difmal cries. This gave great offence to
many, and occafioned difputes. Mr. *Charles Wefley*
mentions this circumftance in his Journal on the
10th of January " At the Society, fays he, We
" had fome difcourfe about agitations . no fign of
" grace, in my humble opinion."

February 21ft, Mr. *Wefley* and his Brother,
thought it prudent to wait on Dr. *Potter*, then

Archbifhop

Archbifhop of *Canterbury*, to prevent any ill impreffion which the various falfe reports of their proceedings might produce on his mind "He fhewed
"us, fays Mr *Wefley*, great affection · fpoke mildly
"of Mr *Whitefield*, cautioned us to give no more
"umbrage than was neceffary for our own defence
"to forbear exceptionable phrafes , to keep to the
"doctrines of the Church ---We told him, we ex-
"pected perfecution would abide by the Church
"till her Articles and Homilies were repealed ----
"He affured us, he knew of no defign in the Gover-
"nors of the Church, to innovate , and neither
"fhould there be any innovation while he lived.
"He avowed juftification by faith alone , and fig-
"nified his gladnefs to fee us, as often as we
"pleafed."

"From him we went to the Bifhop of *London* ;
"who denied that he had condemned, or even
"heard much concerning us. He faid Mr *White-*
"*field's* Journal was tainted with enthufiafm,
"though he himfelf was a pious well-meaning
"youth. He warned us againft Antinomianifm,
"and difmiffed us kindly."

March 28th, "We diffuaded my Brother from
"going to *Briftol*, from an unaccountable fear that
"it would prove fatal to him He offered him-
"felf willingly, to whatever the Lord fhould ap-
"point. The next day he fet out, * recommended
"by us to the grace of God. He left a bleffing
"behind him. I defired to die with him."

* This exactly accords with Mr. *John Wefley's* printed Journal. See his
Works, vol. 27 page 64.

Soon.

Soon after this, a Mr. *Shaw*, began to give fome
difturbance to their little Society, by infifting, that
there is no Priefthood, that is, there is no order of
men in the Chriftian Miniftry, who, properly fpeaking, exercife the functions of a Prieft   that he himfelf had as good a right to Baptize and Adminifter
the Sacrament, as any other man   It appears by his
claiming a right to Baptize, &c that he was a Lay-
Man, and it muft be acknowledged by all parties,
that Chriftian Minifters, confidered as an order in
the Church diftinguifhed by their office from other
believers, are no where, in the New Teftament,
called Priefts. " I tried in vain, fays Mr. *Wefley*,
" to check Mr. *Shaw* in his wild rambling talk
" againft a Chriftian Priefthood.   At laft I told
" him, I would oppofe him to the utmoft, and
" either he or I, muft quit the Society.   In ex-
" pounding, I warned them ftrongly againft Schifm,
" into which Mr. *Shaw*'s notions muft neceffarily
" lead them   The Society were all for my Brother's
" immediate return ---April 19th, I found Mr.
" *Stonehoufe* exactly right (that is, in his notions
" on the Priefthood) warned Mrs. *Vaughan* and
' *Brookmans*, againft *Shaw*'s peftilent errors   I
" fpoke ftrongly at the *Savoy* Society, in behalf of
" the Church of *England*."

April 24th, Mr *Whitefield* preached at *Fetter Lane*,
being returned from *Briftol*, where he firft preached
in the open air, and in fome fenfe opened the way
to an Itinerant Miniftry, which was fure to follow
this ftep, but of which none of them hitherto,
feem to have entertained the leaft conception   It
feems that *Howel Harris* came to *London* with him ;
" A man, fays Mr. *Wefley*, after my own heart.---
" Mr.

" Mr. *Whitefield* related the difmal effects of *Shaw*'s
" doctrine at *Oxford* Both he and *Howel Harris*
" infifted on *Shaw*'s expulfion from the Society.
" April 26th, Mr. *Whitefield* preached in *Iflington*
" Church-Yard the numerous audience, could not
" have been more affected within the walls ----
" Saturday the 28th, he preached out again. After
" him, Mr. *Bowers* got up to fpeak I conjured
" him not but he beat me down, and followed
" his impulfe I carried many away with me."
This laft circumftance, is the more worthy of notice, as it is, fo far as I can find, the firft inftance of
a Lay-Man attempting to preach among the Methodifts It muft be obferved however, that, it was not
with approbation, but by violence. He was not
difcouraged, however, by this oppofition. and it
is probable, that, about this time, feveral other
Lay-Men began to expound or preach, for on the
16th of May, a difpute arofe at the Society in
Fetter-Lane, about Lay-Preaching, which certainly
implies that fome Lay-Men had begun to preach,
and that the practice was likely to become more
general. Mr *Wefley* obferves, that he and Mr. *W.*
declared againft it.

May 25th, Mr *Clagget* having invited Mr. *Wefley*
to *Broadoaks*, he went thither, and preached to four
or five hundred attentive hearers. May 29th, " A
" Farmer, fays he, invited me to preach in his field.
" I did fo, to about five hundred, on, *Repent*
" *for the kingdom of heaven is at hand.* On the
" 31ft, a Quaker fent me a prefling invitation to
" preach at *Thackftead.* I fcrupled preaching in
" another's Parifh, till I had been refufed the
" Church.----Many Quakers, and near feven hun-
                                        " dred

" dred others, attended, while I declared in the
" highways, the Scripture hath concluded all under
" fin."

June the 6th, Two or three, who had embraced
the opinions of *Shaw*, declared themfelves no longer
Members of the Church of *England*. " Now, fays
" Mr. *Wefley*, am I clear of them by renouncing
" the Church, they have difcharged me."---About
this time the *French* Prophets raifed fome difturbance in the Society, and gained feveral Profelytes,
who warmly defended them. June 12th, two of
them were prefent at a meeting, and occafioned
much difputing. At length Mr. *Wefley* afked,
" Who is on God's fide ? Who for the old Pro-
" phets, rather than the new ? Let them follow
" me They followed me into the Preaching-
" room. I expounded the Leffon; feveral gave
" an account of their converfion, dear Brother
" *Bowers* confeffed his errors, and we rejoiced and
" triumphed in the name of the Lord our God."

June the 19th, Mr. *Wefley* was at *Lambeth*, with
the Archbifhop, who treated him with much feverity.
His Grace declared he would not difpute, nor
would he, as yet, proceed to excommunication.---
It does not appear that the Archbifhop condemned
the doctrines Mr. *Wefley* preached, but the manner
of preaching them: it was irregular, and this was
judged a caufe fufficient for condemning him.
Regularity is undoubtedly neceffary, in the government both of Church and State. But when a fyftem
of Rules and Orders purely human, is fo eftablifhed
for the government of the Church, as to be made
perpetual, whatever changes may take place in the
ftate of the people; it muft, in many cafes, become
injurious

injurious rather than useful   And when conformity
to such an establishment, is considered as compre-
hending almost all virtue, and made the only road
to favour and preferment in the Church ; and a de-
viation from it, is marked with disgrace, it becomes an idol, at whose altar many will be tempted
to sacrifice their judgment, their conscience, and
their usefulness.   Civil government knows nothing
of this *perpetual sameness* of its regulations and laws,
in all circumstances of the people   And why should
the Church, in regulations which are purely human,
and prudential? The end of regularity, or conformity to a certain established order in the government of the Church, is, the propagation of christian
knowledge, and the increase of true religion, but if
a Minister be so circumstanced, that, regularity
would obstruct, rather than promote his usefulness
in these respects, irregularity becomes his duty, and
ought not to be condemned by others, when no
essential principle of religion is violated, nor any
serious inconvenience follows from it.   In this case,
the end to be attained, is infinitely more important
than any prudential rules to direct the means of attaining it   which should always admit of such al-
terations as circumstances require, to promote the
end intended

Mr *Wesley* bore the Archbishop's reproof with
great firmness, while in his presence, - but after
leaving him, he fell into great heaviness, and for
several days suffered a severe inward conflict.   He
perceived that it arose from the fear of man.   Mr.
Whitefield, urged him to preach in the fields the
next Sunday : by this step he would break down the
bridge, render his retreat difficult or impossible, and
be

be forced to fight his way forward in the work of the Ministry This advice he followed. June 24th, " I prayed, says he, and went forth, in the *Name of* " *Jesus Christ* I found near a thousand helpless " sinners, waiting for the word in *Moorfields*. I " invited them in my Master's words, as well as " name , *Come unto me, all ye that labour and are* " *heavy laden, and I will give you rest* The Lord " was with me, even me, the meanest of his mef– " sengers, according to his promise At St. *Paul's*, " the Pfalms, Leffons, &c for the day, put new " life into me · and fo did the facrament. My " load was gone, and all my doubts and fcruples. " God fhone on my path, and I knew this was his " will concerning me "---I walked to *Kennington– Common*, and cried to multitudes upon multitudes, *Repent ye and believe the Gofpel* The Lord was my ftrength, and my mouth, and my wifdom. O that all would therefore praife the Lord, for his good– nefs !

June 29th, He was at *Wickham*, in his way to *Oxford*. Here, says he, "I heard of much diftur- ' bance occafioned by *Bowers'* preaching in the ' ftreets " Thus early, it appears that Lay– Preaching had commenced, even beyond the So– cieties in *London*, though not with the confent of any of the Clergymen ---The next day he reached *Oxford*, and waited on the Dean, who fpoke with unufual feverity againft Field-preaching, and Mr. *Whitefield*, who may be called the author or founder of Field-preaching , it is perhaps on this account, that he has fo often been fuppofed to be the founder of Methodifm ---July 1ft, he preached a fermon on Juftification, before the Univerfity, with great bold– nefs.

nefs. All were very attentive · one could not help
weeping.----July 2nd, Mr. *Gambold* came to him,
who had been with the Vice-Chancellor, and well
received. " I waited, fays Mr. *Wefley*, on the Vice-
" Chancellor, at his own defire.   I gave him a full
" account of the Methodifts, which he approved,
" but objected to the irregularity of doing good in
" other men's Parifhes.   He charged Mr. *White-*
" *field* with breach of promife, appealed to the
" Dean, and appointed a fecond meeting there.
" All were againft my fermon, as liable to be mif-
" underftood.----July 3d, Mr. *Bowers* had been laid
" hold of, for preaching in *Oxford*.   To-day the
" Beadle brought him to me.   I talked to him
" clofely ; he had nothing to reply, but promifed
" to do fo no more, and thereby obtained his
" liberty.----At night I had another conference
" with the Dean, who cited Mr *Whitefield* to judg-
" ment *   I faid Mr. Dean, he fhall be ready to
" anfwer the citation   He ufed the utmoft addrefs
" to bring me off from preaching abroad, from ex-
" pounding in houfes, and from finging Pfalms.
" He denied juftification by faith, and all vital re-
" ligion."

July 4th, Mr. *Wefley* returned to *London*   On the
8th, he preached to near ten thoufand hearers, by
computation, in *Moorfields*, and the fame day at
Kennington-Common.   His labours now daily increafed upon him ; and his fuccefs, in bringing
great numbers from darknefs to light, and in roufing
the minds of vaft multitudes to a ferious enquiry
after religion, was beyond any thing we can, at

* I fuppofe for fome breach of order.

prefent,

prefent, eafily conceive.   In fuch circumftances as
thefe, it is almoft impoffible for a Minifter, to keep
his mind quite free from all thoughts of felf ap-
plaufe.   He will be led, at firft almoft infenfibly, to
think more highly of himfelf than he ought, to at-
tribute fome part of his fuccefs to his own fuperior
excellencies, and to think too meanly of others.
If his judgment be rightly informed, and his confcience tender, he is fhocked when he difcovers
thefe workings of his mind, and endeavours to fupprefs them · but he foon finds that the thoughts
and propenfities of his heart, are not under the controul of his judgment ; they prefent themfelves on
every occafion againft his will, and are not a little
ftrengthened by the commendations and praifes of
thofe who have been benefited by him.   The natural
temper of the mind, is fometimes fo far awakened
on thefe occafions, as to produce a fevere inward
conflict, bring on great diftiefs, and make a man
afhamed of himfelf in the prefence of God.   Mr.
Wefley felt the full force of the temptations which
arofe from the fuccefs of his miniftry   July 22nd,
he fays, " Never, till now, did I know the ftrength
" of temptation, and energy of fin. Who, that *con-*
" *fults only the quiet of his own mind,* would covet
" great fuccefs ? I live in a continual ftorm , my
" foul is always in my hand ; the enemy thrufts
" fore at me that I may fall, and a worfe enemy
" than the Devil, is, my own heart. *Miror quemquam*
" *prædicatorem falvari.* I wonder any Preacher of the
" Gofpel is faved.——Auguft 7th, I preached repen-
" tance and faith at *Plaiftow,* and at night expounded
" on *Lazarus* dead and raifed, in a private houfe. The
" next

" next day, called on *Thomas Keen,* a mild and can-
" did *Quaker.*----Preached at *Marybone.*----Too well
" pleafed with my fuccefs, which brought upon me
" ftrong temptations   Auguft 10th, I gave Mr
" *Whitefield* fome account both of my labours and
" conflicts."

" Dear George,

" I forgot to mention the moft material occur-
" rence at *Plaiftow,* namely, that a Clergyman was
" there convinced of fin   He ftood under me, and
" appeared throughout my difcourfe, under the
" greateft perturbation of mind.   In our return
" we were much delighted with an old fpiritual
" Quaker, who is clear in juftification ----Friend
" *Keen* feems to have experience, and is right in
" the foundation.----I cannot preach out on the
" week days, for the expence of coach-hire   nor
" can I accept of dear Mr *Steward's* offer, to which
" I fhould be lefs backward, would he follow my
" advice, but while he is fo lavifh of his Lord's
" goods, I cannot confent that his ruin fhould in
" any degree *feem* to be under my hand ----I am
" continually tempted to leave off preaching, and
" hide myfelf like *J. Hutchins.* I fhould then be
" free from temptation, and have leifure to attend
" to my own improvement   God continues to
" work by me, but not in me, that I perceive.----
" Do not reckon upon me, my Brother, in the
" work God is doing, for I cannot expect that he
" fhould long employ one, who is ever longing and
" murmuring to be difcharged."

" To-day, fays Mr *Wefley,* I took *J. Bray* to Mr.
" *Law,* who refolved all his experience into fits, or
natural

" natural affection or fits , and defired him to take
" no notice of his comforts, which he had better be
" without, than have. He blamed Mr *Whitefield's*
" Journal, and way of proceeding , faid, he had
" great hopes that the Methodifts would have been
" difperfed by little and little, into Livings, and have
" leavened the whole lump. I told him my experi-
" ence then, faid he, I am far below you (if you are
" right) not worthy to wipe your fhoes. He agreed
" to our notion of faith, but would have it, that all
" men held it He was fully againft the *Lay-Man's*
" expounding, as the very worft thing both for
" themfelves and others.   I told him, he was my
" fchool-mafter to bring me to *Chrift*, but the
" reafon why I did not come fooner to *Chrift*, was,
" I fought to be fanctified before I was juftified. I
" difclaimed all expectation of becoming fome
" GREAT ONE ---Among other things he faid, were
" I fo talked of, as Mr. *Whitefield* is, I fhould run
" away, and hide myfelf entirely.   I anfwered, you
" might, but God would bring you back, like
" *Jonah*.   He told me, joy in the Holy Ghoft was
" the moft dangerous thing God could give.   I re-
" plied, but cannot God guard his own gifts ? He
" often difclaimed advifing us, feeing we had the
" Spirit of God but mended on our hands, and at
" laft came almoft quite over to us "

It is really wonderful that Mr. *Law* fhould talk
in this manner ! He who wrote the fpirit of prayer,
the fpirit of love, and an Addrefs to the Clergy,
befides many other pieces, in which he fhews, with
great force of reafoning, that a perfon can have no
true religion, without a fupernatural influence of the

H   Spirit

Spirit of God upon his mind, in which he certainly lays a foundation for chriftian experience.

August 12th, He obferves, " I received great " power to explain the good *Samaritan* commu- " nicated at St *Paul's*, as I do every Sunday . con- " vinced multitudes at *Kennington-Common*, from, " Such were fome of you, but ye are wafhed, &c." " And before the day was paft, felt my own fin- " fulnefs fo great, that I wifhed I had never been " born."

August 13th, Mr *Wefley* wrote to Mr. *Seward* as follows. " I preached yefterday to more than ten " thoufand hearers. I am fo buffeted both before " and after, that were I not forcibly detained, I " fhould fly from every human face. If God does " make a way for me to efcape, I fhall not eafily " be brought back again I cannot love adver- " tifing, it looks like founding a trumpet ---I " hope our Brother *Hutchins* will come forth at " laft, and throw away my mantle of referve, which " he feems to have taken up."

Mr. *Whitefield* was now on the point of returning to *America*, and on the 15th of Auguft Mr *Wefley* wrote to him " Let not *Coffart's* opinion of your " Letter to the Bifhop, weaken your hands. *Abun-* " *dans cautio nocet :* * it is the *Moravian* infirmity. " To-morrow I fet out for *Briftol*. I pray you may " all have a good voyage, and that many poor fouls

---

* *Too much caution is hurtful* Some perfons perhaps may think, that neither Mr *Whitefield*, nor any of them ftood in need of this admonition of this however, we are not very proper judges at this diftance of time. It is evident that on many occafions they did ufe much caution Mr *Wefley* fpeaks as though he had fome thoughts of going again to *America*, and he mentions fuch intentions in feveral places , but they never came to any thing fixed and determined.

" may

" may be added to the Church by your miniftry,
" before we meet again   Meet again I am con-
" fident we fhall, perhaps both here and in *America.*
" The will of the Lord be done, with us and by us,
" in time and in eternity !"

CHAPTER V.

Containing fome Account of Mr Charles Wesley's
Labours as an Itinerant Preacher.

AUGUST 16th, Mr *Wefley* entered on the *Itine-*
rant plan   He rode to *Wickham,* and being denied
the Church, would have preached in a private houfe;
but Mr. *Bowers* having been preaching there in the
ftreets, had raifed great oppofition, and effectually
fhut the door againft him   The next day he went
to *Oxford,* and the day following reached *Evefham.*
After being here two or three days, he wrote to his
Brother as follows.

" Dear Brother,

" We left the Brethren at *Oxford* much edified,
" and two Gowns-Men thoroughly awakened   On
" Saturday afternoon God brought us hither, Mr.
" *Seward* being from home, there was no admiffion
" for us, his wife being an oppofer, and having re-

" fufed

" fufed to fee Mr. *Whitefield* before me.   At feven
" in the evening Mr. *Seward* found us at the Inn,
" and took us home.   At eight I expounded in the
" School-Room, which holds about two hundred
" perfons.----On Sunday morning I preached from
" *George Whitefield's* pulpit, the *Wall*, on, " Repent
" ye and believe the Gofpel "   The notice being
" fhort, we had only a few hundreds, but fuch as
" thofe defcribed in the Morning Leffon, " Thefe
" were more noble than thofe of *Theffalonica*, in that
" they received the word with all readinefs of
" mind "   In the evening I fhewed, to near two
" thoufand hearers, their Saviour in the good *Sama-*
" *ritan* ----Once more God ftrengthened me, at
" nine, to open the new Covenant, at the School-
" Houfe, which was crouded with deeply attentive
" finners."

He goes on. " Auguft 20th, I fpoke from Acts
" ii. 37. to two or three hundred Market people,
" and foldiers, all as orderly and decent as could
" be defired.----I now heard, that the Mayor had
" come down on Sunday, to take a view of us.
" Soon after, an Officer ftruck a Countryman in the
" face, without any provocation. A ferious woman
" befought the poor man, not to refift evil, as the
" other only wanted to make a riot   He took
" patiently feveral repeated blows, telling the Of-
" ficer, he might beat him as long as he pleafed."

" To-day Mr. *Seward's* Coufin told us of a young
" Lady, who was here on a vifit, and had been
" deeply affected on Sunday night under the word,
" feeing and feeling her need of a Phyfician, and
" earneftly defired me to pray for her.----After
" dinner I fpoke with her.   She burft into tears,
                                        " and

" and told us, fhe had come hithei thoughtlefs,
" dead in pleafures and fin, and fully refolved
" againft ever being a Methodift That fhe was
" firft alarmed about her own ftate, by feeing us
" fo happy and full of love · had gone to the
" Society, but was not thoroughly awakened to a
" knowledge of herfelf, till the word came home
" to her foul. That all the following night fhe
" had been in an agony of diftrefs, could not pray,
" could not bear our finging, noi have any reft in
" her fpirit. We betook ouifelves to piayer for
" her, fhe received forgivenefs, and tiiumphed in
" the Lord her God."

Auguft 23d, " By ten laft night we reached
" Gloucefter, through many dangers and difficulties.
" In mounting my horfe I fell ovei him, and
" fpraincd my hand riding in the daik I bruifed
" my foot we loft our way as often as we could:
" there were only two hoifes between thiee of us:
" when we had got to Gloucefter, we weie tuined
" back from a friend's houfe, on account of his
" wife's ficknefs and my voice and ftrength weie
" quite gone To-day they are in fome meafure
" reftoied. At night I with difficulty got into the
" crouded Society, where I preached the Law and
" the Gofpel, which they received with all readi-
" nefs Thiee Clergymen were prefent. Some
" without, attempted to make a difturbance, but
" in vain "

Auguft 25th "Befoie I went into the ftreets and
" high-ways, I fent, according to my cuftom, to bor-
" iow the ufe of the Chuich The Minifter, being one
" of the better difpofed, fent back a civil meffage,
" that he would be glad to drink a glafs of wi.

H 3   " wil

" with me, but durſt not lend me his pulpit for
" fifty guineas   Mr *Whitefield* * however, durſt
" lend me his field, which did juſt as well   For
" near an hour and half, God gave me voice and
" ſtrength to exhort about two thouſand ſinners, to
" repent and believe the Goſpel ---Being invited to
" *Painſwick*, I waited upon the Lord, and renewed
" my ſtrength. We found near a thouſand perſons
" gathered in the ſtreet   I diſcourſed from, God
" was in Chriſt, reconciling the world unto him-
" ſelf.   I beſought them earneſtly to be recon-
" ciled, and the *Rebels* ſeemed inclined to lay
" down their arms   A young Preſbyterian Teacher
" cleaved to us "

On returning to *Gloucester*, Mr *Wesley* received an
invitation from *F. Drummond*, he dined with her,
and ſeveral of the *Friends*, particularly he mentions
" *Josiah Martin*, a ſpiritual man, ſays he, as far as I
" can diſcern   My heart was enlarged, and knit to
" them in love."---Going in the evening, to preach
in the field, Mrs *Kirkman*, an old and intimate acquaintance, whoſe ſon had been with him and his
brother at *Oxford*, put herſelf in his way, and ad-
dreſſed him, with, " What, Mr. *Wesley*, is it you I
" ſee ! is it poſſible that you, who can preach at
" *Chriſt-Church*, St. *Mary's*, &c. ſhould come hither
" after a mob !" He gave her a ſhort anſwer, and
went to his mob, or to put it in the phraſe of the
Phariſees, to this people, which is accurſed. Thou-
ſands heard him gladly, while he explained, the
bleſſings and privileges of the Goſpel, and exhorted
all to come to Chriſt as loſt ſinners that they might

* I ſuppoſe a Brother of the Rev. Mr. *George Whitefield*.

enjoy

enjoy them. I cannot but obferve here, that the
more ignorant and wicked the common people were
at this time, the greater was the charity and kindnefs of thofe, who endeavoured to inftruct them in
their duty to God and man, and by this means reform their manners The reader will eafily perceive, that it required no fmall degree of refolution,
to expofe himfelf to the ignorant rudenefs of the
loweft of the people, to the contemptuous fneers of
thofe of refpectability and influence, and to the fevere cenfures of his particular friends Yet this,
both he, his brother, and Mr. *Whitefield* did, in
adopting the plan of Itinerant preaching It is almoft impoffible to imagine, that, in their circumftances, they could act from any other motive, than
a pure defire of doing good. Travelling from place
to place, and every where preaching in the open air,
was a plan of proceeding well adapted to diffufe
knowledge among the common people, and to
awaken a concern for religion. But it was extraordinary and new, and the novelty of it would naturally engage the attention of the public fo much,
that few perfons would, at firft, form a true judgment of its importance, and the difficulties and
hardfhips attending it Had thefe two points been
confidered and rightly underftood, I am perfuaded
that neither Mr *Charles Wefley*, nor his Brother,
nor Mr *Whitefield*, would have been blamed for
adopting the plan of Itinerancy, and preaching in
the open air, on the contrary they would have
been commended by every perfon of a liberal mind
At prefent, I fhall only hint at one or two particulars, to fhew the importance of their proceedings,
and the hardfhips they had to encounter. The

H 4   labouring

labouring poor, are the moſt numerous claſs of
people in every country. They are not leſs neceſſary
to the happineſs and proſperity of a nation, than
the higher orders of Society. At the period of
which I am now ſpeaking, their education was
almoſt wholly neglected, and as they advanced in
years, they had fewer opportunities of inſtruction
and leſs capacity for it, than thoſe who had received
a better education, and had more leiſure. The public diſcourſes of the *regular* Clergy, had little or no
influence upon this claſs of people, as many of
them never went to Church, and moſt of thoſe who
did, neither underſtood, nor felt themſelves in-
tereſted, in what the Preachers delivered from the
pulpit. Darkneſs covered the earth, and groſs
darkneſs this people. Nor was there any proſpect
of doing them good, except by ſome extraordinary
method of proceeding, as their ignorance and
vicious habits, placed them beyond the reach of any
ſalutary influence from the ordinary means of improvement appointed by Government. But it certainly is a matter of national importance, that ſo
large a body of people as the labouring poor, ſhould
be inſtructed in the principles of religion, and have
the way to happineſs, both here and hereafter,
pointed out to them, in ſuch a manner as to engage
their attention, and inform their underſtandings. A
true knowledge of religion enlarges and ſtrengthens
the faculties of their minds, and prepares them for
a due performance of every duty religious and civil.
It opens to their view ſources of happineſs unknown
to them before, it teaches them to form a true
eſtimate of their privileges and bleſſings temporal
and ſpiritual, to view affliction, not as peculiar to

their

their fituation, but as infinitely diverfified, and
diftributed for wife purpofes, through all the orders
of Society , thus it leads them on to contentment
and happinefs in their humble fituations, and difpofes them to induftry and peace, by which they
largely contribute to the profperity and happinefs
of the nation   Viewing the effects of *Itinerant*
preaching in this point of light, we fee its importance, and muft acknowledge that the authors of it
deferve great praife ; efpecially as they introduced
it by their own example, under many difficulties and
hardfhips.   Their profpects in life, from their
learning, their abilities, and their rank in Society,
were all facrificed to the plan of Itinerancy   In
all human appearance, they had every thing to lofe
by it , reputation, health, and the efteem of their
friends , and nothing in this world to gain, but
great bodily fatigue, ill ufage from the mob, and
general contempt.   As only three perfons united
together at firft in the plan of Itinerancy, they could
not expect to form any extenfive or very permanent
eftablifhment.   It was impoffible to conceive that
the feed they were fowing, would produce fo plen-
tiful a crop of Lay-Preachers as we have feen fpring
up from it, without whom the work muft have
been very limited indeed.   But it is very evident
that thefe three fervants of God, did not look forward to any very diftant confequences of their
prefent proceedings; they contented themfelves
with performing a prefent duty, and doing as much
good as poffible in the way which opened before
them, committing themfelves and their work to
God, who has taken good care of them.

                                                Mr.

Mr *Wesley* pursued his plan, and on the 26th of August was at *Painswick*. The Minister was so obliging as to lend him his pulpit. But the Church would not hold the people, it was supposed there were two thousand persons in the Church-yard. Mr. *Wesley* stood at a window, which was taken down, and preached to the congregation within the walls, and without. They listened with eager attention, while he explained *"God so loved the world that he gave his only begotten Son,"* &c.

"In the afternoon, says he, I preached again to "a *Kennington* congregation. It was the most "beautiful sight I ever beheld. The people filled "the gradually rising Area, which was shut up on "three sides by a vast hill. On the top and bot- "tom of this hill, was a great row of trees. In "this Amphitheatre the people stood deeply at- "tentive, while I called upon them in Christ's "words, *"Come unto me all ye that labour, and are "heavy laden, and I will give you rest."* The tears "of many testified, that they were ready to enter "into that rest. It was with difficulty we made "our way through this most loving people, and "returned amidst their prayers and blessings to "*Ebly*, where I expounded the Second Lesson for "two hours."

A good old Baptist had invited Mr *Wesley* to preach at *Stanley*, in his way to *Bristol*. Accordingly, on the 27th, he rode thither through the rain, and preached to about a thousand attentive hearers, they were so much affected by the sermon, that he appointed them to meet him again in the evening. I mention with pleasure, these instances of persons among the *Friends*, the *Presbyterians*, and the *Baptists*,
who

who shewed a friendly difposition to Mr. *Wefley*, and countenanced his proceedings.   Their conduct difcovers a ftronger attachment to the effential doctrines of the gofpel, than to the peculiarities of opinion and modes of worfhip, in which they differed from him and from one another ; and marks a liberality of fentiment, which reflects honour on the different denominations of chriftians to which they belonged.

He returned to Mr *Ellis's* at *Ebly*   This was a moft agreeable family ; every one having received the faith, except one young man who ftill remained an abandoned finner   His mother mourned and lamented over him, with parental affection and religious concern.   Mr *Oakley*, who travelled with Mr *Wefley*, now informed him that he had been able to faften fome degree of conviction of fin on the young man's mind   His convictions and ferioufnefs were increafed by Mr. *Wefley's* fermon. By perfevering prayer he was brought to the knowledge of God, and received peace and joy in believing   Mr. *Wefley* adds, " *Sing ye heavens for the* " *Lord hath done it , fhout ye lower parts of the earth !* " ---In the morning I had told his mother the " ftory of St *Auftin's* converfion   now I carried " her the joyful news, " *This thy fon was dead and* " *is alive again , he was loft and is found* "

He arrived in *Briftol*, Auguft 28th, and his Brother having fet out for *London*, on the 31ft he entered on his Miniftry at Weaver's-Hall   " I be- " gan, fays he, by expounding *Ifaiah* with great " freedom   They were melted into tears all " around , and again when the Bands met to keep " the Church-Faft.   We were all of one heart " and

" and of one mind I forgot the contradiction
" wherewith they grieved my foul in *London*, and
" could not forbear faying, " *It is good for me to*
" *be here*."

The places where Mr *Wefley* had now to preach,
in *Briftol*, *Kingswood*, and the neighbourhood, were
numerous, and he feldom paffed a day without
preaching or expounding, two or three times The
congregations were large, and his word was with
power, fo that many teftified daily, that the Gofpel
is the power of God to falvation, to all who believe. September the 4th, he preached in *Kingswood* to fome thoufands, Colliers chiefly, and held
out the promifes from *Ifaiah* xxxv, " The wilder-
" nefs and the folitary place fhall be glad for them,
" and the defert fhall rejoice and bloffom as the
" rofe." He adds, " I triumphed in the mercy
" of God to thefe poor outcafts, (for he hath called
" them a people who were not a people) and in the
" accomplifhment of that Scripture, " *Then the*
" *eyes of the blind fhall be opened, and the ears of*
" *the deaf fhall be unftopped, then fhall the lame man*
" *leap as an hart, and the tongue of the dumb fing,*
" *for in the wildernefs fhall waters break out, and*
" *ftreams in the defert*." How gladly do the poor
" receive the gofpel ! We hardly knew how to
" part "

September 5th, " I was much difcouraged by a
" difcovery of the diforderly walking of fome, who
" have given the adverfary occafion to blafpheme.
" I am a poor creature upon fuch occafions, being
" foon caft down Yet I went and talked to them,
" and God filled me with fuch love to their foul.
" as I have not known before. They could not
" ftand

" stand before it. I joined with *Oakley* and *Cen-*
" *nick* in prayer for them"   M. trembled ex-
" ceedingly, the others gave us great cause to hope
" for their recovery."

"September 7th, At *Weaver's*-Hall, I expounded
" the third chapter of *Isaiah*, where the Prophet alike
" condemns, notorious profligates, worldly minded
" men, and *well-dressed* ladies."---By *well-dressed*
ladies, Mr. *Wesley* certainly meant much more than
the phrase imports. He doubtless had in view, a
fanciful, useless, expensive conformity to the change-
able modes of dress, which is unbecoming, if not
criminal, in a person professing godliness   The
Prophet is there speaking of ladies of the first rank
in the kingdom; he mentions paint, a variety of
useless ornaments, and a mode of dress hardly con-
sistent with modesty, *   What added to their guilt
was, that, while they were adorning themselves in
every fanciful and wanton method they could invent, the poor of the land were oppressed beyond
measure, and God denounces heavy judgments
against them for their oppression and wantonness.
It has often been said, by persons too fond of dress,
that religion does not consist in the peculiar shape
or cut of our clothes.   This undoubtedly is true
But when the mode of dress is voluntary, and regulated purely by choice, it is a picture, which gives a
visible representation of the temper and disposition
of the mind. The choice of our dress, like the
choice of our amusements or companions, discovers
what kind of objects are most pleasing and grati-
fying to us   The case is very different where the

* See Bishop *Louth*, on the third chapter of *Isaiah*

mode

mode of drefs is characteriftic of a profeffion, or where a woman is under the controul of hei hufband.

September 11th. He rode with two friends to *Bradford*, near *Bath*, and preached to about a thoufand perfons who feemed deeply affected.----On the 15th he fays, " Having been provoked to fpeak " unadvifedly with my lips, I preached on the " Bowling-Green in great weaknefs, on, " *Lazarus* " *come forth !*" I was furprifed that any good " fhould be done. But God quickens others by " thofe who are dead themfelves A man came " to me and declaied he had now received the " fpiiit of life; and fo did a woman at the fame " time, which fhe openly declared at *Weavei's-* " Hall. We had great power among us while I " difplayed the believer's privileges from the eighth " chaptei of the Epiftle to the *Romans*. On the " 16th, I met between thiity and forty Colliers, " with theii wives, at Mr *Willis*'s, and adminif- " tered the facrament to them , but found no com- " fort myfelf, in that or any other ordinance. I " always find ftrength for the work of the Minif- " try , but when my woik is over, my bodily and " fpiritual ftrength both leave me. I can pray for " others, not for myfelf. God, by me, ftiengthens " the weak hands, and confiims the feeble knees , " yet am I as a man in whom is no ftrength. I " am weary and faint in my mind, continually " longing to be difcharged."----Soon after, however, he found power to pray for himfelf, and confeffed it was good foi him to be in defertion. He was greatly ftrengthened and comforted by opening his Bible on *Ifaiah* liv. 7, 8. " *For a fmall moment* " *have*

" *have I forsaken thee , but with great mercies will I*
" *gather thee   In a little wrath I hid my face from*
" *thee for a moment ; but with everlasting kindness will*
" *I have mercy on thee, saith the* Lord *thy Re-*
" *deemer.*"

Many persons now, came to him for advice
daily, who had been, either awaken or justified
under his ministry   This greatly increased his labour, but it strengthened his hands for the work in
which he was engaged. September 25th. He
preached again at *Bradford*, to about two thousand
hearers   " I described, says he, their state by
" nature and grace. I did not spare those who
" were whole, and had no need of a physician.
" They bore it surprisingly.   I received invitations
" to several neighbouring towns. May I never run
" before God's call, nor stay one moment after it.
" ---We baited at a good Dissenter's near *Bath*,
" who seems to have the root of the matter in
" him."---The next day, two persons came to him
who had been clearly convinced of sin, and received peace and joy in believing , but they had
never been baptized.   On this occasion Mr. *Wesley*
observes, " I now require no further proof, that
" one may be an inward Christian without baptism.
" They are both desirous of it , and who can for-
" bid water ?"

" *Sarah Pearce* declares, that she first received
" comfort on hearing me explain the fifth chapter
" of the *Romans*   She had the witness of her own
" spirit, or conscience, that all the marks I men-
" tioned were upon her , and the spirit of God,
' with his testimony, put it beyond the possibility
" of a doubt.   Some of her words were , " I was
                                      " extremely

" extremely bigotted againſt my brethren the Diſ-
" ſenters, but am now enlarged towards them and
" all mankind, in an inexpreſſible manner. I do
" not depend upon a ſtart of comfort; but find it
" increaſe ever ſince it began. I perceive a great
" change in myſelf, and expect a greater. I feel
" a divine attraction in my ſoul to heavenly things.
" I was once ſo afraid of death that I durſt not
" ſleep, but now I do not fear it at all. I deſire
" nothing on earth; I fear nothing, but ſin. God
" ſuffers me to be ſtrongly tempted; but I know,
" where he gives faith he will try it "---" See
" here the true aſſurance of faith! How conſiſtent!
" An humble, not doubting faith, a filial, not ſer-
" vile fear of offending. I deſire not *ſuch* an aſ-
" ſurance as blots out theſe Scriptures, " *Be not*
" *high-minded, but fear work out your ſalvation*
" *with fear and trembling,*" &c. God keep me in
" conſtant fear, leſt that by any means, when I have
" preached to others, I myſelf ſhould be a caſt-
" away."

" I ſpoke plainly to the women Bands, of their
" unadviſedneſs, their want of love, and not bearing
" one another's burdens. We found an immediate
" effect. Some were convinced they had thought
" too highly of themſelves, and that their firſt
" love, like their firſt joy, was only a foretaſte of
" that temper which continually rules in a new
" heart."

Though there had been no riots, nor any open
perſecution of the Methodiſts in *Briſtol*, yet many
individuals, who became ſerious and changed the
whole courſe of their lives, ſuffered conſiderably.
This was partly occaſioned by the inflammatory
diſcourſes

difcourfes of fome of the Clergy, who reprefented them as Papifts, Jefuits, friends of the Pretender, &c. On this fubject, Mr. *Wefley* makes the following obfervations. " Chriftianity flourifhes under " the crofs None who follow Chrift are without " that badge of Difciplefhip. Wives and children " are beaten and turned out of doors, and the per- " fecutors are the complainers It is always the " Lamb that troubles the waters. Every Sunday, " damnation is denounced againft all who hear " us for we are Papifts, Jefuits, Seducers, and " bringers in of the Pretender The Clergy mur- " mur aloud at the number of communicants, and " threaten to repel them. Yet will not the world " bear that we fhould talk of perfecution no, " for the world now is *chriftian* ! and the offence " of the crofs has ceafed Alas ! what would " they do further ? Some lofe their bread, fome " their habitations One fuffers ftripes, another " confinement, yet we muft not call this per- " fecution. Doubtlefs they will find fome other " name for it, when they fhall think they do God " fervice by killing us "

October 8th, He preached at the Brick-yard. A Mr *Williams*, from *Kidderminfter*, who had written to Mr *Wefley* fome time before to go down thither, was prefent, and much edified and ftrength-ened by the fermon " I know not, fays Mr *W f-* " *ley*, of what denomination he is, nor is it mate- " rial, for he has the mind which was in *Chrift*."

Mr *Wefley's* fermon, when laft at *Braaford*, had been mifunderftood or mifreprefented It was reported that he was a high Calvinift, and great pains had been taken to reprefent him

I   as

as fuch. His brother Mr. *John Wefley*, coming to
Briftol this evening, it was the opinion of both that
he ought to preach again at *Bradford*, and declare
his fentiments openly on this point. The next day,
October the 9th, * they went to *Bradford*, where
Mr *Charles Wefley* preached to a congregation of
about two thoufand people. Mr. *John Wefley* prayed
firft, when Mr *Charles* began abruptly, " If God
" be for us, who can be againft us ? He that fpared
" not his own Son, but delivered him up for us
" ALL, how fhall he not with him alfo freely give
" us all things." He fpake with great boldnefs
and freedom for an hour and a half, holding forth
Chrift a Saviour for all men. He flattered himfelf
that he had done fo much injury to Satan's kingdom, by beating down fin, that he fays, " I believe
" he will no more flander me with being a Predef-
" tinarian" in the modern notion of that word.

October 11th, He preached for the firft time in
the open air by night, in a yard belonging to a
widow *Jones* He obferves, " The yard contained
" about four hundred perfons, the houfe was like-
" wife full Great power was in the midft of us.
" Satan blafphemed without, but durft not venture
" his children too near the gofpel, when I offered
" Chrift Jefus to them. The enemy hurried them
" away, and all we could do, was to pray for
" them."

" October 15th, I waited, with my Brother, on a
" Minifter about baptizing fome of his parifhioners.
" He complained heavily of the multitudes of our
" communicants, and produced the Canon againft

* See the agreement between this account and Mr. *John Wefley*'s printed
Journal in his Works, Vol. 27, Page 142.

" ftrangers.

" ftrangers.   He could not admit as a reafon for
" their coming to his Church, that they had no
" Sacrament at their own.   I offered my affiftance
" to leffen his trouble, but he declined it   He
" told us there were hundreds of new communi-
" cants laft Sunday   We blefs God for *this caufe*
" of offence, and pray it may never be removed."

    " October 19th, I read part of Mr *Law*, on
" Regeneration to our Society   How promifing
" the beginning, and how lame the conclufion!
" Chriftianity, he rightly tells us, is a recovery of
" the Divine image, and a chriftian is, a fallen
" fpirit reftored, and re-inftated in paradife, a
" living mirror of Father, Son and Holy Ghoft.
" After this he fuppofes it *poffible* for him to be in-
" fenfible of fuch a change   to be happy and holy,
" tranflated into Eden, renewed in the likenefs of
" God, and *not to know it*   Nay we are not to ex-
" pect, nor bid others expect any fuch confciouf-
" nefs, if we liften to him.   What wretched in-
" confiftency!"

    When Mr *Wefley* baptized adults, profeffing
faith in Chrift, he chofe to do it by trine immerfion, if the perfons would fubmit to it, judging
this to be the Apoftolic method of baptizing.
October 26th, He fays, "I baptized Mr *Wiggin-*
" *ton* in the river, by *Baptift*-Mills, and went on
" my way rejoicing to *French-Hay*. October 27th,
" I took occafion to fhew the degeneracy of our
" modern Pharifees.   Their predeceffors fafted
" twice a week, but they maintain their character
" for holinefs at a cheaper rate.   In reverence for
" the Church, fome keep their public day on Fri-
" day. none regard it, though enjoined as a Faft.

" Their neglect is equally notorious in regard to
" prayer and the Sacrament   And yet thefe men
" cry out, " THE CHURCH, THE CHURCH ! when
" they themfelves will not hear the Church ; but
" defpife her authority, trample upon her orders,
" teach contrary to her Articles and Homilies, and
" break her Canons, even every man of thofe, who
" of late pretend to enforce their obfervance "

    " October 13th, I wrote to the Bifhop of *Briftol*,
" as follows,

      " My Lord,

    " Several perfons have applied to me for Bap-
" tifm * It has pleafed God to make me inftru-
" mental in their converfion. This has given them
" fuch a prejudice for me, that they defire to be
" received into the Church by my Miniftry   They
" choofe likewife to be baptized by immerfion,
" and have engaged me to give your Lordfhip
" notice, as the Church requires "

    " November 2. I received a Summons from
" *Oxford*, to *refpond* in Divinity Difputations, which,
" together with other concurrent providences, is a
" plain call to that place "

On the 6th, Mr. *Wefley*'s Journal breaks off, and
does not commence again till March 14th, 1740.
Mr. *John Wefley* informs us, that he and his Brother
left *Oxford* on the 15th of November, and taking
Briftol in their way, they arrived at *Tiverton* on the
21ft, a few days after the funeral of their Brother
Samuel.   Having preached at *Exeter* during their
fhort ftay in thefe parts, they returned to *Briftol* on
the 28th of the fame month

                ᴛ He mentioned the names of feven perfons.

                                                    March

March 14th, 1740, Mr. *Wesley* came to *Gloucester*, in company with *Thomas Maxfield*, who travelled with him moft part of this year. The next day he went to *Bengeworth*, in hopes of feeing his old friend, Mr. *Benjamin Seward*. But here he met with a difappointment, which he did not expect. Mr *Seward* had been ill of a fever His relations taking advantage of his fituation, had intercepted all his letters they called his fever madnefs, and now, when he was recovering, placed his fervants over him as fpies, to prevent any Methodift from coming to him. His Brother, Mr *Henry*, came to Mr. *Wesley* and gave him plenty of abufe, calling him fcoundrel, rafcal, pick-pocket, &c. Mr. *Wesley* made little reply, but ordered notice to be given that he would preach next day, March 16th, at the ufual place, which was near Mr. *Seward*'s houfe. Mr. *Henry* came to him to diffuade him from attempting it, telling him that four Conftables were ordered to apprehend him if he came near his Brother's wall Mr. *Wesley* however, was not to be deterred from his purpofe by fuch threatenings, and when the time of preaching drew near, walked forward towards the place. In his way thither, a Mayor's officer met him, and defired he would go with him to the Mayor Mr *Wesley* anfwered, that he would firft wait on his LORD, and then on the Mayor, whom he reverenced for the fake of his office Mr *Henry* now met him with threatenings and revilings Mr *Wesley* began finging, "Shall "I for fear of feeble man," &c. This enraged Mr. *Henry*, who ran about raving like a madman, and quickly got fome fellows fit for his purpofe Thefe laid hold on Mr *Wesley*, who afked, by what autho-

I 3

rity they did it? Where was their warrant? Let
them shew that and he would save them the trouble
of using violence They said they had no warrant,
but he should not preach there, and dragged him
away amidst the cries of the people Mr *Henry*
cried out, "Take him away, and duck him"
" I broke out, says Mr *Wesley*, into singing, with
" *Thomas Maxfield*, and suffered them to carry me
" whither they pleased.   At the bridge in the
" lane they left me then I stood out of the
" Liberty of the Corporation, and gave out,

' Angel of God whate'er betide
 Thy summons I obey!" &c.

" Some hundreds followed, whom they could not
" hinder from hearing me, on, " *If God be for us,*
" *who can be against us ?*"---Never did I feel so
" much what I spoke, and the word did not return
" empty"
   " I then waited on Mr. Mayor, the poor sincere
" ones following me trembling He was a little
" warm at my not coming before.   I gave him the
" reason, and added, that I knew of no Law of God
" or man, which I had transgressed, but if there
" was any such Law, I desired no favour. He said,
" he should not have denied me leave to preach,
" even in his own yard, but Mr *Henry Seward*,
" and the Apothecary, had assured him, it would
" quite cast his brother down again.   I answered,
" it would tend to restore him ---Here a Clergy-
" man spoke much---and nothing.   As far as I
" could pick out his meaning, he grumbled that
" Mr *Whitefield* had spoken against the Clergy in
" his Journal.   I told him, if he were a carnal
                                         " worldly-

" worldly-minded Clergyman, I might do what he
" would call railing, I might warn God's people
" to beware of falfe Prophets. I did not fay, be-
" caufe I did not know, he was one of thofe
" Shepherds who fed themfelves, not the flock ;
" but if he was, I was forry for him, and muft
" leave that fentence of *Chryfoftom* with him, " Hell
" is paved with the fkulls of Chriftian Priefts "----
" I turned from him, and afked the Mayor whether
" he approved of the treatment I had met with ?
" He faid, by no means, and if I complained, he
" would bind the men over to anfwer it at the
" Seffions. I told him, I did not complain, neither
" would I profecute them, as they well knew. I
" affured him, that I waited on him, not from in-
" tereft, for I wanted nothing , not from fear, for
" I had done no wrong , but from true refpect, and
" to fhew him that I believed, " The powers that
" be are ordained of God "

March 17th, He preached again, when a troop
poured in upon him and the quiet congregation, and
made much difturbance " I enjoyed, fays he, a
' fweet calm within, even while I preached the
" gofpel with much contention. Thefe flighter
" conflicts muft fit me for greater "---The next
day, before preaching, he received a meffage from
the Minifter, informing him that if he did not immediately quit the Town, Mr. *Henry Seward* could
eafily raife a mob, and then he muft look to himfelf Mr *Canning*, and others of his friends, diffuaded him from going to the Society, for his enemies were determined to do him a mifchief, which
they thought he fhould avoid by going out of the
way for awhile. But Mr. *Wefley* was not intimi-

dated

dated by threatenings. He adds, " I went, and
" set upon the oppofers   I bid them to rejoice
" and glory, for now they had terrified me , I was
" really afraid---to leave *Evefham*   I durft no
" more do it, than forfake my Captain, or deny
" my Mafter, while any one of them opened his
" mouth againft the truth.   No man anfwered a
" word, or offered to difturb me in my following
" exhortation.-----I received great comfort from
" thofe words in the firft Leffon, " *Then the men of*
" *the city faid unto Joafh, bring out thy fon, that he may*
" *die, becaufe he hath caft down the altar of Baal---*
" *and Joafh faid unto all that ftood againft him, will*
" *ye plead for Baal ? If he be a god let him plead for*
" *himfelf, becaufe one hath caft down his altar.*"   In
" the afternoon there was none to plead for him,
" or to moleft me in the work of God, while I
" fhewed God's method of faving fouls , " *For he*
" *maketh fore and bindeth up , he woundeth and his*
" *hand maketh whole* "   The tears that were fhed
" gave comfortable evidence that I had not laboured
" in vain "

Mr. *Wefley* went from hence to *Weftcot, Idbury,*
and *Oxford,* where he laboured with his ufual fuccefs.   He then returned to *Evefham,* faw his friend
Mr *Benjamin Seward,* and preached without moleftation.   April 3d, he arrived in *London,* and preached
at the Foundery, on, " *The kingdom of God is not*
" *meat and drink, but righteoufnefs, peace and joy in*
" *the Holy Ghoft* '   He obferves, " My heart was
" enlarged in prayer for the Infant Society."

The Society in *London* was at this time terribly
diftracted with foolifh and hurtful difputations.
Mr. *Bray,* one *Bell,* and feveral others who had in-
                                                    fluence

fluence among the people, had imbibed a notion from *Molther*, the *Moravian*, that there are no degrees of faith, that he who has any doubt has no faith at all that there are no means of grace, but Chrift, that a believer is under no obligation to ufe the ordinances that an unbeliever ought to be *fill*, and neither read the Scriptures, nor pray, nor ufe any of the ordinances, becaufe he cannot do thefe things without trufting in them, and that would hinder him from receiving faith, &c. Mr. *Wefley* oppofed thefe teachers with great firmnefs and perfeverance. His Journal, during his ftay in *London*, is filled with difputations on thefe fubjects, which I fhall not tranfcribe. The following particulars, as they throw fome light on the ftate of things at this time, and on the fuccefs of Mr. *Wefley*'s Miniftry, feem worthy of being preferved.

April 16th, He received the following Letter. " I beg leave to afk your opinion about my ftate. " I do not doubt myfelf, for through the grace " given me, I am confident, God for Chrift's fake " has forgiven my fins, and made me free. But " it has been queftioned whether I have faith or " not "

" I was brought up an Heathen in the houfe of " a D. D. After that I went to the Lord's table, " and then thought myfelf a good Chriftian But " bleffed be God I now fee that I was an abomi- " nable Pharifee For my pride God caft me out " of his houfe, and I fell into the fouleft crimes I " could commit After fome time I had a fight " of my damnable eftate, and that I was nothing " but fin I daily dreaded God's vengeance I " durft not offer to pray, knowing my prayer was " an

" an abomination to that God who is of pure eyes
" than to behold iniquity   I could not think it
" poffible there fhould be forgivenefs for me .

> " I had my punifhment in view
> I felt a thoufand hells my due."

" I went twice to hear Mr. *Whitefield*, but thought
" it did not fignify.   My mifery ftill increafed
" But it pleafed God, that the laft time you
" preached at *Kennington*, my bleffed Saviour was
" revealed in me, in fo glorious a manner, that I
" rather thought myfelf in heaven than on earth
" I thought I could meet death with boldnefs.   I
" was ready to cry out to every one, O ! tafte and
" fee how good the Lord is   I would not for a
" thoufand worlds be in my former ftate again
" May God prolong your life and health, in his
" kingdom and fervice '

Hitherto the government of the Society had been
vefted wholly in the people.   At their different
meetings, they made fuch rules and orders as they
thought neceffary and proper, without paying any
particular deference to the Minifters   In one or
two inftances, mentioned in thefe Journals, they
threatened to expel Mr *Wefley* himfelf, when he
did not conform to the rules they had made   But
on the 20th of April this year, it was agreed, 1
That no order fhould be valid unlefs the Minifter
be prefent at the making of it   2 That, whofoever
denies the ordinances to be commands, fhall be expelled the Society.

One or two of the leaders in this new doctrine
concerning ordinances and means of grace, thinking Mr *John Wefley* more favourable to their
                                                    opinions

opinions than Mr *Charles*, wrote to him at *Briftol*, defiring him to come immediately to *London*. He arrived on the 22nd, * and on the 24th, Mr. *Charles Wefley* wrote to a friend at *Briftol* as follows. " My Brother came moft critically. The " fnare we truft will now be broken, and many " fimple fouls be delivered Many here infift, " that a part of their chriftian calling is liberty " from obeying, not liberty to obey. The unjuf- " tified, fay they, are to *be ftill;* that is, not to " fearch the Scriptures, not to pray, not to com- " municate, not to do good, not to endeavour, not " to defire , for it is impoffible to ufe means with- " out trufting in them. Their practice is agreeable " to their principles Lazy and proud themfelves, " bitter and cenforious towards others, they trample " upon the ordinances and defpife the commands " of Chrift. I fee no middle point wherein we " can meet "

May 2nd, Mr. *Wefley* received the following Letter.

" My Reverend Father in Chrift,

" I firft received the gift of faith after I had feen " myfelf a loft finner, bound with a thoufand chains, " and dropping into hell Then I heard his voice, " Be of good cheer, thy fins are forgiven thee I " faw the Son of God loved me, and gave himfelf " for me I thought I faw him at the right-hand " of the Father, making interceffion for me. I " went on in great joy for four months Then " pride crept in, and I thought the work was

---

* See alfo Mr *John Wefley's* printed Journal in his Works, Vol 27 Page 205.

" finifhed,

" finifhed, when it was but juft begun.   There I
" refted, and in a little time, fell into doubts and
" fears, whether my fins were really forgiven me,
" till I plunged myfelf into the depth of mifery.
" I could not pray, neither had I any defire to do
" it, or to read the word   Then did I fee my own
" evil heart, and feel my helpleffnefs, fo that I
" could not fo much as think a good thought. My
" love was turned into hatred, paffion, envy, &c
" I felt a thoufand hells my due, and cried out in
" bitter anguifh of fpirit, " Save Lord, or I perifh "
" In my laft extremity I faw my Saviour full of
" grace and truth for me, and heard his voice
" again, whifpering, Peace be ftill   My peace re-
" turned, and greater fweetnefs of love than I ever
" knew before.   Now my joy is calm and folid,
" my heart drawn out to the Lord continually.   I
" know that my Redeemer liveth for me   He is
" my ftrength and my rock, and will carry on his
" work in my foul to the day of redemption
" Dear Sir, I have fpoken the ftate of my heart as
" before the Lord   I beg your prayers, that I
" may go on from ftrength to ftrength, from con-
" quering to conquer, till death is fwallowed up in
" victory "

G. MURRAY.

May 8, H Harris being in Town, Mr Wefley obferves, " He declared his experience before the So-
" ciety   O! what a flame was kindled   No man fpeaks
" in my hearing as this man fpeaketh   What a
" nurfing father God has fent us !   He has indeed
" learned of the good fhepherd to carry the lambs
" in his bofom.   Such love, fuch power, fuch fim-
                              ' plicity,

" plicity, was irresistible " At this meeting *H.*
Harris invited all lost sinners, justified or not jus-
" tified, to the Lord's table   " I would not, said
" he, for ten thousand worlds, be the man who
" should keep any from it.   There I first found
" him myself   that is the place of meeting." " He
" went on, adds Mr. *Wesley*, in the power of the
' Most High.   God called forth his witnesses ;
" several declared they had found Christ in the
" ordinances "

May 29th, " I dined, says Mr. *Wesley*, at friend
" *Keen*'s, a Quaker, and a Christian, and read over
" *George Whitefield*'s account of God's dealings with
" him.   The love and esteem he expressed for me,
" filled me with confusion, and brought back my
" fear, lest after having preached to others, I my-
" self should be a cast-away."

June 11th, To put an end to vain disputings,
and to stop the further progress of the hurtful
opinions which then prevailed, Mr *John Wesley*
proposed to new model the Bands, and to put those
by themselves, who were still for the ordinances.
This proposal raised a great clamour   " The noisy
" ill ones, adds Mr *Wesley*, well knew, that
" hitherto they had carried their point, by wearying
" out the sincere ones scattered among them, one
" or two in a Band of disputers, who had harassed
" and sawn them asunder, so that a remnant scarcely
" was left Mr *Ingham* seconded us, and we ob-
" tained that the names should be called over, and
" as many as were aggrieved, should be put into
" new Bands. We gathered up our wreck, *rari*
" *nantes in gurgite vasto*, floating here and there on
" the vast abyss, for nine out of ten, were swal-
                                         " lowed

" lowed up in the dead fea of ftillnefs   O why
" was not this done fix months ago !   How fatal
" was our delay and falfe moderation   I told them
" plainly, I fhould continue with them fo long as
" they continued in the Church of *Fngland* "

June 17th, " We had an extraordinary meeting
" of the Society, increafed from *twelve*, to three
" hundred.   I took my leave of them with hearty
" prayer "---The next day he fet out for *Briftol*,
where he arrived on the 21ft, having called at
Oxford in his way thither   " My firft greeting at
" *Kingswood*, fays he, was by a daughter of one of
" our Colliers.   In the evening was at the *Malt*-
" Room, and addreffed myfelf to thofe in the wil-
" dernefs.   O what fimplicity is in this childlike
" people ! A fpirit of contrition and love ran
" through them   Here the feed has fallen upon
" good ground "

" Sunday, June 22nd, I went to learn Chrift
" among our Colliers, and drank into their fpirit.
" We rejoiced for the confolation.   O that our
" *London* brethren, would but come to fchool to
" *Kingswood !* Thefe are, what they of *London* pre-
" *tend* to be.   God knows their poverty , but they
" are rich, and daily entering into his reft   They
" do not hold it neceffary to deny weak faith,
" in order to get ftrong.   Their fouls truly
" wait upon God, in his ordinances   Ye many
" Mafters, come learn Chrift of thefe outcafts,
" for know, that except ye be converted, and be-
" come like thefe little children, ye cannot enter
" into the kingdom of heaven.---I met feveral of
" thofe whom I had baptized, and found them
" growing in grace,"

" June

" June 30, I now fpent a week at *Oxford*, to
" little purpofe, but that of obedience to man,
" for the Lord's fake   In the Hall I read my
" two Lectures on the cxxxth Pfalm, preaching
" repentance towards God, and faith in Chrift
" Jefus   But learned *Gallio*, cared for none of
" thefe things "

July 16th, Being returned to *Briftol*, he obferves,
" While I was meeting the Bands, my mouth was
" opened to reprove, rebuke, and exhort, in words
" not my own.   All trembled before the prefence
" of God   I was forced to cut off a rotten mem-
" ber, but felt fuch love and pity at the time, as
" humbled me into the duft.   It was, as if one
" criminal was executing another   We betook
" ourfelves to fervent prayer for him, and the So-
" ciety   The fpirit of prayer was poured out upon
" us, and we returned to the Lord, with weeping
" and mourning "---See here, the true *Apoftolical*
Spirit of Church Difcipline

Many of the Colliers, who had been abandoned
to every kind of wickednefs, even to a Proverb,
were now become pious and zealous for the things
of God.   A great number of thefe, at this time,
came to the Churches in *Briftol* on a Lord's-day,
for the benefit of the Sacrament   But moft of the
Briftol Minifters repelled them from the table, becaufe they did not belong to their Parifhes   Setting
religion afide, common humanity would have taught
them to rejoice in fo remarkable a reformation
among thefe wretched people.   But thefe watchmen
of *Ifrael* did not choofe to have any increafe of
trouble.   Can we wonder, that the Methodifts had
fuch great fuccefs in preaching the gofpel to the
middling

middling and lower orders of the people, when
such lazy drones as these, had the care of most of
the Parishes in *England?* The case, I believe, is
now greatly altered.   At present, there is more
religious knowledge, more candour, and greater attention to propriety of conduct, both among the
Clergy and the people, than there was at that time;
and the Methodists have been the principal means
of producing the change.

July 25, He began to speak to every Member of
the Society in particular   A woman came to him,
crying out, that she was born of God, that she had
a new heart, &c. But on examination, she could
give no account of her faith; no satisfactory proof
of her pretensions   Mr *Wesley* observes on this
occasion, " How exceedingly cautious ought we to
" be, in receiving people's testimony of them-
" selves "   Another came to him, who seems to
have been puffed up with her religious comforts
and enjoyments   " I plainly see, says he, why
" many lose their first comfort, it is expedient for
" them that it should go away "   In this case, as
he observes, nature will feed on the gift, instead of
the giver.   We see some, who look at their joy,
and compare their state with others, till they become high-minded, lose sight of Christ, and then
sink into great darkness and distress, without perceiving the reason of it   One part of these, generally recover their former experience, after much
suffering   another part, content themselves with
the externals of religion, and much religious talk,
while their passions have the same dominion over
them, they formerly had   and a third, look upon
all experience as mere imagination, ridicule it in
the

the terms they had been accuftomed to ufe, and caft
off religion altogether   Thefe cafes therefore, require the moft ferious and early attention of every
experienced Minifter of the gofpel

July 27   " I heard a miferable fermon, fays Mr.
" Wefley, at Temple Church, recommending religion
" as the moft likely way to raife a fortune.   After
" Sermon, proclamation was made, that all fhould
" depart who were not of the parifh   While the
" Shepherd was driving away the lambs, I ftaid,
" fufpecting nothing till the Clerk came to me and
" faid, " Mr. Beacher bids you go away, for he will
" not give you the facrament."   I went to the
" Veftry door, and mildly defired Mr Beacher to
" admit me. He afked, " Are you of this parifh ?"
" I anfwered, Sir, you fee that I am a Clergyman.
" Then dropping his firft pretence, he charged me
" with rebellion in expounding the Scripture with-
" out authority, and faid in exprefs words, " I
" repel you from the facrament "   I replied, I cite
" you to anfwer this, before Jesus Christ at the
" day of judgment   This enraged him above
" meafure. he called out, " Here, take away this
" man.'   The Conftables were ordered to attend,
" I fuppofe, left the furious Colliers fhould take the
" facrament by force, but I faved them the trouble
" of taking away, " This man," and' quietly re-
" tired "---Thefe things are but poor evidences,
that the Briftol Minifters were the true fucceffors of
the Apoftles !

In Auguft Mr. Wefley had a very dangerous
fever   It was reported, and publifhed in the papers,
that he was dead   Upon his recovery, he obferves,
" I found myfelf after this gracious vifitation, more

K   " defirous

" defirous and able to pray, more afraid of fin,
" more earneftly longing for deliverance, and the
" fulnefs of chriftian falvation ' ---Soon afterwards
two or three of the Society died, in the triumph of
faith, and full affurance of hope, which ftrengthened the hands and comforted the hearts of thofe
who were left behind

September 22nd, Mr *Wefley* was informed that the
Colliers were rifen, and riding out from *Briftol*, he
met about a thoufand of them at *Lawrence*-Hill
The occafion of their rifing was, the dearnefs of
corn. He went up to an eminence, and began to
talk to them   Many feemed inclined to go back
with him to the School, which fome of the moft
defperate perceiving, they rufhed violently upon the
others, beating, tearing, and driving them every way
from Mr *Wefley*. He adds, " I rode up to a
" rufhan, who was ftriking one of our Colliers, *
" and prayed him rather to ftrike me   He an-
" fwered, no, not for all the world, and was quite
" overcome   I turned upon another, who ftruck
" my horfe, and he alfo funk into a lamb   Where-
" ever I turned, Satan's caufe loft ground, fo that
" they were obliged to make one general affault,
" and the violent Colliers forced the quiet ones in-
" to the Town   I feized one of the talleft, and
" earneftly befought him to follow me   yes, he
" faid, that he would, all the world over   I preffed
" about fix into Chrift's fervice.   We met feveral
" parties, and ftopt and exhorted them to follow
" us, and gleaning fome from every company, we
" increafed as we marched on finging, to the School.

* He means a Collier, who was in the Methodift's Society

" From

" From one till three o'clock, we fpent in prayer,
" that evil might be prevented, and the lion chained.
" Then news was brought us, that the Colliers
" were returned in peace They had walked quietly
" into the City, without fticks or the leaft violence.
" A few of the better fort of them, went to the
" Mayor, and told their grievance then they all
" returned as they came, without noife or diftur-
" bance All who faw it were amazed Nothing
" could more clearly have fhewn the change wrought
" among them, than this *e* *e'n't on fuch an occafion."

" I found afterwards, that all our Colliers to a
" man, had been forced away. Having learned of
" Chrift not to refift evil, they went a mile with
" thofe who compelled them, rather than free
" themfelves by violence One man the rioters
" dragged out of his fick bed, and threw him into
" the Fifh Ponds Near twenty of Mr *Willis* 's
" men they had prevailed on, by threatening to fill
" up their pits, and bury them alive, if they did not
" come up and beat them company "---It was a
happy circumftance that they forced fo many of the
Methodift Colliers to go with them, as thefe, by
their advice and example would reftrain the favage
fury of the others This undoubtedly was the true
caufe, why they all returned home without making
any difturbance

November 6th, He fet out for *Wine* Here, vain
difputings and janglings about predeftination, had
done much harm in feveral Societies even *H.*
Harris, embracing this doctrine, had been greatly
eftranged from his friend Any doctrine comes
poorly recommended to us, when it almoft uniformly diminifhes chriftian love and friendfhip, in

the

the minds of those who embrace it This is an effect so contrary to the general end, and manifest tendency of the gospel, that the doctrine which produces it, should be viewed with suspicion and approached with caution.   That the diminution of christian love was on the part of H Harris, is evident from the following letter, which Mr. Wesley sent him from Cardiff, on the 10th of November.

" My dearest Friend and Brother,

" In the name of Jesus Christ, I beseech you, if
" you have his glory and the good of souls at heart,
" to come immediately to meet me here.   I trust
" we shall never be two, in time or eternity.   O!
" my Brother, I am grieved that Satan should get
" a moment's advantage over us , and am ready to
" lay my neck under your feet for Christ's sake.
" If your heart be as my heart, hasten, in the name
" of our dear Lord, to your second self."---This
letter shews a mind susceptible of the strongest attachments of friendship, and does Mr Wesley great honour   Howel Harris however, did not come to him till the 18th, when he was at Lantrissant, and preparing to leave Wales.   Mr Wesley adds, " All
" misunderstanding vanished at the sight of each
" other, and our hearts were knit together as at the
" beginning   Before the Society met, several per-
" sons were with me, desiring that as I had now
" got him, I would reprove him openly.   Some
" wanted me to preach against Lay-preaching ,
" some against Predestination, &c. In my discourse,
" a gentleman, who had come thither on purpose,
" interrupted me by desiring I would now speak
" to Mr Harris, since I was sent for to disprove
                                                    " his

" his errors I quashed all further importunity by
" declaring, I am unwilling to speak of my brother
" *Harris*, becaufe when I begin, I know not where
" to leave off, and fhould fay fo much good of him
" as fome of you could not bear "

Before Mr *Wefley* left *Wales*, a violent oppofition
was raifed againft him, which threatened danger.
During the Sermon on Sunday, while Mr. *Wefley* was
defcribing the ftate of the Pharifee, a Phyfician of
the place found himfelf hurt, and got up and walked
out of the church On the Tuefday following,
being unufually heated with wine, and urged on by
a company of Players, determined on mifchief, he
came to the houfe were the people were affembled,
to demand fatisfaction for the injury he fuppofed
that he had received. He ftruck Mr *Wefley* and
feveral of the women with his cane, and raged like
a madman, till the men forced him out of the room,
and fhut the door.   Soon after, it was broke open
by a Juftice of the Peace, and the Bailiff, or head
Magiftrate " The latter began expoftulating with
" me, fays Mr. *Wefley*, upon the affront offered the
" Doctor He faid, as it was a public injury, I
" ought to make him a public fatisfaction I an-
" fwered Mr. Bailiff, I honour you for your Office
" fake , but were you, or his Majefty King *George*
" among my hearers, I fhould tell you both,
" that you are by nature finners, *or, children of*
" *wrath, even as others* In the Church while
" preaching, I have no fuperior but God, and fhall
" not afk man leave to tell him of his fins As a
" Ruler it is your duty to be a terror to evil doers,
" but a praife to them that do well Upon this
" fpeaking to him, he became exceedingly civil,

K 3   " affured

" affured me of his good will, and that he had
" come to prevent me from being infulted, and no
" one fhould touch a hair of my head "

" While we were talking, the Doctor made
" another attempt to break in and get at me, but
" the two Juftices and others, with much trouble
" got him away, and we continued our triumph
" in the name of the Lord our God The fhout
" of a King was among us. We fang unconcerned,
" though the Players had befet the houfe, were
" armed, and threatened to burn it The ground
" of their quarrel with me was, that the preaching
" of the Gofpel had ftarved them We prayed
" and fang with great tranquility till one in the
" morning then I lay down till three I rofe
" again, and was fcarcely got into the room when
" they difcovered a Player juft by me, who had
" ftolen in unobferved They feized him, and
" F Ic 'ey wrefted the fword from him There
" was no need of drawing it, for the point and
" blade were ftript of the fcabbard, about an hand's
" breadth. Great was our rejoicing within, and
" the uproar of the Players without My female
" advifers were by no means for my venturing out,
" but wifhed me to defer my journey I preferred
" Mr. Wells's advice, of going with him through
" the midft of our enemies We called on the
" poor creature they had fecured. On fight of me
" he cried out, " Indeed Mr. Wefley, I did not
" intend to do you any harm " That, I anfwered,
" was beft known to God and his own heart, but
" told him that my principle was to return good
" for evil, and therefore defired he might be re-
" leafed. I afured him of my good wifhes, and
" with

" with Mr. *Wells* walked down to the water fide,
" no man forbidding me "---The next day, November the 20th, he arrived fafe in *Briftol*

He goes on " November 30th, I gave the
" facrament to our fifter *Taylor*, dying in triumph.
" Here is another witnefs to the truth of the
" gofpel we preach Commend me to a religion,
" upon which I can truft my foul, while entering
" into eternity."

December 2nd, " I preached on the three-fold
" office of Chrift, at *Kingfwood*, but never with
" greater power. It conftrained even the fepara-
" tifts (the Calvinifts) to own that God was with
" us of a truth. I rode back in a glorious ftorm
" of thunder, lightening and rain, my fpirit re-
" joicing in hope of the glory of God He opened
" my mouth again in the Society, and I fpoke in
" much grief, of our defolate Mother, the Church
" of *England*. My heart yearns towards her, when
" I think upon her ruins, and it pitieth me to fee
" her in the duft "

December 5th, " I was much refrefhed in fpirit
" among fome of my friends the *Quakers*, by a
" writer of theirs who ftrongly infifts on the perfect
" death unto fin, and life unto righteoufrefs, which
" every chriftian experiences Death muft precede
" life, and condemnation, juftification. This he as
" clearly teaches as any of our firft Reformers "

December 24th, He fet out, with *Thomas Marfield*,
for *London*, where they arrived the next day On
the 27th, he fays, " Six or feven hundred of us met
" from eleven o'clock till one, to praife God with
" the voice of joy and thankfgiving He hath
" done great things for us already, but we fhall

' fee greater things than thefe ---I dined at the
" houfe of a Diflenter, who was armed cap-a-pee
" with her faith of adherence, brimfull of the Five
" Points, and going on to the perfection defcribed
" in *Romans* the feventh " On the 28th, I earneftly
" warned the Bands not to fancy they had new
" hearts before they had feen the deceitfulnefs of
" the old, not to think they would ever be above
" the neceffity of prayer, not to yield for one mo-
" ment to the fpirit of judging.----Mr *Afpernel*,
" told me ftrange things, and I fear true, of fome
" new creatures of their own making, who have
" been caught in grofs lies."

April 4th, 1741 Mr *Wefley* fet out for *Briftol*,
and arrived there in fifety the next day April 7th,
He fays, " I prayed by one fuppofed to be at the
" point of death He rejoiced to meet the king
" of terrors, and appeared fo fweetly refigned, fo
" ready for the Bridegroom, that I longed to change
" places with him April 11th, Found a dying
" finner rejoicing in God her Saviour. At fight
" of me, fhe cried out, O how loving is God to me !
" But he is loving to every man. he loves every
" foul as well as he loves mine Many like words
" fhe uttered in triumphant faith, and witneffed in
' death the univerfal love of Jefus Chrift ---April
" 12th, To-day he called forth another of his
" dying witneffes. The young woman whom at
" my laft vifit, I left in utter defpair, this morning
" broke out into the following expreffions, " I fee,
" I fee it now, that Jefus Chrift died for me, and
" for all the world " Some of her words to me
" were, death ftares me in the face, but I fear him
" not, he cannot hurt me. and again, death may
" fhake

" fhake his dart in vain, God is love, pure love,
" love to every man!---The next I faw, was our
" brother S--- "

> " With joyful eyes, and looks divine,
> Smiling and pleafed in death."

April 13th, "I gave the facrament to the Bands
" of *Kingswood*, not of *Briftol*, in obedience, as I
" told them, to the Church of *England*, which re-
" quires a weekly facrament at every Cathedral.
" But as they had it not there, and as on this par-
" ticular Sunday, they were refufed it, at *Temple-*
" Church, (I myfelf, with many of them, having
" been repelled,) I therefore adminiftered it to them
" in our fchool, and had we wanted a houfe,
" would juftify doing it in the midft of the wood.
" I ftrongly urged the duty of receiving it, as often
" as they could be admitted to the Churches
" Such a facrament, I never was prefent at before.
" We received the fure pledges of our Saviour's
" dying love, and were moft of us, filled with all
" joy and peace in believing "---This it feems, was
the beginning of the practice of adminiftering the
facrament at *Kingswood*

April 20th, " Returning from *Baptift*-Mills, I
" heard that our Sifter *Richardfon* had finished her
" courfe My foul was filled with ftrong con-
" folation, and ftruggled, as it were, to go out after
" her, " as heaven-ward endeavouring." Jefu, my
" time is in thy hand only let me follow her, as
" fhe has followed Thee! The voice of joy and
" thankfgiving was in the congregation, while I
" fpake of her death "---April 22nd, " I haftened
" to the joyful funeral. The New Room was
                                   " crouded

" crouded within and without. I fpake largely
" of her whofe faith they might fafely follow.
" Great was my glorying and rejoicing over her
" She being dead, yet fpake in words of faith and
" love, which ought to be had in remembrance
" We were in a meafure, partakers of her joy, a
" a joy unfpeakable and full of glory   The whole
" Society followed her to the grave, through all
" the city   Satan raged exceedingly in his chil-
" dren, who threw dirt and ftones at us   After the
" burial we joined in the following hymn,

" Come let us, who in Chrift believe,
    With Saints and Angels join," &c.

May 1ft, " I vifited a Sifter dying in the Lord
" Then two others, one mourning after, the other
" rejoicing in, God her Saviour   I was now in-
" formed that another of our Sifters, I. Smith, is
" gone home in triumph   She witneffed a good
" confeffion of the univerfal Saviour, and gave up
" her fpirit with thefe words, " I go to my heavenly
" Father," &c May 4th, I rejoiced over our Sifter
" Hooper   The outward man decayeth, but the
" inner man is renewed.   For one whole night fhe
" had wreftled with all the powers of darknefs
" but having done all, fhe ftood unfhaken   From
" henceforth fhe was kept in perfect peace, and
" that wicked one touched her not ---I faw her
" again in great bodily weaknefs, but ftrong in the
" Lord, and in the power of his might   I fpoke
" with her Phyfician, who faid he had little hope
" of her recovery   only, added he, fhe has no dread
" upon her fpirits, which is generally the worft
" fymptom.   Moft people die for fear of dying,
                                " but

" but I never met with such people as yours They
" are none of them afraid of death , but calm, and
" patient, and refigned to the laft   He had faid to
" her, " Madam be not caft down " She an-
" fwered, fmiling, " Sir, I fhall never be caft
" down "

May 6th, " Found our Sifter *Hooper* juft at the
" haven She expreffed, while able to fpeak, her
" fulnefs of confidence and love , and her defire to
" be with Chrift.   At my next vifit, I faw her in
" the laft conflict   The angel of death was come,
" and there were but a few moments between her
" and a bleffed eternity   We poured out our fouls
" to God, for her, her children, ourfelves, the
" Church and Minifters, and for all mankind. My
" foul was tenderly affected for her fufferings, but
" the joy fwallowed up the forrow   How much
" then did her confolations abound ! The fervants
" of Chrift, *comparatively fpeaking*, fuffer nothing.
' I afked her, whether fhe was not in great pain ?
" Yes, fhe anfwered, but in greater joy   I would
" not be without either."   But do you not prefer,
" life or death ? She replied, all is alike to me ;
" let Chrift choofe, I have no will of my own.
" Her fpirit afcended to God, and we kneeled
" down and gave God thanks from the ground of
" our heart   Then we had recourfe to the book
" of comfort, and found it written, " *Let us there-*
" *fore labour to enter into that reft* " even fo, come
" Lord Jefus, and give us an inheritance among all
" them that are fanctified."

May

May 8th, " We folemnized the funeral * of our
" Sifter *Hooper*, and rejoiced over her with finging
" A great multitude attended her to the grave.
" There we fang another hymn of triumph. I found
" myfelf preffed in fpirit to fpeak to thofe who
" contradicted and blafphemed While I reafoned
" on death and judgment to come, many trembled,
" one woman cried out in horrible agony. We re-
" turned to the Room, and continued our folemn
" rejoicings, all defiring to be diffolved and to be
" with Chrift."

May 14th, He now vifited Mrs. *Lellington*,
drawing near the end of her journey through life
She had received peace and joy in believing, and all
fear of hell, death and fin, were fled away He
adds, " I faw two more of our fick Sifters, then
" two of the brethren in *Kingswood*, who were all
" rejoicing in hope of a fpeedy diffolution Preached
" at *Kendalfhire*, and vifited one of the Bands there,
" who walked through the valley of the fhadow of
" death, and feared no evil I prayed by a feventh
" in *Briftol*, who triumphed over the King of ter-
" rors If God be not with us, who hath begotten
" us thefe ?"

May 20th, " I was called to a dying woman, who
" confeffed fhe had often railed at me in her health,
" but was now conftrained to fend for me, and afk
" my pardon, or fhe could not die in peace. We
" prayed our Lord to fpeak peace and pardon to
" her foul. Several fuch inftances we have had of
" fcoffers, when their *feet flumble on the dark moun-*
" *tains.*----May 22nd, I preached a funeral fermon

---

* This was a very early interment, but I fuppofe the ftate of the body made it neceffary.

" for

" for our Sister *Lellington*, and attended the corpse
" to the grave, where we rejoiced in hope of quickly
" following her.   I gave an exhortation to repen-
" tance, though Satan greatly withstood me ; there-
" by teaching me, never to let go unwarned, the
" poor sinners that come on such occasions.-----
" Passed the night with my Brother at *Kingswood*,
" in watching unto prayer   I wish this primitive
" custom were revived among all our brethren.
" The word of God encourages us, to be in watch-
" ings often.   By two o'clock I returned to *Bristol*,
" and at five found strength to expound in the New
" Room.----May 30th, He observes, "I passed an
" hour with a spiritual Quaker, and rejoiced to
" find, we were both of the same religion."----I apprehend that all men, who have true christian
experience, are of the *same religion;* however
they may differ in opinion or modes of worship.
They are the one fold, under the one true Shepherd   If all true christians would consider this
point as they ought, there would soon be an end
of disputation among them, and brotherly love
would take place.

May 31st, " Throughout this day, I found my
" strength increase with my labour   I read in the
" Society, my account of *Hannah Richardson* *   She
" being dead, yet spake so powerfully to our hearts,
" that my voice was lost in the sorrowful sighing
" of such as be in captivity   To several God
" shewed himself the God of consolation , par-
" ticularly to two young *Welchmen*, whom his pro-
" vidence sent hither from *Caermarthen.*   They had

* This Account was printed   See Mr. *John Wesley's* Works, Vol 12.
Page 213

" heard

" heard moſt dreadful ſtoiies of us, *Arminians, Free-*
" *willers, Perfectioniſts, Papiſts*, which all vaniſhed
" like ſmoke, when they came to hear with theii
" own eais   God applied to their hearts the woid
" of his powei.   I took them to my lodgings, and
" ſtocked them with books, then ſent them away,
" recommended to the grace of God, which biingeth
" ſalvation to all men "

June 16th, " I pieached in *Kingswood*, on the
" dieadful woid, " SHIL ALL " How has the
" Devil baffled thoſe teacheis, who foi feai of
" ſetting men upon woiks, forbear urging this firſt
" *univerſal duty !* li enforcing Chiiſt's words be to
" preach woiks, I hope I ſhall pieach works as
" long as I live "---It is certain howevei, that Mr.
Weſley did not undeiſtand our Loid's woids liteially,
but as teaching us to put away eveiy thing we know
to be ſinful, how advantageous ſoevei it may be to
oui temporal inteieſt, oi agreeable to oui inclination, and that we ſhould omit no opportunity of
doing all the good in oui powei

July 11th, Mi *Weſley* pieached five times this
day   at *Biiſtol*, twice at *Kingswood*, at a place called
Sawfoid, and at *Both*.   He obſeives, " Satan took
" it ill to be attacked in his head quaiteis, that
" *Sodom* of oui land, *Bath*   He iaged horribly in
" in his children   They went out, and came back
" again, and mocked, and at laſt ioaied, as if each
" man's name had been Legion.   The ſincere,
" were melted into teais, and ſtiong deſiies of ſal-
" vation "---It is pleaſing to ieflect on the change
which has taken place in *Bath*, ſince the time of
which Mr. *Weſley* is heie ſpeaking   God has iaiſed
up many faithful witneſſes of his tiuth, both among
the

the Methodifts, and among Lady *Huntingdon*'s people, who have been ornaments to the chriftian profeffion: and at prefent the gofpel is preached there, without moleftation

July 13th, He fet out for *Cardiff*, and on the 15th, rode on with Mr. *Wells*, Mr. *Hodges*, and others to *Fonmon*-Caftle Mr *Wefley* adds, " Mr. *Jones*, who " had fent for me, received me very courteoufly. " He civilly apologized for the firft queftion, " which he afked me as a Magiftrate " Whether " I was a Papift? or whether I was a Member of " the Eftablifhed Church of *England?* He was fully " fatisfied with my anfwers, and I found we were " cotemporaries at the fame College. After din- " ner he fent to *Porthkerry*, where, at his defire, " Mr. *Richards* the Minifter lent me his pulpit. " I preached, on, " *God fo loved the world,"* &c. " Never hath he given me more convincing words. " The flock, and their fhepherd, were deeply af- " fected After fermon, Mr *Richards* begged my " pardon for having believed the ftrange reports " circulated concerning me. God had now fpoken " the contrary to his heart, and to the hearts of " his people. I yielded to Mr. *Jones's* impor- " tunity, and agreed to delay my return to *Briftol*, " that I might preach here once more, and fpend " a night at the Caftle "

July 17th, He met Mr and Mrs *Jones* at Mr. *Richards's*, where he again preached, and in the evening went to the Caftle. Mr *Wefley* adds, " We ate our bread with gladnefs and fingle- " nefs of heart, and at feven o'clock I preached " to fome hundreds in the Court-Yard My three " brethren, the Rev. Meffrs. *Richards*, *Wells*, and " *Hodges*,

" *Hodges*, ftood in the midft of the people, and
" kneeled on the ground in prayer, and cried after
" the Son of *David*. He breathed into our fouls
" ftrong defires O ! that he may confirm, in-
" creafe, and fatisfy them ---The voice of thankf-
" giving was heard in this place Before and after
" fupper, we fang, and bleffed God with joyful
" lips. They in the parlour, and kitchen, were
" continually honouring him, by offering up praife
" I thought it looked like the houfe of faithful
" *Abraham*. The next day, July 18th, I took
" fweet counfel with Mr *Jones* alone The feed
" is fown in his heart, and will bring forth fruit
" unto perfection His wife joined us, and I com-
" mended them to the grace of God in earneft
" prayer, and then went on my way rejoicing "

Mr. *Wefley* now returned to *Briftol*, and on
Auguft the 3d, he preached the funeral fermon for
Mrs. *Peacock*, who died in the Lord moft trium-
phantly. He obferves, " She was always praifing
" God for giving her fuch patience. All her de-
" fires were unto the Lord, and fhe continued
" calling upon him, in all the confidence of love,
" till he received her into his more immediate
" prefence At the fight of her coffin, my foul
" was moved within me, and ftruggled as a bird to
" break its cage Some relief I found in tears,
" but ftill was fo overpowered, that, unlefs God
" had abated the vehemence of my defires, I could
" have had no utterance. The whole congregation
" partook with me, in the bleffednefs of mourning.
" ---Auguft 6th, Coming to pray by a poor *Welch*
" woman, fhe began with me, " Bleffed be God
" that ever I heard you ! Jefus, my Jefus, has
" heard

" heard me on a bed of ficknefs. He is in my
" heart, he is my ftrength, none fhall pluck
' me out of his hands. I cannot leave him, and
" he will not leave me O! do not let me afk for
" death, if thou wouldft have me live. I know
" thou canft keep me. If thou wouldft have me
" live, let me live humbly with thee all my days."
" I fat and heard her fing the new fong, till even my
" hard heart was melted She glorified the Saviour
" of the world, who would have all men to be
" faved " I know it, faid fhe, he would not have
" one finner loft Believe, and he will give you
" all that, which he has given me "—Surely the
doctrine which thefe men preached, was the true
gofpel of God our Saviour. It not only improves the underftanding, but it gives ftrength
and firmnefs of mind to the moft weak and ignorant,
enabling them to triumph over the fevereft afflictions to which human life is fubject Here is a
poor illiterate *Welch* woman, who not only rifes
fuperior to ficknefs and death, but talks in a rational
fcriptural manner, of the deep things of God! Shew
me any fyftem of philofophy, any mere fpeculative
notions of divinity, any other way of preaching the
gofpel, which produces the fame effects on the human mind in the fame circumftances then I may
doubt, whether this be the true gofpel.

On the 24th of this month Mr. *Wefley*, in company with F. *Farley*, paid another vifit to his friends
in *Wales*, and again in September, ftaying only a few
days each time. Mr. *Jones*, of *Fonmon-Caftle*, accompanied him in his return from the laft vifit;
being defirous to fee the wonderful effects of the
gofpel among the wild ignorant Colliers of *Kingswood* Thither Mr *Wefley* took him on the 20th
of September, and fays, " It was a glorious time at
the Society, where God called forth his witneffes,

L   Our

Our guest was filled with confolation, and acknowledged that God was with us of a truth   I met the
Bands, and ftrongly urged them to prefs towards the
mark.   Read them a letter full of threatenings to
take our houfe by violence.   We laughed our enemies to fcorn   faith faw the mountain full of horfe-
men and chariots of fire.   Our brother from *Wales*
was compelled to bear his teftimony, and declare
before all what God had done for his foul.   He
warned us to prepare for the ftorm which would
furely fall upon us, if the work went on.   His artlefs words were greatly bleffed to us all , and our
hearts were bowed and warmed by the fpirit of love,
as the heart of one man."

September 22,   " Mr *Jones* wifhed to take me
to fome of his great friends in the city ; particularly
to a Counfellor, about the threatened feizure of our
fchool   I feared nothing but trufting to an arm of
flefh .   our fafety is, to be ftill   However, at his
importunity I went with him a little way, then turned
back, and at laft agreed to go with him to Juftice
C—, the moft forward of our adverfaries.   He
received us courteoufly.   I faid, I came to wait
upon him in refpect to his office, having heard his
name mentioned among fome, who were offended at
the good we did to the poor Colliers   that I fhould
be forry to give any juft caufe of complaint, and was
willing to know if any had been made . that many
idle reports were fpread, as if he fhould countenance
the violence of thofe who had feized the houfe of
Mr. C— and now threatened to take away the Collier's fchool.   He faid it would make a good
Workhoufe.—I caught hold of the expreffion, and
replied, it is a Workhoufe already.   Ay, faid he,
but what work is done there ? I anfwered, we work
the works of God, which man cannot hinder   ' But
you occafion the increafe of the poor.'   Sir, you are
misinformed ,

misinformed, the reverse of that is true None of
our Society are chargeable to you even those who
were so, before they heard us, are not so now,
the men who spent all their wages at the Alehouse,
now never go there at all, but keep their money to
maintain their families, and have to give to those
who want. Notorious swearers, have now only the
praises of God in their mouths. The good done
among them is indisputable, our worst enemies
cannot deny it No one who hears us, continues
either to swear or drink. If I thought so, he hastily,
replied *(in eodem luto hæsitans)* I would come and
hear you myself I desired he would, and said,
the grace of God was as sufficient for him as for
our Colliers, and who knew but he might be
converted among us?

" I gave him to understand, that Mr. *Jones* was
in the Commission of the Peace, who then asked him,
on what pretence they had seized Mr. C—'s
house? He utterly denied having had any hand in
it, and said he should not at all concern himself. ' For
if what you do, you do for gain, you have your re-
ward if for the sake of God, he will recompense
you. I am of *Gamaliel's* mind, if this Counsel or
work be of men, it will come to nought, but if it be
of God.'—I proceeded, ye cannot overthrow it, lest
haply ye be found to fight against God. Follow
therefore *Gamaliel's* advice, take heed to yourselves, refrain from these men, and let them alone.
He seemed determined so to do, and thus, through
the blessing of God, we parted friends.

" In our way home I admired the Hand which
directs all our paths. In the evening at *Bristol*, we
found under the word, that there is none like unto
the God of *Jeshurun*. It was a time of sweet re-
freshment. Just when I had done, my Brother
came in from *London*, as if sent on purpose to be

L 2   comforted

comforted together with us * He exhorted and
prayed with the congregation for another half hour.
Then we went to our friend *Vigers*, and for an hour
or two longer, our souls were satisfied as with marrow and fatnefs, while our mouth praifed God with
joyful lips "

I find no account of Mr *Wefley's* labours for the
year 1742. In the beginning of February 1743,
he was employed with his brother Mr. *John Wefley*,
in vifiting the Claffes in *London*, † and makes an
obfervation, which deferves the moft ferious confideration both of Preachers and people. " One
among the Claffes, fays he, told my brother, that fhe
had a conftant fenfe of forgivenefs, and he let her
pafs I could not help proving her further; and
then the juftified finner appeared full of the gall of
bitternefs. She faid again and again, of a Sifter
prefent, I do not love her, I hate her, &c. I
affured her that if an angel from heaven told me *fhe*
was juftified, I would not believe him, for fhe was
a murderer As fuch we prayed for her, and fhe
was convinced of unbelief, I fear we have *many
fuch believers* among us "—Mr. *Wefley* was no friend
to an over hafty admiffion of members into the
Society, which he thought hurtful. He clearly faw
two errors, into which the Methodift Preachers are
continually in danger of falling. Every affiftant is
defirous of making the *numbers* in the different
Societies over which he has prefided, appear as high
as poffible, at the yearly Conference. This becomes
a ftrong temptation to take improper perfons into
the Society, whofe life and converfation do no
credit to religion Every Preacher in the Metho-

* This exactly accords with Mr *John Wefley's* printed Journal See
his Works, vol xxviii page 5
† See again, vol xxxvii page 133

dift

dift connection, is defirous of making as many friends to himfelf as poffible, among the people, and this becomes a temptation to omit reproof where it is neceffary, to flatter the profeffions of fome, who deferve no credit, and to fpeak of others as being in a ftate of grace, to which they have no claim. I fincerely wifh that every Preacher may carefully avoid thefe dreadful precipices, where he is in conftant danger of deftroying both himfelf and others.

In the latter end of February, Mr *Wefley* went down to *Bath* and *Briftol* and here, and in the neighbouring places, perhaps alfo in *Wales* (for his Journal does not mention particulars) he continued his labours till the 17th of May, when he fet out for the North He preached at *Painfwick*, admitted twelve new members into the Society, and then vifited *Stroud*, *Evefham*, and feveral other places; and on the 20th, he obferves, " I got once more to our dear Colliers at *Wednefbury* Here the feed has taken root, and many are added to the church A Society of more than three hundred, are feeking full redemption in the cleanfing blood of *Chrift* The enemy rages exceedingly, and preaches againft them. A few here have returned railing for railing, but the generality have behaved as the followers of Chrift Jefus. May 21, I fpent the morning in conference with feveral who have received the atonement under my Brother's miniftry. I faw the piece of ground to build a chapel upon, given us by a Diffenter I walked with many of our brethren to *Walfol*, finging as we went. We were received with the old complaint, *Behold thefe that turn the world upfide down, are come hither alfo.* We walked through the town, amidft the noify greetings of our enemies. I ftood on the fteps of the Market-Houfe An hoft of men came againft us, and they lifted up their voice and raged horribly. I preached from thefe words, *But none*

*of thefe things move me; neither count I my life
dear unto myfelf, fo that I might finifh my courfe with
joy,* &c. The ftreet was full of fierce *Ephefian* beafts,
(the principal man letting them on) who roared,
and fhouted, and threw ftones inceffantly. At the
conclufion a ftream of ruffians was fuffered to beat
me down from the fteps, I rofe, and having given
the bleffing, was beat down again, and fo a third
time   When we had returned thanks to the God of
our falvation, I then from the fteps bid them depart
in peace, and walked through the thickeft of the
rioters. They reviled us, but had no commiffion
to touch a hair of our head. May 22, I preached
to between one and two thoufand peaceable people,
at *Birmingham,* and again at *Wednefbury* in the evening   On the 23d, I took my leave in thofe words,
*Confirming the fouls of the difciples, and exhorting them
to continue in the faith, and that we muft through much
tribulation enter into the kingdom of heaven.* With
many tears, and bleffings, they fent me away, recommended to the grace of God."

May 24, Mr. *Wefley* reached *Nottingham,* having
preached at two or three places in his way thither
from *Wednefbury.* At two o'clock, he went to the
Market-Crofs, and proclaimed the Saviour of all
men, and in the evening expounded, at their requeft,
to Mr *Howe's* Society. The next day he was at the
crofs again, he obferves, " There was not a breath
of oppofition, but a ftorm muft follow this calm.
Several perfons joined me at the Inn, in prayer and
thankfgiving   One gave me a kind caution, for
which I fincerely thanked him. ' Mr. *Rogers* did
run well, and preached the truth, as you do here,
but what a fad end has he made of it' Take care you
do not leave the Church like him.' In the afternoon I came to the flock in *Sheffield,* who are as
fheep among wolves, the Minifter having fo ftirred up
                                                    the

the people, that they are ready to tear the Methodifts
in pieces. At fix o'clock, I went to the Society
houfe, next door to our brother *Bennet's* Hell
from beneath was moved to oppofe us   As foon as
I was in the defk, with *David Taylor*, the floods began to lift up their voice. An Officer in the Army,
contradicted and blafphemed. I took no notice of
him, but fang on. The ftones flew thick, ftriking
the defk and the people. To fave them, and the
houfe from being pulled down, I gave out, that I
fhould preach in the ftreet, and look them in the
face   The whole army of the alien *Chaldeans* followed me. The Captain laid hold on me, and began rioting· I gave him for anfwer, *A word in feafon, or advice to a Soldier.* I then prayed, particularly for his Majefty King *George*, and preached the
gofpel with much contention   The ftones often
ftruck me in the face. I prayed for finners, as
fervants of their Mafter, the Devil, upon which the
Captain ran at me with great fury, threatening revenge for abufing, as he called it, " *The King his
Mafter.*" He forced his way through the brethren,
drew his fword, and prefented it to my breaft. I immediately opened my breaft, and fixing my eye on
his, and fmiling in his face, calmly faid, ' I fear God
and honour the King.' His countenance fell in a moment, he fetched a deep figh, and putting up his
fword, quietly left the place. He had faid to one of
the company who afterwards informed me, ' You
fhall fee if I do but hold my fword to his breaft, he
will faint away ' So perhaps I fhould, had I only his
principles to truft to, but if at that time I was not
afraid, no thanks to my natural courage.—We returned to our brother *Bennet's*, and gave ourfelves
up to prayer. The rioters followed, and exceeded
in outrage, all I have feen before. Thofe at *Moorfields, Cardiff,* and *Walfal,* were lambs to thefe.

As there is no King in *Israel,* I mean no Magistrate
in *Sheffield,* every man doth as seemeth good in his
own eyes."—The mob now formed the design of pull-
ing down the Society house, and set upon their work,
while Mr *Wesley* and the people were praying and
praising God within. " It was a glorious time, says
he, with us   every word of exhortation sunk deep,
every prayer was sealed, and many found the spirit of
glory resting upon them "—The next day the house
was completely pulled down, not one stone being left
upon another " Nevertheless, said Mr *Wesley* to a
friend, the foundation standeth sure, and our house
not made with hands, eternal in the heavens "—This
day he preached again in the street, somewhat more
quietly than before. In the evening the rioters became very noisy again, and threatened to pull down
the house, where Mr *Wesley* lodged He went out
to them , read the Riot-Act, and made a suitable exhortation, and they soon afterwards separated, and
peace was restored.

   May 27   At five in the morning, he took leave
of the Society in these words, *Confirming the souls of
the disciples, and exhorting them to continue in the
faith, and that we must through much tribulation enter
into the kingdom of God* He observes, " Our hearts
were knit together, and greatly comforted we rejoiced in hope of the glorious appearing of the great
God, who had now delivered us out of the mouth of
the lions. *David Taylor* informed me, that the people of *Thorpe,* through which we should pass, were
exceedingly mad against us.   So we found them as
we approached the place, and were turning down the
lane to *Barley-Hall* The ambush rose, and assaulted
us with stones, eggs, and dirt My horse flew from
side to side, till he found his way through them.
They wounded *D. Taylor* in the forehead, and the
wound bled much. I turned back, and asked, what
                                                        was

was the reason, a Clergyman could not pass without
such treatment? At first the Rioters scattered, but
their Captain rallying them, answered with horrible
imprecations and stones   My horse took flight, and
turned away with me down a steep hill   The enemy pursued me from afar, and followed shouting.
Blessed be God, I received no hurt, only from the
eggs and dirt   My clothes indeed abhorred me, and
my arm pained me a little from a blow I received at
Sheffield."—This conduct is undoubtedly disgraceful
to humanity   I hope the present inhabitants of these
towns will endeavour to retrieve their character, by
a peaceable and obliging behaviour on all occasions.
Mr. *Wesley* now spent an hour or two, with some
quiet sincere persons, assembled at *Barley-Hall*   By
four o'clock in the afternoon he reached *Bristal*, a
land of rest.   Here they had peace in all their bor-
ders.   Great multitudes were bowed down, by the
victorious power of gospel truth   " It was, says Mr.
Wesley, a time much to be remembered, for the gracious rain, wherewith our God refreshed us."—The
next day he preached again, in the morning and at
noon, to this child-like people, and again in the afternoon at *Ormsby*, in his way to *Leeds*.   May 29,
he informs us in his Journal, that, not a year before,
he had come to *Leeds*, and found no man who cared
for the things of God   " but, he observes, a spark
has now fallen in this place also, and it will kindle a
great flame.   I met the Infant Society, about fifty
in number, most of them justified, and exhorted them
to walk circumspectly   At seven o'clock, I stood
before Mr. *Shent*'s door, and cried to thousands,
Ho! every one that thirsteth, come ye to the waters.
The word took place   They gave diligent heed to
it, and seemed a people prepared for the Lord.   I
went to the great Church, and was shewed to the
Ministers pew.   Five Clergymen were there, who a
                                        little

little confounded me, by making me take place of my elders and betters. They obliged me to help in administering the sacrament. I assisted with eight more Ministers, for whom my soul was much drawn out in prayer But I dreaded their favour, more than the stones at *Sheffield.*"—What Mr. *Wesley* here speaks respecting the Clergymen present, must not be understood as implying either disrespect or reproach. If he had any fault in his judgment of the Clergy, it was that he thought too highly of the Clerical office The fear which he here speaks of, concerned himself only He was fully convinced, that the *manner* in which he now preached the Gospel, was not contrary to any written law of God or man from the circumstance of being excluded from the Churches, from the satisfaction he experienced in himself, in carrying the Gospel to those who would not come to it, and from the effect of his labours on multitudes of the people, he was fully satisfied that his present plan of proceeding was agreeable to the will of God. But he found, that the favours and friendly attentions of those who disapproved of it, tended to weaken his resolution to persevere in it.   Kindness has a wonderfully assimilating influence on the human mind it melts down opposition in a generous heart, and while a man feels nothing but the most agreeable sensations from it, he is insensibly changed into a conformity with those who shew him favour. Many have been turned from their duty, by kindness and favour, who could not be moved by persecution. Mr. *Wesley* felt the force of this assimilating principle, and hence he says, that he dreaded their favour more than the stones at *Sheffield*

At two o'clock, he found a vast multitude waiting for the word, and strongly exhorted them to repent and believe the gospel, that their sins might be blotted out.   He preached again at *Bristol*, calling upon the poor

poor and maimed, the halt and blind, to come to the
great supper. He observes, " My Lord disposed
many hearts, I doubt not, to accept the invitation.
He shewed me several witnesses of the truth, which
they have now received in the love of it. I had a
blessed parting with the society. May 30, my horse
threw me, and fell upon me My companion thought
I had broken my neck, but my leg only was bruised,
my hand sprained, and my head stunned, which
spoiled me from making hymns, or thinking at all
till the next day, when the Lord brought us safe to
Newcastle At seven o'clock I went to the Room,
which will contain about two thousand persons. We
rejoiced for the consolation of our mutual faith."

Many persons at *Newcastle*, had been greatly agitated during the preaching, falling into convulsive
motions with strong cries. At their first preaching
of the Gospel, many, as he justly observes, were undoubtedly struck down into the deepest distress,
which affected both soul and body Mr. *Wesley* believed, that such instances might still continue to occur. But he soon perceived, that these natural affections, and the outward expressions of them, were
easily imitated, and the persons at first so affected,
being much noticed and talked of, this became a
temptation to others to imitate their state He says,
" I have already detected many counterfeits." I
recollect two instances, mentioned in his Journal before this period A woman at *Kingswood* was greatly
agitated under his preaching, and cried much: he
turned to her and said, I do not think the better of
you, for crying, &c. and she presently became quite
calm A young girl at *Bristol* fell into fits, and
seemed like one in a trance She continued this
practice for some time, but at length acknowledged
she had done it, that Mr *Wesley* might take notice
of her No man ever had a more tender sympathy
with

those in diftrefs, than Mr. *Charles Wefley*, but no
man abhorred hypocrify, or a mere affumed appearance of religious concern more than he did.
Yet he did not judge perfons who appeared to be fo
affected, till he had the proper evidences on which
he could form a true judgment, but he thought it
prudent to give them no encouragement, until fome
evidence of their fincerity appeared   June 4, " To
day, fays he, one came who was pleafed to fall into
a fit for my entertainment. He beat himfelf heartily
I thought it a pity to hinder him, fo, inftead of finging over him, as had often been done, we left him to
recover at his leifure   A girl, as fhe began her cry,
I ordered to be carried out   Her convulfions were
fo violent, as to take away the ufe of her limbs, till
they laid her without at the door, and left her, then,
fhe immediately found her legs, and walked off.
Some very unftil Sifters, who always took care to ftand
near me, and tried who fhould cry loudeft, fince I
have had them removed out of my fight, have been
as quiet as lambs   The fiift night I preached here,
half my words were loft, through the noife of their
outcries.   Laft night before I began, I gave public
notice, that whofoever cried, fo as to drown my
voice, fhould, without any man's hurting or judging
them, be gently carried to the furtheft corner of the
room   But my Porters had no employment the
whole night! Yet the Lord was with us, mightily
convincing of fin and of righteoufnefs "

June 5. " My foul was revived by the poor people at *Chowden*, and yet more at *Tanfield*, where I
called to great numbers, *Behold the Lamb of God*, &c.
At *Newcaftle* I preached in the crowded fquare,
chiefly to the backfliders, whom I befought with
tears to be reconciled to God. Surely Jefus looked
upon fome of them as he looked upon *Peter* June 6,
I had the great comfort of recovering fome of thofe
                                        who

who have drawn back I truſt we ſhall recover them
again for ever. On the 8th, I ſpake to the Bands
ſeparately, and tried their faith. We certainly have
been too raſh and eaſy in allowing perſons for believers on their own teſtimony nay, and even per-
ſuading them into a falſe opinion of themſelves.
Some ſouls it is doubtleſs neceſſary to encourage;
but it ſhould be done with *prudence* and caution.
To tell one in darkneſs that he has faith, is to keep
him in darkneſs ſtill, or to make him truſt in a falſe
light, a faith that ſtands in the words of men, not in
the power of God.—June 13, I wrote thus to a Son
in the goſpel, Be not over ſure that ſo many are
juſtified By their fruits ye ſhall know them. You
will ſee reaſon to be more and more deliberate in
the judgment you paſs on perſons. Wait for their
converſation. I do not know whether we can infallibly pronounce at the time, that any one is
juſtified. I once thought ſeveral in that ſtate, who,
I am now convinced were under the drawings of the
Father Try the ſpirits therefore, leſt you ſhould lay
the ſtumbling-block of pride in their way, and by ſup-
poſing them to have faith before they have it, you
keep them out of it for ever "

We may perceive by theſe obſervations, that Mr
Weſley was a diligent attentive watchman over the
people. He carefully explored the unfrequented
road through which he had to guide them, and ho-
neſtly pointed out the flattering by-paths which led
to miſery and danger But experience hath repeat-
edly ſhewn, that they who moſt want theſe ſalutary
cautions, are the leaſt diſpoſed to receive them.
Few perſons have ſincerity enough to be thankful
for advice which tends to undeceive them, to ſtrip
them of ſome imaginary comforts, and make them
think worſe of themſelves than they did before.
Profeſſors of religion are commonly the moſt impatient

tient of fuch advice   It is certain, that thefe cautions require great prudence and difcernment, in
applying them to particular perfons , but in a large
body of people, and among a great number of Preachers, there is much more danger of flattering individuals into a falfe confidence, under a pretence of
giving them encouragement, than of hindering their
progrefs by putting them upon a clofe and fevere
felf-examination.   In the one cafe we tread a flip-
pery path, in the other we ftand on firm ground
At this early period of the prefent revival of religion,
Mr. *Wefley* faw the neceffity of making thefe remarks.
He repeated them frequently afterwards, and has
been cenfured for fo doing.   I wifh the neceffity of
urging fuch advice on the Preachers and people,
may not greatly increafe, while the practice of doing
it is daily diminifhed.

Mr *Wefley* obferves, that firce he had preached
the gofpel it never had greater fuccefs than at this
time at *Newcaftle*.   " Yet, fays he, we have no fits
among us, and I have done nothing to hinder them,
only declared that I do not think the better of any
one for crying out — June 16, I fet out for *Sunder-
land* with ftrong averfion to preaching.   I dragged
myfelf to about a thoufand wild people, and cried,
*O Ifrael, thou haft deftroyed thyfelf, but in me is thy
help*   Never have I feen greater attention in any
people at their firft hearing the word.   We rode to
Shields, went to Church, and the people flocked in
crowds after me.   The Minifter fpake fo low that
he could not be heard in reading prayers, but I heard
him loud enough afterwards, calling to the Church-
Wardens to quiet the difturbance, which none but
himfelf had raifed   I fancy he thought I fhould
preach in the Church were I flood, like fome of the
firft Quakers.   The Clerk came to me bawling out,
' It was confecrated ground, and I had no bufinefs

to preach on it. That I was no Minister,' &c.
When he had cried himself out of breath, I whispered in his ear that I had no intention to preach
there. He stumbled on a good saying, ' If you
have any word of exhortation to the people, speak
to them without.' I did so, to an huge multitude
waiting in the church-yard many of them very
fierce, threatening to drown me, and what not! I
walked through the midst of them, and discoursed
in strong awakening words on the *Jailor's* question,
What must I do to be saved. The Church-Wardens and
others laboured in vain to interrupt me, by throwing
dirt, and even money among the people. Having
delivered my message, I rode to the Ferry, crossed
it, and met as rough friends on the other side. The
mob of *North Shields* waited to salute me, with the
Minister at their head. He had got a man with a
horn instead of a trumpet, and bid him blow, and
his companions shout. Others were almost as violent in their approbation. We went through honour
and dishonour, but neither of them hurt us, and by
six o'clock with God's blessing we came safe to *Newcastle.*

June 19 Mr. *Wesley* took leave of the Society at
Newcastle, who parted from him with tears and many
prayers. Wherever he came, he preached or exhorted
as opportunity offered, and on the 22d, reached *Epworth,* his native place " All who met me, says
he, saluted me with hearty joy. At eight in the
evening I preached in *Edward Smith's* yard. July
23, waking, I found the Lord with me, even my
strong helper, the God of whom cometh salvation.
I preached and guarded some new converts against
spiritual pride."—The next day, June 24, he arrived at *Nottingham,* and adds, " I found my brother in the market-place,* calling lost sinners to him

* See also Mr *John Wesley's* works, vol xxviii page 151

who

who juftifieth the ungodly. He gave notice of my
preaching in the evening. At feven, many thoufands attended in deep filence.   Surely the Lord
hath much people in this place.   We began a fociety of nine members   June 25, I came to *Birmingham*, and the next day, being Sunday, feveral of our
perfecuted brethren from *Wednefbury*, came to me,
whom I endeavoured to comfort.   I preached at
eight and at one o'clock, no man forbidding me
I expounded in the evening to feveral thoufands   In
the name of the Lord *Jefus Chrift*, I began our fociety.   The number at prefent is thirteen "

June 27. He fet out for *London*, where he arrived on the evening of the 28th, having vifited *Oxford* in his way thither.   July 3, he fays, " Mr
Hall, poor moravianized Mr. *Hall*, met me at the
Chapel.   I did him honour before the people.   I
expounded the Gofpel, as ufual, and ftrongly avowed my intolerable attachment to the church of *England*.   Mr *Meriton* and *Graves* affifted at the facrament.—July 6, I fhewed from Romans the 5th, the
marks of Juftification, and overturned the *vain* confidence of feveral.   I ftrongly warned them againft
feducers, and found my heart knit to this people.
July 8, *I Bray* came to perfuade me, not to preach
till the Bifhops fhould bid me   They have not yet
forbid me, but by the grace of God I fhall preach
the word, in feafon and out of feafon, though they
and all men forbid me '—July 11, he left *London*,
and the day following arrived in *Briftol*.   He ftayed
there only one night, and then fet out for *Cornwall*,
and on the 16th, came fafe to *St Ives*. July 17, he
fays, " I rofe and forgot that I had travelled from
Newcaftle.   I fpake with fome of this loving fimple
people, who are as fheep in the midft of wolves
The Priefts ftir up the people, and make their minds
                                              evil

evil affected towards their brethren Yet the sons of violence are much checked by the Mayor, an honest Presbyterian, whom the Lord hath raised up

Mr *Wesley* continued preaching the Gospel at *St. Ives* and the places adjacent, till the beginning of August During this time, he and the people passed through many difficulties and dangers, the rioters being numerous, and almost as desperate as those at *Sheffield* The Mayor informed Mr. *Wesley* that the ministers were the principal authors of all the mischief In their sermons they continually represented Mr. *Wesley* and the preachers, as Popish Emissaries, and urged the enraged multitude to take all manner of means to stop them While he was preaching at *St Ives* on the 26th, he observes, " All was quiet, the Mayor having declared his resolution to swear twenty more Constables, and suppress the rioters by force of arms. Their drum he had seized. All the time I was preaching he stood at a little distance to awe the rioters. He has set the whole town against him, by not giving us up to their fury. But he plainly told Mr *Hoblin*, that fire and faggot Ministers, that he would not be perjured to gratify any man's malice He informed us, that he had often heard Mr. *Hoblin* say, they ought to drive us away by blows, not by arguments."

During the riots he one day observes, " I went to church, and heard that terrible chapter, *Jeremiah* the 7th, enough, one would think, to make even this hardened people tremble Never were words more applicable than those, *Stand in the gate of the Lord's house, and proclaim there this word, and say, Hear the word of the Lord, all ye of Judah, that enter in at the gates to worship the Lord. Thus saith the Lord of hosts, the God of Israel, amend your way and your doings, and I will cause you to dwell in this place. Trust ye not in lying words, saying, The* TEMPLE OF

M   THE

THE LORD, *The* TEMPLE OF THE LORD, *The*
TEMPLE OF THE LORD, *are these —Behold ye trust
in lying words that cannot profit. Will ye steal, murder, and commit adultery, and swear falsely—and come
and stand before me in this house? &c*

His brother having summoned him to *London,* to
confer with the heads of the *Moravians* and *Calvinists,*
he set out on the 8th of August. " We had, says
he, near three hundred miles to travel in five days.
I was willing to undertake the labour for the sake
of peace, though the journey was too great for us
and our beasts, which we had used almost every day for
three months. August 12, hardly reached the
Foundery by nine at night. Here I heard that the
Moravians would not be present at the Conference.
Spangenberg indeed said he would, but immediately
left *England.* My brother was come from *Newcastle, I. Nelson* from *Yorkshire,* and I from the Land's
End, for good purpose!"

October 17. He set out to meet his brother at
Nottingham, who had escaped with his life, almost by
miracle, out of the hands of the mob at *Wednesbury.*
On the 21st, Mr *Charles Wesley* observes, " My
brother came, delivered out of the mouth of the
Lions! His clothes were torn to tatters—He looked
like a soldier of Christ. The mob of *Wednesbury,
Darlaston,* and *Walsal,* were permitted to take and
carry him about for several hours, with a full intent
to murder him but his work is not yet finished, or
he had been now with the souls under the Altar.
October 24, I had a blessed parting from the Society, and by night came wet and weary to *Birmingham.* On the 25th, was much encouraged by the
patience of our brethren from *Wednesbury.* They
pressed me to come and preach to them in the midst
of the town. It was agreed between my brother
and me, that if they asked me I should go. Accordingly

ingly we set out in the dark, and came to *Francis Ward's*, from whence my brother had been carried last Thursday night * I found the brethren assembled, standing fast in one mind and spirit, in nothing terrified by their adversaries. The word given me for them, was, " Watch ye, stand fast in the faith, quit yourselves like men, be strong " *Jesus* was with us in the midst, and covered us with a covering of his spirit Never was I before, in so primitive an assembly We sang praises with courage, and could all set out seal to the truth of our Lord's saying, *Blessed are they that are persecuted for righteousness sake* We laid us down and slept, and rose up again, for the Lord sustained us As soon as it was light, I walked down the town and preached boldly. It was a most glorious time our souls were satisfied as with marrow and fatness, and we longed for our Lord's coming to confess us before his Father, and before his holy Angels —We now understood what it was to receive the word in much affliction, and yet with joy in the Holy Ghost

" I took several new members into the Society; and among them, the young man whose arm had been broke, and *Munchin*, upon trial, the late captain of the mob He has been constantly under the word, since he rescued my brother I asked him what he thought of him? 'Think of him, said he, that he is a man of God, and God was on his side, when so *many of us* could not kill *one man*'—We rode through the town unmolested on our way to *Birmingham*, where I preached I rode on to *Evesham*, and found *John Nelson* preaching, and confirmed his word October 27, preached at five in the morning, then read prayers and preached twice at *Quinton*, and the fourth time at Evesham, with great liberty "

* See Mr *John Wesley's Works*, vol xxviii page 175

October 29, he came once more to *Bristol*, where, he observes, that he had only spent one day for six months   On the 31st, he set out for *Wales*, and reached *Cardiff* on the first of November "The gentlemen, says he, had threatened great things if I ever came there again   I called in the midst of them, ' Is it nothing to you, all ye that pass by,' &c   The love of God constrained me to speak and them to hear   The word was irresistible. After it one of the most violent opposers took me by the hand, and pressed me to come and see him   The rest were equally civil all the time I staid, only one drunkard made some disturbance, and when sober, sent to ask my pardon —The voice of praise and thanksgiving was in the Society   Many are grown in grace and in the knowledge of our Lord and Saviour *Jesus Christ*   I passed an hour with the wife and daughter of the Chief Bailiff, who are waiting as little children for the kingdom of God."

November 6   Mr *Wesley* returned to *Bristol*. On the 16th he preached at *Bath* in his way to *Cirencester*, and the Lord gave testimony to his word. He travelled on, and preached at *Evesham*, *Gutherton*, *Quinton*, and *Oxford*, and on the 23d, at the *Foundery*   He staid in *London*, labouring in public and private, for the good of the people, till January 30, 1744, when he again set out for the North, recommended to the grace of God by all the brethren. On the first of February, he came to *Birmingham*. He observes, " A great door is opened in the country, but there are many adversaries.' The preacher at *Dudley* had been cruelly abused by a mob of Papists and Dissenters, the Dissenters being stirred by Mr *Hinting* their minister   " It is probable, says Mr *Wesley*, that he would have been murdered, but for an honest Quaker, who favoured his escape by disguising him in his broad hat and *drab coloured coat.*

coat *Staffordshire*, at present, seems the seat of war." Mr. *Wesley* here uses the word *Dissenters* in the common acceptation, as denoting either *Presbyterians, Independents*, or *Baptists*, but which of these denominations is here intended I do not know. No men have cried out with more vehemence against persecution, when under the rod, than the Dissenters, and yet we find that their principles and practices have sometimes been at variance. I am inclined to think, that the *Friends*, or Quakers, as they are commonly called, are the only denomination of Christians in *England*, of any long standing, who have never been guilty of persecution, in some form or other. Candour must acknowledge that this is greatly to their praise.

February 2. " I set out with brother *Webb*, for *Wednesbury*, the field of battle. We met with variety of greetings on the road. I cried in the street, ' Behold the Lamb of God, which taketh away the sins of the world.' Several of our persecutors stood at a distance, but none offered to make the least disturbance. I walked through the blessings and curses of the people (but the blessings exceeded) to visit Mr. *Egerton's* widow. Never have I observed such bitterness as in these opposers. February 3, I preached, and prayed with the Society, and beat down the fiery self-avenging spirit of resistance, which was rising in some to disgrace, if not to destroy the work of God." Mr. *Wesley* preached within sight of *Dudley*, and then waited on the friendly Captain *Dudley*, who had stood in the gap, and kept off persecution at *Tippen-Green*, while it raged all around. He then returned in peace through the enemy's country.

The rioters now gave notice that they would come on the Tuesday following, and pull down the houses and destroy the goods of the Methodists. " One

would

would think, says Mr. *Wesley*, there was no king in
Israel There is certainly no Magistrate, who will
put them to shame in any thing.   Mr. *Constable* offered to make oath that their lives were in danger,
but the Justice refused it, saying that he could do nothing   Other of our complaining brethren met
with the same redress, being driven away with revilings   The Magistrates do not themselves tear off
their clothes and beat them, they only stand by and
see others do it   One of them told Mr *Jones*, it
was the best thing the mob ever did, so to treat the
Methodists, and he himself would give five pounds
to drive them out of the country   Another, when
our brother *Ward* begged his protection, delivered
him up to the mercy of the mob, who had half-mur-
dered him before, and throwing his hat round his
head, cried, huzza boys, well done, stand up for the
church.'—Such Magistrates, sworn to maintain the
public peace, and such defenders of a national
church, are a lasting disgrace to any government.
Mr *Wesley* adds, " No wonder that the mob, so encouraged, should say there is no law for the Methodists   Accordingly, like outlaws they treat them,
breaking open their houses, and taking away their
goods at pleasure extorting money from those who
have it, and cruelly beating those who have it not.
February 4, I spoke with those of our brethren who
have this world's goods, and found them entirely resigned to the will of God, all thoughts of resistance,
blessed be God, are over The chief of them said to
me, ' Naked came I into the world, and I can but
go naked out of it ' They are resolved, by the
grace of God, to follow my advice, and to suffer all
things. Only I wished them to go round again to
the Justices and give information of their danger.
Mr. *Constable* said he had just been with one of them,
who redressed him only by bitter reproaches, that
the

the reft were of the fame mind, and could not plead
ignorance, becaufe the rioters had the boldnefs to fet
up papers inviting all the country to rife with them
to deftroy the Methodift. —At noon I returned to *Birmingham*, having continued two days in the lion's
den unhurt."

Mr *Wefley* now fet out for *Nottingham*, where he
arrived on the 6th, and found that here alfo, the
monfter perfecution was lifting up its deftructive
head   " Our brethren, fays he, are violently driven from their place of meeting, pelted in the ftreets,
&c and mocked with vain promifes of juftice by
the very man who underhand encourages the rioters
An honeft Quaker has hardly reftrained fome of our
brethren from refifting evil   but henceforth I hope,
they will meekly turn the other check "

Mr. *Wefley* and his friends at *Nottingham* fent a
perfon to *Litchfield*, to get intelligence of what mifchief had been done in *Staffordfhire*, by the rioters
in their threatened infurrection. He returned on
the ninth, and Mr *Wefley* gives the following account. " He met our brother *Ward*, who had fled
thither for refuge   The enemy had gone to the
length of his chain   all the rabble of the county were
gathered together, and laid wafte all before them.
I received a note from two of the fufferers, whofe
lofs amounts to two hundred pounds   My heart rejoiced in the great grace which was given them, for
not one refifted evil, but they took joyfully the
fpoiling of their goods   We gave God glory, that
Satan was not fuffered to touch their lives   they
have loft all befides, and rejoice with joy unfpeakable "

Mr *Wefley* now went on to *Newcaftle*, preaching
every where, as he had opportunity The year forty-
four, was confidered as a time of public danger
There was much talk of the *Pretender*, and the

M 4   *Fren b*

French threatened an invasion in support of his pretensions to the Crown of England   In this critical
situation of affairs, it was thought proper by many, that
Mr *John Wesley* should write an address to the King
in the name of the Methodists   This address was accordingly drawn up * but not delivered   On the 6th
of March Mr *Charles Wesley,* wrote to his brother
on this subject, as follows. " My objection to
your address in the name of the Methodists, is, that
it would constitute us a sect · at least it would *seem to
allow* that we are a body distinct from the *National*
church, whereas we are only a found part of the
church   Guard against this, and in the name of the
Lord   address to-morrow "—March 14, being at
Bristol, a person informed him there was a Constable
who had a warrant in which his name was mentioned.
Mr *Wesley* sent for him, and found it was, " To
summon witnesses to some treasonable words said to
be spoken by one *Wesley* " He was just leaving
Bristol when this information was given him, but he
now determined not to go forward for *London* as he
intended, thinking it better to appear before the Justices at *Wakefield* the next day, and look his enemies
in the face   Accordingly, he rode to *Wakefield* the
next morning, and waited on Justice *Burton* at his
Inn, with two other Justices, Sir *Rowland Wynn,*
and the Rev Mr *Zouch.* He informed Mr *Burton,*
that he had seen a warrant of his, summoning witnesses of some treasonable words, said to be spoken
by one *Wesley*   that he had put off his journey to
London, that he might answer whatever should be
laid to his charge   Mr. *Burton* replied, he had nothing to say against him, and he might depart.   Mr
Wesley answered, " That is not sufficient without

* See Mr *John Wesley's* Works, vol xxviii. page 209, where the
Address itself is inserted

clearing my character, and that of many innocent
people, whom their enemies are pleased to call Methodists. ' Vindicate them, said my brother Clergyman, that you will find a very hard task.' I answered, as hard as you may think it, I will engage
to prove that all of them, to a man, are true members of the church of *England*, and loyal subjects of
his Majesty King *George*. I then desired they would
administer to me the oaths, and added, I wish, gentlemen, that you could send for every Methodist in
England, and give them all the same opportunity you
do me, of declaring their loyalty upon oath. Justice *Burton* said, he was informed that we constantly
prayed for the *Pretender* in all our societies, or noc-
turnal meetings, as Mr *Zouch* called them. I answered the very reverse is true. We constantly pray
for his Majesty King *George*, by name. Here are
such hymns (shewing them) as we sing in our societies. Here is a sermon which I preached before the
University, and another preached there by my brother. Here are his appeals and a few more tracts,
containing an account of our principles and practices.
Here I gave them our books, and was bold enough
to say, I am as true a church of England man, and
as loyal a subject as any man in the kingdom. They
all cried that was impossible. But it was not my business to dispute, and as I could not answer till the
witnesses appeared, I withdrew without further delay.

" While I waited at a neighbour's house, the Constable from *Bristol*, whose heart the Lord had touched, was brought to me by one of the brethren. He
told me he had summoned the principal witness,
Mary Castle, on whose information the warrant was
granted. She was setting out on horseback when the
news came that I was not gone forward to *London*,
as they expected, but had returned to *Wakefield*.
Hearing this she turned back, and declared to him
                                                    that

that she did not hear the treasonable words herself, but another woman had told her so. Three more witnesses, who were to swear to my words retracted likewise, and knew nothing of the matter. The fifth, Mr *Woods*, an Alehouse-keeper, is forth-coming, it seems, in the afternoon I now plainly see the consequence of not appearing here to look my enemies in the face. Had I gone on my journey, there would have been witnesses enough, and oaths enough, to stir up a persecution against the Methodists. I took he witnesses names, and a copy of the warrant as follows.

" West Riding of *Yorkshire.*

" To the Constable of *Birstal*, of the said Riding, or Deputy,

" THESE are, in his Majesty's Name, to require and command you to summon *Mary Castle*, of *Birstal* aforesaid, and all other such person or persons as you are informed can give any information against one *Westley*, or any other of the Methodist Preachers, for speaking any treasonable words or exhortations, as praying for the *banished*, or the *Pretender*, &c. to appear before me, and other of his Majesty's Justices of the Peace for the said Riding, at the *White Hart* in *Wakefield*, on the 15th of March instant, by ten o'clock in the forenoon, to be examined, and to declare the truth of what they and each of them know touching the premises and that you likewise make a return hereof, before us on the same day. Fail not Given under my hand the tenth of March 1744   E BURTON "

" Between two and three o'clock, Mr *Woods* came, and started back on seeing me, as if he had trod upon a serpent. One of the brethren took hold
of

of him, and told me he trembled every joint of him. The Justices Clerk had bid the Constable bring *Woods* to him as soon as ever he came But not-withstanding the Clerk's instructions, *Woods* frankly confessed, now he was come, he had nothing to say, and would not have come at all, if they had not forced him.

" I waited at the door till seven in the evening, while they were examining the disaffected I took public notice of *Okershousen*, the *Moravian* teacher; but not of Mr *Kendrick* When all their business was over, and I had been insulted at their door from eleven in the morning till seven at night, I was sent for and asked, what would Mr *Wesley* desire? *Wesley* I desire nothing but to know what is alleged against me Justice *Burton* said, what hope of truth from him? Then addressing himself to me, ' Here are two of your brethren, one so silly it is a shame he should ever set up for a teacher, and the other has a thousand lies and equivocations upon oath. He has not wit enough, or he would make a compleat *Jesuit* ' I looked round, and said, I see none of my brethren here, but this Gentleman, pointing to the Reverend Justice, who looked as if he did not thank me for claiming him *Burton* " Why do you not know this man? pointing to *Kendrick*. *Wesley* Yes Sir, very well for two years ago I expelled him from our Society in *London*, for setting up for a Preacher. To this poor *Kendrick* assented, which put a stop to further reflections on the Methodists. Justice *Burton* then said, I might depart, for they had nothing against me. *Wesley* Sir, that will not satisfy me, I cannot depart till my character be fully cleared It is no trifling matter even my life s concerned in the charge *Burton* I did not summon you to appear *Wesley* I was the person meant by one *Stiles*, and my supposed words were the occasion

cafion of your order, which I read figned with your
name   *Burton*   I will not deny my orders, I did
fend to fummon the witneffes   *Wefley*   Yes, and I
took down their names from the Conftable s paper.
The principal witnefs, *Mary Caftle*, was fetting out,
but hearing I was here, fhe turned back, and declared
to the Conftable, fhe only heard another fay, that I
fhould fpeak treafon.   Three more of the witneffes
recanted for the fame reafon   and Mr. *Woods*, who
is here, fays he has nothing to fay, and fhould not
have come, had he not been forced by the Minifter
Had I not been here, he would have had enough to
fay, and you would have had witneffes and oaths
enough, but I fuppofe, my coming has prevented
them   One of the Juftices added, ‘ I fuppofe fo
too ’

“ They all feemed fully fatisfied, and would have
had me to have been fo too.   But I infifted on their
hearing Mr *Wood.*   *Burton.*   Do you defire he may
be called as an evidence for you?   *Wefley*   I defire
he may be heard as an evidence againft me, if he has
ought to lay to my charge   Then Mr *Zouch* afked
Mr *Woods*, what he had to fay?   What were the
words I had fpoken   *Woods* was as backward to
fpeak as they to hear him   but was at laft compelled
to fay, ‘ I have nothing to fay againft the Gentleman, I only heard him pray, that the Lord would
call home his banifhed ones ’   *Zouch*   But were there
no words before or after, which pointed to thefe
troublefome times?   *Woods.* No   none at all   *Wefley*
It was on February the 12th, before the earlieft news
of the invafion.   But if folly and malice may be in-
terpreters, any words, which any of you Gentlemen,
may fpeak, may be conftrued into treafon.   *Zouch.*
It is very true   *Wefley*   Now, Gentlemen, give me
leave to explain my own words   I had no thoughts
of praying for the *Pretender*, but for thofe who con-

3   fefs

lefs themfelves ftrangers and pilgrims upon earth;
who feek a country, knowing this is not their home.
The fcriptures, yes Sir (to the Clergyman) know
that the fcriptures fpeak of us as captive exiles, who
are abfent from the Lord, while prefent in the body.
We are not at home till we are in heaven Zouch.
I thought you would fo explain the words, and it is
a fair interpretation—I afked if they were all fatisfied? They faid they were, and cleared me as fully
as I defired I then afked them again, to adminifter
to me the oaths. Mr. Zouch, looked on my fermon,
and afked who ordained me. I anfwered, the
Archbifhop, and Bifhop of London, in the fame week.
He faid, with the reft, it was quite unneceffary,
fince I was a Clergyman, and ftudent of Chrift
Church, and had preached before the Univerfity,
and taken the oaths before. Yet I mentioned it
again, till they acknowledged in explicit terms,
' That my loyalty was unqueftionable.' I then
prefented Sir Rowland and Mr Zouch, with the ap-
peal, and took my leave "

Mr Wefley now returned to Briftal, where he
preached, and then left Yorkfhire He came to
Derby, and Nottingham, at the laft of which places,
the mob was become outrageous, under the patronage of the Mayor The Methodifts prefented a petition to the Judge, as he paffed through the town,
and he gave the Mayor a fevere reprimand, and encouraged them to apply for relief if they were further molefted But the Mayor paid no regard to the
Judge, any longer than while he was prefent. On
the 22d of March Mr Wefley arrived late in London
Here he continued his labours till the beginning of
May, when he went down to Briftol, and returned in
about eight days There was at this time a Thomas
Ball ars, who had been admitted to preach in the
Foundery, and who had acquired confiderable influence

ence among the people. He applied for ordination,
was difappointed, and laid the blame chiefly on Mr.
Wefley, who had been as a father to him, and rendered him every friendly office in his power. He
now fhewed himfelf unworthy of fuch friendfhip.
Mr *Wefley* obferves, "He anfwers the character one
of his inmates gave me of him. 'I never thought him
more than a fpeaker I can fee no grace he has.
His converfation is quite contrary to the Gofpel,
light and vain He is haughty, revengeful, head-
ftrong, and unmanageable' June 15, I was grieved
to hear more and more of *W*—s ingratitude A lying fpirit feems to have taken full poffeffion of him
There is nothing fo grofs or improbable which he
does not fay "—By lies and infinuating arts, he was
too fuccefsful in prejudicing fome of Mr *Wefley's*
friends againft him. Alas! how little ufe do the
people make of their underftanding! how eafily do
they fuffer their eyes to be blinded, and their hearts
to be imbittered by artful men, againft thofe who are
honeftly labouring to do them good! It is truly wonderful to obferve, how foon they give themfelves up
to believe the moft improbable ftories which malice
can invent, againft their beft friends, how quickly
they drink deep into the fpirit of religious perfecution, even of thofe very perfons, whom a little before
they loved as their own fouls This was in fome
meafure the cafe at prefent, and I wifh it was the
only inftance among the Methodifts, in which the
people have fuffered themfelves to become the dupes
of artful and defigning men Mr *Wefley's* mind was a
good deal affected on this occafion, and he wrote
thus to a friend "Be not weary of well doing, or
overcome of evil. You fee, that our calling is to
fuffer all things Pray for me, that I alfo may endure unto the end for a thoufand times I cry out,
the burden of this people is more than I am able to
bear.

bear O my good friend, you do not know them!
Such depth of ingratitude I did not think was possible among the devils in hell "—" At night I was
informed that a friend had entertained the deepest
prejudice against me, on supposition that I meant her
in a late difcourfe Lord, what is man! what is
friendfhip!

"June 24. Our brethren *Hodges*, *Taylor*, and
Merton, affifted us at the Sacrament. At one Love
Feaft we were fix ordained Minifters. Monday the
25th, we opened our Conference,* with folemn
prayer and the Divine Blefling I preached with
much affiftance. We continued in Conference the
reft of the week, fettling our doctrines, practice, and
difcipline, with great love and unanimity."

Mr. *Wefley* fpent the remaining part of this year in
travelling, and preaching the Gofpel, with great
zeal, diligence, and fuccefs in many parts of the
kingdom, from the Land's End to *Newcaftle*. July
9th, he left *London*, and arrived in *Briftol* the next
day. On the 13th, he fet out for *Cornwall*, where
I c had the pleafure of feeing the word of God greatly
profper under his miniftry The joy which the Society expreffed, at his arrival in *St Ives*, is beyond
the power of words to defcribe and every where he
was received by great numbers of the people, as the
meffenger of God, for good Such was the fuccefs
of the Gofpel in *Cornwall*, this year, that in fome
places the inhabitants of a whole parifh feemed entirely changed in their amufements and morals. Perfecution raged in other places with great bitternefs;
but this did not much obftruct the progrefs of the
work It quickened the zeal of thofe who had experienced the power of gofpel truth, and united them
together in brotherly love it made them attentive

---

* This was the firft Conference. See the Minutes

to their conduct, and diligent in the means of grace, left they should give the enemy, watching for their halting, any cause of triumph When professors of religion are daily in danger, by persecution, of losing every thing they have in this world, and perhaps their lives too, they more sensibly feel the importance of the good things of another life, and more earnestly endeavour to secure them as their eternal inheritance Mr. *Wesley*, as usual, went through evil report and good report, was abused and caressed, by different classes of the people, but being intent on his work he was little affected by either. Having laboured in *Cornwall*, as a faithful Minister of *Christ*, near four weeks, during which time he had preached the Gospel in most parts of the county, he left it, and coming to *Minehead* passed over into *Wales*, and came safe to *Bristol* on the 17th of August

August 22. Mr *Wesley* arrived at *Oxford*, where he met his brother, the Rev Messrs *Piers* and *Me-riton*, and a great company of the brethren Mr. *John Wesley*, was to preach before the University, at St. Mary's, on the 24th He says, " My brother bore his testimony before a crowded audience, much increased by the races Never have I seen a more attentive congregation they did not suffer a word to slip them Some of the Heads of Colleges stood up the whole time, and fixed their eyes upon him If they can endure sound doctrine, like his, he will surely leave a blessing behind him. The *Vice Chancellor* sent after him, and desired his Notes, which he sealed up and sent immediately.' *

He now returned to *Bristol*, and on the 26th of September came up to *London* *Thomas Williams*, had invented so many stories, to injure him in the

* See Mr *John Wesley's* Works vol. xxvii p 233 where the agreement between the two accounts is striking and pleasing.

opinion of the people, and affected them with fo
much confidence, that they had made an ill impreffion on the minds of many of his friends. Thefe calumnies, however, were fo directly contrary to Mr.
Wefley's habits of life, being always in the company
of one friend or other, and almoft conftantly travelling from place to place, that they were altogether
incredible, and nothing but the confidence with
which they were afferted, could poffibly have made
an impreffion on any member of the Society Thofe
who wifh to propagate flander with fuccefs, are unufually confident in their affertions, and zealous in
their endeavours They invent a number of plaufi-
ble pretences for their zeal, and by this and the
boldnefs of their affertions, impofe on thofe who are
unacquainted with the arts of defigning men to
deceive

Mr *Wefley*, confcious of his innocence, and thinking the circumftances of this cafe fo clear that he
wanted no public defence, appointed a day when thofe
who had been troubled with any reports concerning
him, or his brother, might meet him In this conference, one who had been led away by the lies of
Thomas Williams, afked pardon of God and of Mr.
Wefley He obferves, " O! how eafy and delightful
it is, to forgive one who fays, I repent Lord grant
me power as truly to forgive them, who perfift to injure me "—I apprehend, that he has reference here
to *Williams*, and perhaps to a few others, too much
prejudiced to come to him

October 10, he fet out for the North, travelling
through the Societies to *Newcaftle*, and every where
ftrengthening the brethren, and convincing gain-
fayers with great fuccefs He laboured fome time
in *Newcaftle* and the neighbouring places, and having fuftained great bodily fatigue, and efcaped many
dangers in travelling through deep fnow, at this un-

N   favourable

favourable feafon of the year, he again reached *London* in fafety, on the 29th of December

In 1745   Mr *Wefley* confined his labours chiefly to *London*, *Briftol*, (including the neighbouring places) and *Wales*. Auguft 1, he obferves, " We began our conference, with Mr. *Hodges*, four of our affiftants, *Herb. Jenkins*, and Mr. *Gwynne*. We continued it five days, and parted in great harmony and love."—On the 25th, he was in *Wales*, and Mr. *Gwynne* fent his fervant, to fhew him the way to *Garth*, but having fome time before fprained his leg, and having taken too much exercife after the accident, he was unable to go, and at length left *Wales*, without vifiting that agreeable family —The following is a remarkable inftance of his zeal in doing good to the vileft and moft wretched of human beings.   October 9, " After preaching at *Bath*, a woman defired to fpeak with me   She had been in our Society, but left it through offence, and fell by little and little into the depth of vice and mifery.   I called Mrs. *Naylor* to hear her mournful account She had lived fome time in a wicked houfe, in *Avon-Street*, confeffed it was hell to her, to fee our people pafs by to the preaching, but knew not what to do, nor how to efcape.   We bid her fly for her life, and not once look behind her.   Mis *Naylor* kept her with herfelf till the morning, and then I carried her with us in the coach to *London*, and delivered her to the care of our fifter *Davey*.   Is not this a brand plucked out of the fire!"

February 3, 1746. He opened the new Chapel in *Wapping*, and preached from 1 Cor   xv. 1   *Moreover brethren, I declare unto you the Gofpel which I preached unto you, which alfo ye have received, and wherein ye ftand* —The next day he wrote to a friend, expreffing his apprehenfions that God was about to pour out heavy judgments on the nation. He fays to

his

his friend, " You allow us one hundred years to fill up the meafure of our iniquity, you cannot more laugh at my vain fear, than I at your vain confidence."—This, and the preceding year, were times of danger and national alarm, and it is obfervable that religious people are more apprehenfive of divine judgments, at fuch feafons, than other perfons. Thofe fearful apprehenfions have been falfely attributed to fuperftition; but I think they arife from a more rational and laudable principle Religious perfons have a more clear knowledge than others, of the enormity and guilt of national fins, they fee more clearly the mercies enjoyed, and know more perfectly the holinefs and vengeance of God againft fin, when once a nation has filled up the meafure of its iniquity, and hence arifes their fear, in any public danger, left this fhould then be the cafe   We have not indeed, any certain rule of judging when a nation has filled up the meafure of its iniquity, and is ripe for divine vengeance, and therefore may often be miftaken in applying a general principle, in itfelf true, to a particular inftance.   But every good man will rejoice, when, in times of public difturbance and danger, God is better to us than our fears and confcious guilt fuggefted   This was the cafe of Mr. *Wefley* —Being at *Briftol* when he firft heard the news of the victory at *Culloden*, over the rebel army, he obferves, " I fpoke at night on, *He that glorieth, let him glory in the Lord*   We rejoiced unto him with reverence, and thankfully obferved the remarkable anfwer of that petition,

> All their ftrength o'erturn, o'erthrow,
>   Snap their fpears and break their fwords
> Let the daring Rebels know,
>   The Battle is the Lord's.

Oh! that in this repiieve, before the tide is turned, we may know the time of our vifitation."

May 29. He obferves, " In Conference, I found many of our children in a thriving condition, not one of thofe who are juftified, dreams that he is fanctified at once, and wants nothing more "—Mr *Charles Wefley* was an uniform and fteady oppofer of the opinion of his brother, that a perfon is fanctified at once, by a fimple act of faith, in the manner he is juftified or pardoned   And there are many among the Methodifts who think the Scriptures give no countenance to this opinion   Such a method of proceeding, is certainly not analogous to the operations of Divine Power, in the productions of nature, nor does it accord with the common order in which the mind acquires knowledge and experience, and which appears to be founded on the nature of our faculties.—But this fubject will be more fully difcuffed, in explaining the religious opinions of Mr *John Wefley*.

What has already been faid of Mr *Charles Wefley*, fufficiently demonftrates, that he was animated with a difintereſted and laudable zeal for the promotion of chriftian knowledge, among the middling and lower clafſes of the people   Both his doctrines and practice, tended to difcourage a party fpirit, and to promote brotherly-love among all denominations of Chriftians in the kingdom   Thofe who differ from him in judgment, and are difpofed to cenfure what has been called his irregularity, muft notwithftanding, acknowledge the goodnefs of his motives, and admire his indefatigable diligence.   He feldom ftaid long in one place, but preached the Gofpel in almoft every corner of the kingdom   In fatigues, in dangers, and in minifterial labours, he was, for many years, not inferior to his brother, and his fermons were generally more awakening and uſeful   Neither he nor his brother travelled alone, fome perfon always accompanying them, whom they treated rather as a companion, than as a fervant.   This

plan

plan was not adopted merely for the fake of convenience, but that they might conftantly have perfons
about them who might be witnefles of their conduct
and behaviour This was prudent, confidering the
falfe reports which were propagated concerning
them —June 2, Mr. *Charles Wefley* left *Briftol*, accompanied with a Mr. *Waller;* intending to vifit
the brethren in *Cornwall.* He took a large circuit
in his way thither, preaching fometimes in a houfe,
and occafionally in the ftreet, where he met with
various treatment from the people. At *Taviftock,*
he found great oppofition, the people behaving almoft like wild beafts they were reftrained however,
from doing any mifchief Here, fome of Mr.
Whitefield's fociety at *Plymouth,* met him, and importuned him to come and preach among them, and
he complied with their requeft, Mr *Whitefield* was
his particular friend and no man, perhaps, ever felt
the attachment of friendfhip, in a ftronger degree,
than Mr. *Charles Wefley* yet on account of fome
difference in opinion he determined to preach, not
in their houfe, but in the ftreets, or fields only. He
might perhaps be afraid, left he fhould fay fomething
in the warmth of an extempore difcourfe, which
would give offence, or promote difputings among
them.   At length, however, their importunity
overcame his refolution and caution. He met them
in their houfe, prayed with them, and endeavoured
to provoke them to love and good works. He foon
found that God was with them, who does not make
thofe diftinctions among his true worfhippers, for
fpeculative errors, which men are apt to imagine.
Mr *Wefley* obferves, " I found no difference between them and our children at *Kingswood,* or the
Foundery." He continued a few days, till the 23d,
with this earneft artlefs people, who feemed ready to
devour the word. During his ftay here, he went over

to the *Dock*, and preached *Chriſt* crucified to a great multitude of hearers. The word was as a fire, melting down all it touched He adds, " we mourned and rejoiced together in him that loved us. I have not known ſuch a refreſhing time ſince I left *Briſtol* " Sunday, June 22, he preached again on a hill in *Stoke* Church-yard, to upwards of four thouſand perſons by computation. Some reviled at firſt, but Mr. *Weſley* turning to them and ſpeaking a few words, ſilenced them, the generality behaving as men who feared God When he had finiſhed his diſcourſe they followed him with bleſſings, only one man curſed, and called him *Whitefield* the ſecond.

He now prepared to leave them. " Our own children, ſays he, could not have expreſſed greater affection to us at parting If poſſible, they could have plucked out their own eyes, and have given them to us Several offered me money, but I told them I never accepted any Others would have per-ſuaded Mr. *Waller* to take it, but he walked in the ſame ſteps and ſaid their love was ſufficient "

Mr *Weſley* reached *Gwennup*, in the Weſt of *Corn-wall*, on the 26th of June, and he gives the following account of the ſtate of the people. " Upon examina-tion of each ſeparately, I found the Society in a proſ-perous way their ſuffering had been for their fur-therance, and for the furtherance of the Goſpel. The oppoſers behold and wonder, at their ſtedfaſt-neſs and godly converſation —June 29, my evening congregation was computed to be upwards of five thouſand They all ſtood uncovered, kneeled at prayer, and hung, *Narrantis ab ore* * For an hour and a half, I invited them back to their Father, and felt no hoarſeneſs, or wearineſs afterwards. I ſpent

---

* *On the mouth of the Speaker.* A ſtrong metaphorical expreſſion for attention

an hour and a half more with the Society, warning
them againft pride, and the love of the creature, and
ftirring them up to univerfal obedience."

Monday, June 30, " Both fheep and fhepherds,
had been fcattered in the late cloudy day of perfecution but the Lord gathered them again, and kept
them together by their own brethren, who began to
exhort their companions, one, or more in every
Society.   No lefs than four have fprung up in
Gwennap I talked clofely with each, and found no
reafon to doubt that God had ufed them thus far   I
advifed, and charged them, not to ftretch themfelves
beyond their line, by fpeaking out of the Society, or
fancying themfelves public teachers.   If they keep
within their bounds as they promife, they may be
ufeful in the Church and I would to God, that all
the Lord's people were prophets like thefe."

July 3   " At *Lidgeon*, I preached *Chrift* crucified, and fpake with the Claffes, who feem much in
earneft.   Shewed above a thoufand finners at *Sithney*, the love and compaffion of *Jefus*, towards them.
Many who came from *Helftone*, a town of rebels and
perfecutors, were ftruck, and confeffed their fins,
and declared they would never more be found fighting againft God — July 6, At *Gwennup*, near two
thoufand perfons liftened to thofe gracious words
which proceeded out of his mouth, *Come unto me all
ye that travel and are heavy laden, &c.* Half of them
were from *Redruth*, which feems on the point of fur-
rendering to the Prince of Peace The whole country finds the benefit of the Gofpel.   Hundreds, who
follow not with us, have broke off their fins, and are
outwardly reformed, and the perfecutors in time
paft, will not now fuffer a word to be fpoken
againft this way   Some of thofe who fell off in the
late perfecution, defired to be prefent at the Society

" At

" At *St Ives*, no one offered to make the leaſt diſturbance indeed the whole place is outwardly changed in this reſpect. I walk the ſtreets with aſtoniſhment, ſcarcely believing it is *St Ives* All oppoſition falls before us, or rather is fallen, and not yet ſuffered to lift up its head again This alſo hath the Lord wrought "

July 19. " Rode to *Sithney*, where the word begins to take root The rebels of *Helſtone* threatened head—they ſay all manner of evil of us. Papiſts we are, that is certain and are for bringing in the Pretender Nay the vulgar are perſuaded that I have brought him with me, and *James Waller* is the man But law is to come from *London* to-night to put us all down, and ſet *a price* upon my head " It is hardly poſſible to conceive the danger of Mr. *Weſley's* ſituation, when ſuch an opinion as this prevailed among the fierce Tinners of *Cornwall*. But he truſted in God and was protected. He obſerves, " We had notwithſtanding, a numerous congregation, and ſeveral of the perſecutors. I declared my commiſſion to open their eyes, to turn them from darkneſs to light, &c Many appeared convinced, and caught in the Goſpel net "

The next day, being Sunday, Mr *Weſley* preached again, and near one hundred of the fierceſt rioters were preſent. A ſhort time before, theſe men had cruelly beat the ſincere hearers, not ſparing the women and children It was ſaid, the miniſter of the pariſh had hired them for that purpoſe. But now, theſe very men, expecting a diſturbance, came to protect Mr *Weſley*, and ſaid they would loſe their lives in his defence The whole congregation was attentive and quiet.

It is not eaſy, perhaps impoſſible, to give a ſatisfactory reaſon, on natural principles, for that ſudden and entire change which ſometimes takes place on
theſe

thefe occafions, in the minds of the moft viol. nt op-
polers of the Golpel I believe the moft attentive
obferver could never difcover any external circumftance, fufficient to produce the change If we admit a particular providence, and a divine fupernatural influence on the mind of man, the matter becomes
plain and eafy , but without taking thefe into the account, both this and many other things appear inex-
plicable myfteries. I believe the chief objections
which philofophers, who make high pretenfions to
reafon, have made to many Chriftians on thefe two
points, have originated in a fuppofition, that a particular providence, and a fupernatural influence on
the mind, are not directed by fixed laws, analogous
to the operations of Divine power in the works of
nature, and that a fupernatural influence muft fu-
percede or derange the operations of our natural faculties But in both thefe things, I apprehend, they
are miftaken It appears to me, that the interpofi-
tions of Providence in the affairs of men, and a Divine influence on the human mind, are under regulations, or laws, according to the œconomy of the
Golpel, which are as wifely adapted to attain the
end propofed, in the circumftances of the fubjects to
which they are applied, and operate with as much
certainty, under thefe circumftances, as the laws by
which the heavenly bodies are preferved within their
refpective orbits, and directed in their various motions The fubjects of a particular providence, and
of divine influence, in this view of them, are moral
agents, poffeffed of active powers, which I apprehend are effentially different from the re-action, or
the repulfive force of inanimate bodies But were
moral agents to be conformable to thefe laws of a
particular providence, and of divine influence, in
the œconomy of the Golpel, I have no doubt but
they would operate with as much regularity and certainty,

tainty, as the laws of motion   Nor is it neceſſary
that a ſupernatural influence on the mind, ſhould
either ſuperſede or derange the operations of our
natural faculties.   It gives efficacy to the external
means of inſtruction, and co-operates with them;
it gives vigour and ſtrength to the ſoul, in the ac-
quiſition of knowledge and virtue on the goſpel
plan, and enables us to attain ſuch degrees of them,
as could not be attained under any circumſtances,
by our merely natural powers.   Indeed, when I
conſider the Goſpel, not only as a revelation from
God, of truths uſeful to man, but as the means divinely appointed, of redeeming him from ſin and
death, and by a reſurrection reſtoring him to im-
mortal life and glory   when I conſider the connected
ſeries of prophecies, which for ages prepared the
world for its reception as an univerſal bleſſing, the
manifeſtations of divine power at its promulgation
and eſtabliſhment, the glory attributed to *Jeſus
Chriſt*, in the Scriptures, as our Redeemer and Ad-
vocate, and the relation which he conſtantly bears
to his people, as their Captain, and the Head of his
Church, it appears to me, altogether derogatory
from the wiſdom and goodneſs of God to ſuppoſe,
that the Goſpel, connected with all theſe circumſtances, ſhould now be left in the world as a de-
ſerted orphan, to ſhift for itſelf in the beſt manner
it can, without any divine influence, or ſuperin-
tending care.   This ſuppoſition renders the Goſpel
unworthy of the ſublime deſcriptions given of it in
the Old and New Teſtament, and reduces it to a
mere ſyſtem of Ethics, or moral precepts, as in-
adequate to the great and noble purpoſe of man's
redemption, as the moral teachings of *Socrates* or
Plato.

Whatever may be ſaid of theſe reaſonings, Mr.
Weſley thought he was in the way of his duty, and
under

under the protection of a *particular* Providence;
and pursued his labours with great diligence, confidence, and success He was informed that the
people of *St Just*, being scattered by persecution,
had wandered into by-paths of error and sin, and
had been confirmed therein by their exhorter. He
visited them, and spake with each member of the
Society; and adds, "I was amazed to find them
just the reverse of what they had been represented.
Most of them had kept their first love, even while
men were riding over their heads, and while they
were passing through fire and water. Their exhorter appears a solid humble Christian, raised up
to stand in the gap, and keep the trembling sheep
together." The next day he again talked with
some of the Society, and says, "I adored the
miracle of grace, which has kept these sheep in the
midst of wolves Well may the despisers behold
and wonder. Here is a bush, burning in the fire
yet not consumed! What have they not done to
crush this rising sect, but lo! they prevail nothing!
For one Preacher they cut off, twenty spring up.
Neither persecutions nor threatening, flattery nor
violence, dungeons, or sufferings of various kinds,
can conquer them. Many waters cannot quench
this little spark which the Lord hath kindled, neither
shall the floods of persecution drown it."

" Monday, July 28. I began my week's experiment of leaving off tea but my flesh protested
against it I was but half awake and half alive, all
day and my head-ach so increased towards noon,
that I could neither speak nor think So it was for
the two following days, with the addition of a violent
diarrhœa, occasioned by my milk diet. This so
weakened me, that I could hardly sit my horse.
However, I made a shift to ride to *Gwennap*, and
preach and meet the Society. Being very faint and
weary,

veary, I would afterwards have eat something, but could get nothing proper.'

The congregations had been large in most places, during his stay in the West of *Cornwall* but it being generally known that he was now preparing to leave it, they were greatly increased.   Sunday August 10, being at *Gwennap*. He observes, "Nine or ten thousand, by computation, listened with all eagerness, while I recommended them to God, and the word of his grace.   For near two hours I was enabled to preach Repentance towards God, and faith in our Lord *Jesus Christ*   I broke out, again and again, into prayer and exhortation, believing, not one word would return empty   Seventy years sufferings would be overpaid, by one such opportunity   Never had we so large an effusion of the spirit, as in the Society, I could not doubt at that time, either of their perseverance, or my own and still I am humbly confident, that we shall stand together among the multitude which no man can number.

The next day, August 11, being filled with thankfulness to God, for the mercies shewn to himself and the people, he wrote a thanksgiving hymn, which begins thus,

> All thanks be to God,
> Who scatters abroad
> Throughout every place,
> By the least of his servants, his favour of grace
> Who the victory gave
> The praise let him have
> For the work he hath done,
> All honour and glory to Jesus alone¹ &c.

He now travelled forward to St *Endys*, and preached on, *Repent and believe the Gospel* His friends, the Rev. Messrs *Bennet* and *Tomson*, were present.   "As I was concluding, says he, a Gentleman rode up to me very fiercely, and bid me
come

come down We exchanged a few words, and talked together more largely in the houfe The poor drunken Lawyer went away in as good a humour as he was then capable of I had more difficulty to get clear of a different antagonift, one *Adams*, an old Enthufiaft, who travels through the land, as overfeer of all the Minifters '

Having received many letters from Mr *Kinf-man's* family, Mr. *Jenkins*, and others at *Plymouth*, importuning him to favour them with another vifit on his return, he complied with their requeft, on the 14th of Auguft, and on the 18th, he took boat at the Dock, accompanied by feveral friends, to meet a congregation at fome diftance He ob-ferves, " The rough ftormy fea tried our faith. None ftirred, or we muft have been overfet. In two hours, our invifible Pilot brought us fafe to land, thankful for our deliverance, humbled for our littlenefs of faith, and more endeared to each other by our common danger We found thou-fands waiting for the word of life The Lord made it a channel of grace. I fpoke and prayed alter-nately, for two hours. The moon-light added to the folemnity. Our eyes overflowed with tears, and our hearts with love fcarce a foul but was af-fected with grief or joy We drank into one fpirit, and were perfuaded, that neither life nor death, things prefent, nor things to come, fhall be able to feparate us *from the love of God which is in Chrift Jefus our Lord.*"

Mr *Wefley* continued his labours daily, vifiting various places in his way to *Briftol*, where he ar-rived on the 28th, and came fafe to *London* on the 2d of September He ftaid here a fortnight, during which he became acquainted with Mr. *Edward Perronet*, a fenfible, pious, and amiable young man. September the 16th, they fet out, accompanied

accompanied by feveral friends, to pay a vifit to
the Rev Mr. *Perronet*, Vicar of *Shoreham* in *Kent*,
a man of a moft artlefs child-like fpirit, and zealous
for the doctrines of the Gofpel   But his preaching
and godly converfation, had, as yet, but little influence on the minds of the people, who, through
ignorance, oppofed the truth with great violence.
It is probable, notice had been given, that Mr
Wefley would preach in the church.   "As foon,
fays he, as I began preaching, the wild beafts be
gan roaring, ftamping, blafpheming, ringing the
bells, and turning the church into a bear-garden.
I fpoke on for half an hour, though only the neareft
could hear.   The rioters followed us to Mr. *Perronet's* houfe, raging, threatening, and throwing
ftones.   *Charles Perronet* hung over me, to in-
tercept the blows   They continued their uproar,
after we got into the houfe."   Mr. *Wefley* returned
to *London*, with Mr. *E Perronet*, and October the 9th,
being appointed as a day of public thankfgiving
for national mercies, the Foundery was filled at
four in the morning   Mr. *Wefley* preached from
thofe words, *How fhall I give thee up Ephraim?*
He adds, "Our hearts were melted by the long-
fuffering love of God, whofe power we found dif-
pofing us to the true thankfgiving   It was a day
of folemn rejoicing.   O that from this moment, all
our rebellions againft God might ceafe!

Though the winter was now approaching, and
travelling far North is both difficult and dangerous
at this feafon, yet Mr. *Wefley*, in a poor ftate of
health, determined to take his Northern journey
as far as *Newcaftle-upon-Tyne*   October 10, he tells
us, "I fet out for *Newcaftle* with my young companion and friend, *E. Perronet*, whofe heart the
Lord hath given me.   His family has been kept
from us fo long by a miftaken notion, that we were
                                                          againft

against the Church." He visited the brethren in *Staffordshire*, and on the 15th, preached at *Tippen-Green*. After preaching in the evening, a friend invited him to sleep at his house at no great distance from the place. Soon after they were sat down, the mob beset the house, and beating at the door, demanded entrance. Mr. *Wesley* ordered the door to be set open, and the house was immediately filled. "I sat still, says he, in the midst of them for half an hour. I was a little concerned for *E. Perronet*, lest such rough treatment at his first setting out, should daunt him. But he abounded in valour, and was for reasoning with the wild beasts, before they had spent any of their violence. He got a deal of abuse thereby, and not a little dirt, both of which he took very patiently. I had no design to preach; but being called upon by so unexpected a congregation, I rose at last, and read, ' When the Son of man shall come in his glory, and all the holy angels with him, then shall he sit on the throne of his glory.' While I reasoned with them of judgment to come, they grew calmer by little and little. I then spake to them, one by one, till the Lord had disarmed them all. One who stood out the longest, I held by the hand, and urged the love of Christ crucified, till in spite of both his natural and diabolical courage, he trembled like a leaf. I was constrained to break out into prayer for him — Our leopards were all become lambs, and very kind we were at parting. Near midnight the house was clear and quiet. We gave thanks to God for our salvation, and slept in peace."

October 21, Mr *Wesley* preached at *Dewsbury*, where *John Nelson* had gathered many stray sheep, and formed a Society. The Minister did not condemn them unheard, but talked with them, examined into the doctrine they had been taught,

and

and its effects on their lives When he found, that
as many as had been affected by the preaching,
were evidently reformed, and brought to Church
and Sacrament, he testified his approbation of the
work, and rejoiced that sinners were converted to
God This conduct certainly deserves great praise;
and had all the Ministers of the Established Church
acted with the same candour, it is probable they
would have served the interests of the Church better
than they have done, and the work would have been
much more extended than we have yet seen it

October 25 They arrived at *Newcastle*, where
Mr *E. Perronet* was immediately taken ill of the
small pox, and had a very narrow escape for his
life October 31, Mr *Wesley* observes, " Rode to
Wickham, where the Curate sent his love to me,
with a message that he was glad of my coming, and
obliged to me for endeavouring to do good among
his people, for none wanted it more, and he heartily
wished me good luck in the name of the Lord He
came, with another Clergyman, and staid both
preaching and the meeting of the Society" As
such instances of liberality and candour are not very
common among Ministers of the Gospel, they deserve the greater commendation, who have resolution to set so good an example

Mr *Wesley* continued his labours in, and about
Newcastle, till the 27th of November, when he rode
to *Hexham*, at the pressing request of Mr *Wardrobe*,
a Dissenting Minister, and others He observes,
" I walked directly to the Market-place, and called
sinners to repentance A multitude of them stood
staring at me, but all quiet The Lord opened
my mouth, and they drew nearer and nearer, stole
off their hats, and listened none offered to interrupt, but one unfortunate Squire, who could get no
one to second him. His servants and the con-

3   stables,

stables hid themselves   one he found and bid him
go and take me down   The poor Constable simply
answered, 'Sir, I cannot have the face to do it,
for what harm does he do?' Several Papists attended, and the Church Minister, who had refused
me his pulpit with indignation   However he came
to hear with his own ears   I wish all who hang us
first, would, like him, try us afterwards"

"I walked back to Mr *Ord's*, through the people,
who acknowledged, 'It is the truth and none can
speak against it' A Constable followed, and told me,
'Sir *Edward Blacket* orders you to *disperse* the
'town' (depart, I suppose he meant) and not raise a
disturbance here   I sent my respects to Sir *Edward*,
and said, if he would give me leave I would wait
upon him and satisfy him   He soon returned with
an answer, that Sir *Edward* would have nothing to
lay to me   but if I preached again and raised a
disturbance, he would put the law in execution
against me   I answered, that I was not conscious
of breaking any law of God or man, but if I did,
was ready to suffer the penalty   that, as I had not
given notice of preaching again at the Cross, I
should not preach again *at that place*, nor cause a
disturbance any where   I charged the Constable,
a trembling, submissive soul, to assure his worship,
that I reverenced him for his office sake   The only
place I could get to preach in was a Cock-pit, and I
expected Satan would come and fight me on his
own ground   Squire *Roberts*, the Justice's son,
laboured hard to raise a mob, for which I was to
be answerable; but the very boys ran away from
him, when the poor Squire persuaded them to go
down to the Cock-pit and cry fire   I called, in
words then first heard in that place, *Repent and be
converted, that your sins may be blotted out*   God
struck the hard rock, and the waters gushed out.

O   Never

Never have I feen a people more defirous of knowing the truth, at the firft hearing. I paffed the evening in confeience with Mr *Wardrobe*. O that all our Diffenting Minifters were like-minded, then would all diffentions ceafe for ever!*

---

* It is uncertain, whether Mr *Wardrobe* was at this time fettled as a Diffenting Minifter at *Hexham* He was afterwards, however, fixed at *Bethgate*, in *Scotland*, where he laboured as a faithful Minifter of Chrift, till his death He was a man of great piety, and of more liberality of mind than was commonly found among the *Scotch* Minifters at that time He cultivated an acquaintance with the *Methodifts*, and on the 22d of May 1755, preached in their houfe at *Newcaftle*, to the no fmall amazement and difpleafure of fome of his zealous countrymen He died on the 7th of May 1756, and Mr *Adams*, Minifter at *Falkirk*, gives the following account of his death, in a letter to Mr *Gilles* " On Friday night, about ten, I witneffed Mr *Wardrobe's* entrance into the joy of his Lord But ah! who can help mourning the lofs of the Church of Chrift? His amiable character gave him a diftinguifhed weight and influence, which his Lord had given him to value, only for its fubferviency to his honour and glory He was fuddenly taken ill on the laft Lord's day, and from the firft moment believed it was for death I went to fee him on Thurf-day evening and heard fome of the livelieft expreffions of triumphant faith, zeal for the glory of Chrift and the falvation of fouls, mixed with the moft amiable humility and modefty Yet a little while, faid he, *and this mortal fhall put on immortality Mortality fhall be fwallowed up of life this vile body fafhioned like to his glorious body! O for victory! I fhall get the victory! I know in whom I have believed* Then with a remarkably audible voice, lifting up his hands he cried out, *O for a draught of the well of the water of life, that I may begin the fong before I go off to the Church triumphant! I go forth in thy name, making mention of thy righteoufnefs, even of thine only I die at the feet of mercy* Then ftretching out his arms, he put his hand upon his head, and with the moft ferene and fteady majeftic eye, I ever faw, looking upward, he faid, *Crowns of grace, Crowns of grace, and palms in their hands! O Lord God of truth, into thy hands I commend my fpirit!* He fays to me, *You that are Minifters, bear a proper teftimony againft the profeffors of this age, who have a form of godlinefs without the power* Obferving fome of his people about his bed, he faid, *May I have fome feals among you! O where will the ungodly and finners of Bathgate appear? Labour all to be in Chrift* Then he ftretched out his hand to feveral, and faid, *Farewell, Farewell, Farewell* and to, *O Ita, what want I for? My hope is in thee!* Once or twice he faid, *Lay me to lead acrofs the bed to expire, where I have fometimes prayed, and fometimes meditated with pleafure* He expreffed his grateful fenfe of the affiduous care which Mr *Wardrobe*, of Cult, had taken of him, and on his replying, " Too much could not be done for fo valuable a life," faid, *O fpeak not fo, or you will provoke God Glory be to God, that I have ever had any regard paid me for Chrift's fake I am greatly funk under the wind O help me by your prayers, to get the proper fubmiffion and improvement*"

November

November 28, at fix, we affembled again in our Chapel, the Cock-pit   I imagined myfelf in the *Pantheon*, or fome *Heathen* Temple, and almoft fcrupled preaching there at firft, but we found the earth is the Lord's, and the fulnefs thereof   His prefence confecrated the place.   Never have I found a greater fenfe of God, than while we were repeating his own prayer.   I fet before their eyes, Chrift crucified   The rocks were melted, and gracious tears flowed.   We knew not how to part   I diftributed fome books among them, which they received with the utmoft eagernefs, begging me to come again, and to fend our Preachers to them."

December 6   He fays, "I vifited one of our fick children, and received her bleffings and prayers. December 18, I waked between three and four, in a temper of mind I have rarely felt on my birth-day   My joy and thankfulnefs continued the whole day, to my own aftonifhment—19th, called on Mr. ——— (one of the friendly Clergymen) at *Wickham*, whofe countenance was changed   He had been with the Bifhop, who forbid his converfing with me. I marvel the prohibition did not come fooner "

Towards the end of the month, Mr *Wefley* quitted thefe cold regions of the North, and began to move Southward. January 6, 1747, he came to *Grimfby*, where he was faluted by a fhouting mob.   In the evening he attempted to preach at the Room, but the mob was fo violent he could not proceed   At length one of the rioters aimed a fevere blow at Mr *Wefley*, which a friend who ftood near him, received.   Another of them cried out, "What, you dog, do you ftrike a Clergyman? and fell upon his comrade.   Immediately every man's hand was againft his fellow   they began fighting and beating one another, till, in a few minutes, the room was

O 2   cleared

cleared of all difturbers, when Mr. *Wefley* preached
for half an hour, without further moleftation. On
the 9th, at *Hainton*, he talked feparately with the
members of the little Society, who were as fheep
encompaffed with wolves. The Minifter of the place
had repelled them from the facrament, and laboured
to ftir up the whole town againft them. It is probable they would have been worried to death, but
for the chief man of the place, a profeffed Papift,
who hindered thefe *good Proteftants* from deftroying
their innocent brethren.

Mr. *Wefley* continued his labours for the good of
the people, and the propagation of Chriftian knowledge, in *Yorkfhire*, *Derbyfhire*, *Loncafhire*, and *Staffordfhire*, till the 8th of February, and on the 10th,
he arrived fafe in *London* * He continued here till
the 23d, when he again commenced his peregri-
nations, in which he had new troubles and diff-
culties to encounter, even greater than any he had
before experienced. On the 24th, he reached the
Devizes in his way to *Briftol*, in company with
Mr *Mintor*. They foon perceived that the enemies of religion had taken the alarm, and were
muftering their forces for the battle. They began
by ringing the bells backward, and running to and
fro in the ftreets, as lions roaring for their prey.
The Curate's mob went in queft of Mr *Wefley* to
feveral places, particularly to Mr *Philips's*, where
it was expected he would preach. They broke
open, and ranfacked the houfe; but not finding
him there, they marched off to a Mr. *Rogers's*,
where he, and feveral others being met together,
were praying and exhorting one another to continue ftedfaft in the faith, and through much tribulation to enter the kingdom. The zealous

---

* See the exact correfpondence between this account and Mr *John
Wefley's* printed Journal in his Works, vol. xxix. page 9.

Curate,

Curate, Mr. *Innys*, ftood with them in the ftreet dancing for joy "This, fays Mr. *Wefley*, is he, who declared in the pulpit, as well as from houfe to houfe, ' That he himfelf heard me preach blaf-phemy before the Univerfity, and tell them, if you do not receive the Holy Ghoft while I breathe upon you, ye are all damned ' He had been about the town feveral days, ftirring up the people, and can-vaffing the Gentry for their vote and intereft , but could not raife a mob while my Brother was here : the hour of darknefs was not then fully come." What a difgrace to the Governors of any Church, that fuch a man as this fhould be fupported as a Minifter in it But we may obferve, that it is a general rule, with all perfecutors, to make thofe whom they perfecute, appear to the people as ab-furd, or as wicked as poffible. To accomplifh their end, perfecutors give full fcope to invention and fufpicion , and propagate with confidence, fuch things as they imagine will anfwer their purpofe, without wifhing to bring them to the teft of reafon and truth In the prefent inftance, Mr *Innys* well knew, that what he afferted of Mr *Wefley*, was falfe I fear, we may fix it as a general rule, with very few exceptions, that any man, who has been a little practifed in the ways of perfecution, will not fcruple to utter a falfehood, which feems very convenient for his purpofe. Let us then, learn to judge truly of men and things , and when we fee a man deeply prejudiced againft another, or in-fluenced by a fpirit of perfecution, let us give no credit to any thing he may fay, from the pulpit, from the prefs, or in converfation, till we have further evidence on the fubject than his affertions This will be the beft method of fuppreffing per-fecution, and its concomitant, flander O how careful fhould all Minifters be, to avoid this fnare

of

of the Devil! The Methodist Preachers, in particular, who have no fhadow of claim to our
efteem, as Preachers, but in proportion to their
integrity, piety, and zeal to do good

Mr *Innys*, by affiduity, and falfehood boldly
afferted as truth, had engaged the Gentlemen of
the town in his party, and prevailed with them to
encourage the mob. While they befet the houfe
where Mr *Wefley*, and the company with him, were
affembled, he often heard his own name mentioned,
with, "Bring him out, bring him out." He obferves, "The little flock were lefs afraid than I
expefted, only one of our Sifters fainted away '—
It being now dark, the befiegers blocked up the
door with a waggon, and fet up lights left Mr
Wefley fhould efcape   One of the company however, got out unobferved, and with much entreaty
prevailed on the Mayor to come down   He came
with two Conftables, and threatened the rioters,
but fo gently that no one regarded him   Having
tore down the fhutters of the fhop, and broken the
windows, it is wonderful they did not enter the
houfe   but a fecret hand feemed to reftrain them.
After a while they hurried away to the inn, where
the horfes were put up, broke open the ftable door,
and turned out the beafts   "In the mean time,
fays Mr. *Wefley*, we were at a lofs what to do,
when God put it into the heart of our next door
neighbour, a Baptift, to take us through a paffage
into his own houfe, offer us his bed, and engage
for our fecurity. We accepted his kindnefs and
flept in peace "

February 25. "A day never to be forgotten   At
feven o'clock, I walked quietly to Mrs *Philip:'s,*
and began preaching a little before the time appointed   For three quarters of an hour, I invited
a few liftening finners to Chrift. Soon after, *Satan s*
whole

whole army affaulted the houfe. We fat in a little
ground room, and ordered all the doors to be
thrown open They brought a hand engine and
began to play into the houfe. We kept our feats,
and they rufhed into the paffage. juft then Mr.
Borough, the Conftable, came and feizing the fpout
of the engine carried it off They fwore if he did
not deliver it, they would pull down the houfe.
At that time they might have taken us prifoners;
we were clofe to them, and none to interpofe but
they hurried out to fetch the larger engine. In
the mean time we were advifed to fend for the
Mayor, but Mr. Mayor was gone out of town, in
the fight of the people, which gave great encouragement to thofe who were already wrought up
to a proper pitch by the Curate, and the Gentlemen of the town, particularly Mr. *Sutton* and Mr.
Willy, Diffenters, the two leading men. Mr *Sutton*,
frequently came out to the mob, to keep up their
fpirits He fent word to Mrs *Philips*, that if fhe did
not turn that fellow out to the mob, he would fend
them to drag him out Mr *Willy*, paffed by again
and again, affuring the rioters, he would ftand by
them, and fecure them from the law, do what they
would "——What fhall we fay to thefe proceedings?
There is no clafs of people, who cry out more loudly
againft perfecution, than the Diffenters, when it
happens to be their turn to be perfecuted The
truth feems to be, that moft denominations of Chriftians difavow, and condemn perfecution in theory,
and yet fall into the practice of it, when power
and opportunity occur How far the *Roman Catholics*, who have hitherto been confiftent, and perfecuted on principle, will now contradict the former
practice of their own Church (if they fhould obtain
the power of perfecuting in thefe kingdoms) time
only can difcover; but there feems a very general

inclination

inclination at prefent, to give them an opportunity,
either of doing a great deal of mifchief, or, of re-
trieving their character in this refpect, by fetting
an example of moderation to other bodies of pro-
feffing Chriftians

The rioters " now began playing the larger
engine, which broke the windows, flooded the
rooms, and fpoiled the goods. We were withdrawn
to a fmall upper room, in the back part of the
houfe, feeing no way to efcape their violence, as
they feemed under the full power of the old murderer   They firft laid hold on the man who kept
the Society houfe, dragged him away, and threw
him into the horfe-pond, and it was faid, broke his
back —We gave ourfelves unto prayer, believing
the Lord would deliver us, how, or when, we faw
not, nor any poffible way of efcaping we therefore
ftood ftill to fee the falvation of God —Every now
and then, fome or other of our friends would venture to us, but rather weakened our hands, fo that
we were forced to ftop our ears, and look up
Among the reft, the Mayor's maid came, and told
us her miftrefs was in tears about me, and begged
me to difguife myfelf in womens clothes, and try
to make my efcape. Her heart had been turned
towards us by the converfion of her fon, juft on the
brink of ruin   God laid his hand on the poor
prodigal, and inftead of running to fea, he entered
the Society.—The rioters without, continued playing
their engine, which diverted them for fome time,
but their number and fiercenefs ftill increafed, and
the Gentlemen fupplied them with pitchers of ale,
as much as they would drink.   They were now on
the point of breaking in, when Mr *Borough*, thought
of reading the Proclamation   he did fo at the
hazard of his life   In lefs than the hour, of above
a thoufand wild beafts, none were left, but the guard.

3   Our

Our Constable had applied to Mr. *Street*, the only Justice in town, who would not act. We found there was no help in man, which drove us closer to the Lord, and we prayed, with little intermission, the whole day.

"Our enemies at their return, made their main assault at the back door, swearing horribly, they would have me if it cost them their lives. Many seeming accidents concurred to prevent their breaking in The man of the house came home, and instead of turning me out, as they expected, took part with us, and stemmed the tide for some time. They now got a notion, that I had made my escape; and ran down to the inn, and played the engine there They forced the inn-keeper to turn out our horses, which he immediately sent to Mr *Clark*'s; which drew the rabble and their engine thither. But the resolute old man, charged, and presented his gun, till they retreated.—Upon their revisiting us, we stood in jeopardy every moment Such threatenings, curses, and blasphemies, I have never heard They seemed kept out, by a continual miracle. I remembered the *Roman* Senators, sitting in the *Forum*, when the *Gauls* broke in upon them; but thought there was a fitter posture for Christians, and told my companion, they should take us off our knees —We were kept from all hurry, and discomposure of spirit, by a Divine Power resting upon us. We prayed and conversed as freely, as if we had been in the midst of our brethren, and had great confidence that the Lord would, either deliver us from the danger, or in it.—In the height of the storm, just when we were falling into the hands of the drunken enraged multitude, Mr. *Maton* was so little disturbed that he fell fast asleep.

"They

" They were now clofe to us on every fide, and
over our heads untiling the roof. A ruffian cried
out, ' Here they are, behind the curtain ' At this
time we fully expected their appearance, and retired
to the furthermoſt corner of the room, and I faid,
THIS IS THE CRISIS In that moment, Jesus rebuked the winds and the fea, and there was a great
CALM. We heard not a breath without, and wondered what was become of them.   The filence lafted
for three quarters of an hour, before any one came
near us, and we continued in mutual exhortation and
prayer, looking for deliverance. I often told my
companions, Now God is at work for us he is continuing our efcape he can turn thefe leopards into
lambs, can command the heathen to bring his children on their fhoulders, and make our fierceſt enemies
the inſtruments of our deliverance About three
o clock Mr *Clark* knocked at the door, and brought
with him the perfecuting Conſtable. He faid, ' Sir,
if you will promife never to preach here again, the
Gentlemen and I will engage to bring you fafe out of
town.' My anfwer was, I fhall promife no fuch
thing—fetting afide my office, I will not give up my
birth-right as an *Englifhman*, of vifiting what place
I pleafe of his Majefty's dominions. ' Sir,' faid the
Conſtable, ' we expect no fuch promife, that you will
never come here again only tell me, that it is not
your *prefent* intention, that I may tell the Gentlemen, who will then fecure your quiet departure.' I
anfwered, I cannot come again at this time, becaufe
I muſt return to *London* a week hence But, *obferve,*
I make no promife of not preaching here, when the
door is opened, and do not you fay, that I do.

" He went away with this anfwer, and we betook
ourfelves to prayer and thankfgiving We perceived it was the Lord's doing, and it was marvellous in our eyes. The hearts of our adverfaries

were turned Whether pity for us, or fear for themselves, wrought strongest, God knoweth, probably
the latter, for the mob were wrought up to such a
pitch of fury, that their Masters dreaded the confequence, and therefore went about appeasing the multitude, and charging them not to touch us in our
departure

" While the Constable was gathering his *posse*, we
got our things from Mr *Clark's*, and prepared to go
forth The whole multitude were without, expecting us, and saluted us with a general shout The
man Mrs. *Naylor* had hired to ride before her was,
as we now perceived, one of the rioters This hope-
ful guide was to conduct us out of the reach of his
fellows Mr. *Minton* and I took horse in the face of
our enemies, who began clamouring against us the
Gentlemen were difperfed among the mob, to bridle
them We rode a flow pace up the fheet, the whole
multitude pouring along on both fides, and attending
us with loud acclamations—fuch fierceness and diabolical malice I have not before feen in human faces.
They ran up to our horfes as if they would fwallow
us, but did not know which was *Wefley* We felt
great peace and acquiefcence in the honour done us,
while the whole town were fpectators of our march.
When out of fight, we mended our pace, and about
seven o clock came to *H. vall* The news of our danger was got thither before us, but we brought the
welcome tidings of our deliverance. We joined in
hearty prayer to our Deliverer, finging the hymn,

" Worfhip, and thanks, and blefling," &c

Ichiuary 26, I preached at *Bath*, and we rejoiced
like men who take the fpoil We continued our
triumph at *Brifls'*, and reaped the fruit of our labours
and fuflerings '

Iа

In the beginning of March, Mr. *Wesley* returned to *London*, and on the 24th preached at *Shoreham*, without molestation. The next day he met with and stopt a Travelling Preacher, "who, he says, had crept in among our Helpers, without either *discretion* or *veracity*." We may well suppose, that such instances as this did not frequently occur at this early period of the work, when the Lay-Preachers were few in number, no provision made for their subsistence, and their labours and dangers very great. It is not easy to imagine, what motive a Preacher could have, in going out to travel under these circumstances, but a desire of doing good.

About this time Mr. *Charles Perronet* attached himself to Mr. *Wesley*, and attended him as a companion, both in *England* and *Ireland*, the whole of this year. On the 4th of May they left *London*, and the next day arrived in *Bristol*. On the 9th, Mr *Wesley* observes, "My name-sake and charge was taken ill of a fever, which soon appeared to be the small-pox. On the 12th I administered the sacrament to my patient, who grows worse and worse. May 19, expecting the turn of the distemper, I sat up with *Charles* the Lord is pleased to try our faith and patience yet further."—On the 23d, he was out of danger.

Mr. *Wesley* continued his labours in *Bristol*, *London*, and the places adjacent, till *August* the 24th, when he set out for *Ireland* with Mr *Charles Perronet*, being strongly importuned by his brother, Mr. *John Wesley*, to come and supply his place in *Dublin*. On the 27th, they reached Mr *Phillips's*, in *Wales*, and his brother not being come from *Ireland*, according to appointment, they concluded he was detained by contrary winds, and had an opportunity of refreshing themselves and their weary beasts. On the 28th, he observes, "Mr *Gwynne* came to see me, with two of his family. My soul seemed pleased to take acquaintance

quaintance with them. We rode to *Maifmynis* church, where I preached, and Mr. *Williams*, after me, in *Welfh*. I preached a fourth time (the fame day) at *Garth*. The whole family received us as the meffengers of God, and, if such we are, they received him that fent us "

August 29, Mr. *John Wefley* arrived from *Ireland*, and came to them at *Garth* *. On the 30th, Mr. *Charles Wefley* preached on a tomb-ftone in *Builth* church-yard; and again in the afternoon in the evening he preached at *Garth*, on the marks of the *Meffias*, from Matthew xi. 5. September 2, he obferves, " I took horfe with Mr. *Phillips*, Mr. *Gwynne*, and a brother from *Anglefea*, as a guide, and found the feven miles to *Radnor* four good hours ride. I preached in the church, and laboured to awaken the dead, and to lift up the hands that hung down. The Minifter feemed a man of a fimple heart, and furely not eager for preferment, or he would not be content with his falary of three pounds a year. September 3, their friends left them · on the 4th, early in the morning, they fet out for *Holyhead*, which place they reached the next day at feven in the morning, having travelled on horfeback twenty-five hours. Sunday, September 6, he fent an offer of his affiftance to the Minifter, who was ready to beat the meffenger He preached, however, at the requeft of fome Gentlemen, who behaved with great propriety.— September the 9th, they reached *Dublin* in fafety.

Dublin had long been remarkable for a bad police. Frequent robberies, and fometimes murder, were committed in the ftreets at an early hour in the evening with impunity. The *Ormond* and *Liberty* mob, as they were called, would fometimes meet, and fight till one or more perfons were killed. It was

---

* This accords with Mr. *John Wefle*s printed Journal

faid

fud the mob had beat a Conſtable to death in the ſtreet, and hung the body up in triumph, without any of them being brought to puniſhment for the murder There was no vigour in the Magiſtrates, and their power was deſpiſed It is no wonder that the Methodiſts, at their firſt coming, were roughly handled in ſuch a place as this but it is wonderful that they ſo ſoon got a firm footing, and paſſed through their ſufferings with ſo little injury On Mr. *Wiſley's* arrival here, he obſerves, "the laſt news we heard was, that the little flock ſtands faſt in the ſtorm of perſecution, which aroſe as ſoon as my brother left them The Popiſh mob broke open their room, and deſtroyed all before them Some of them are ſent to Newgate, others bailed What will be the event we know not, till we ſee whether the Grand Jury will find the bill" He afterwards informs us that the Grand Jury threw out the bill, and thus gave up the Methodiſts to the fury of a licentious *Popiſh* mob He ſays, "God has called me to ſuffer affliction with his people. I began my miniſtry with, 'Comfort ye, comfort ye, my people,' &c. September 10, I met the Society, and the Lord knit our hearts together in love ſtronger than death. We both wept and rejoiced for the conſolation God hath ſent me, I truſt, to confirm theſe ſouls, and to keep them together in the preſent diſtreſs"

Mr *Wiſley* ſpent no time in idleneſs He was daily employed in preaching, expounding, viſiting the people, and praying with them September 20, after commending their cauſe to God, he went forth to the Green adjoining to the *Barracks,* believing the Lord would make bare his arm in their defence He called in his Maſter's name and words, "Come unto me all ye that are weary," &c The number of hearers was very great, and a religious awe kept down all oppoſition. He ſpoke with great freedom

to

to the poor Papifts, and, like St *Paul* at *Athens*, quoted their own authors to convince them, particularly *Kempis* and their *Liturgy*. None lifted up his voice or hand to oppofe, all liftened with ftrange attention, and many were in tears.   He advifed them to go to their refpective places of worfhip they exprefled general fatisfaction, efpecially the Papifts, who now maintained that he was a good *Catholic*.

The two following inftances, together with others of a fimilar kind which have already been brought forward, may fhew the liberality of his fentiments towards other denominations of Chriftians, who did not unite with him, or with the Methodifts. " September 25, I paft the evening very agreeably at a Baptift s, a woman of fenfe and piety, and a great admirer of my father's life of Chrift.   September 28 had an hour's conference with two ferious Quakers, who hold the head with us, and build on the one foundation. '

At this early period of the work, when the Societies were in their infancy, the Two Brothers, and the Lay-Preachers, fuffered great inconveniences at the places where they lodged, even in large towns, and we may fuppofe that both their accommodations and provifions were worfe in country Societies.   The rooms, alfo, where they affembled when they could not preach in the open air, began to be much too fmall for the number of people who attended.   This being the prefent ftate of things in *Dublin*, Mr. *Charles Wefley* purchafed a houfe near the place called *Dolphin's Barn*.   The whole ground floor was 42 feet long, and 24 broad   This was to be turned into a preaching-houfe, and the Preachers were to be accommodated in the rooms over it, but before he completed the purchafe, he wrote to his brother for his opinion on the matter.   His letter is dated October 9, in which he fays, one advantage of the houfe was,

was, that they could go to it immediately, and then adds, " I must go there, or to some other lodgings, or take my flight, for here I can stay no longer. A family of squalling children, a landlady just ready to lie in, a maid who has no time to do the least thing for us, are some of our conveniences * Our two rooms for four people (six when J. Healy, and Haughton, come) allow no opportunity for retirement Charles and I groan for elbow-room in our press-bed our diet answerable to our lodgings no one to mend our clothes and stockings, no money to buy more. I marvel that we have stood our ground so long in these lamentable circumstances. It is well I could not foresee, while on your side of the water " October 17, he observes, " I passed the day at the house we have purchased, near Dolphin's Barn, in writing and meditation. I could almost have set up my rest here but I must not look for rest on this side eternity "

Mr Wesley continued his labours in Dublin, till February 9, 1748, when he took an excursion into the country. His brother, Mr John Wesley, had spent fourteen or fifteen days in Dublin, the preceding August, and then returned to England, without visiting any of the country places There were, however, a few Preachers in Ireland, who had already introduced the Gospel into several country towns Mr Wesley came to Tyrrel's Pass, where he soon met a large and well-disposed congregation. " Few such feasts," says he, " have I had since I left England, it refreshed my body more than meat or drink God has begun a great work here. The people of Tyrrel's Pass were wicked to a proverb · swearers, drunkards, Sabbath-breakers, thieves, &c. from time immemorial. But now the scene is

* He seems to mean, these are some of the best things in our present accommodations.

changed;

changed, not an oath is heard, nor a drunkard seen
among them, *aperto æstatis horto*   They are turned
from darkness to light, and near one hundred are
joined in Society

February 11, Mr. *Wesley*, *J. Healy*, and five
others set out for *Athlone*, where, it is probable, notice had been given of their coming   On the road
some persons overtook them, running in great haste,
and one horseman riding full speed   It soon appeared that the Papists had laid a plan to do them
some violent mischief, if not to murder them, at the
instigation of their Priest, Father *Terrill*, who had
sounded the alarm the Sunday before.   They spoke
of their designs with so much freedom, that a report
of them reached *Athlone*, and a party of dragoons being quartered there, were ordered out to
meet Mr *Wesley* and his friends on the road, and
conduct them safe to the town   But of this they
were ignorant, and being earlier than was expected,
the Papists were not assembled in full force, nor did
the dragoons meet them at that distance from the
town which was intended.   They rode on, suspect-
ing nothing, till within about half a mile of *Athlone*, when, rising up a hill, several persons appeared
at the top of it, and bid them turn back   " We
thought them in jest, says Mr. *Wesley*, till the
stones flew," one of which knocked *J. Healy* off his
horse, and laid him senseless on the ground, and it
was with great difficulty the Papists were hindered
from murdering him.   The number of these barba-
rians was soon greatly increased, and though the Protestants began to rise upon them, they kept their
ground till the dragoons appeared, when they immediately fled   Mr. *Wesley* and his little company,
their wounded friend having recovered his senses,
were now conducted in safety to *Athlone*, where the
soldiers flocked about them with great affection, and

the

the whole town expressed the greatest indignation at the treatment they had met with. *J Healy* was put under the care of a surgeon, and at length recovered of his wounds.

February 15, Mr *Wesley* returned to *Dublin*, and continued his labours with great success, the Society being greatly increased, and many testifying publicly, that they had received *the knowledge of salvation by the remission of their sins*, under his word. March 8, his brother, Mr *John Wesley*, arrived from *England*, which gave him a release from his present situation. He did not, however, leave *Dublin* till the 20th, when he entered the packet-boat at two o clock in the afternoon, and by three the next day reached *Holy-head*, from whence he wrote to his brother as follows.

Teneo te Italiam !
Per tantos casus, per tot discrimina rerum—

" In twenty-five hours exactly, as before, the Lord brought us hither. To describe our voyage were, *renovare dolorem.* But here we are, after all, God be praised, even God that heareth the prayer. Thanks, in the second place, to our praying bre-thren. The Lord return it into their bosom. But let them pray on for us, and we for them. And I pray the Father, in the name of our Lord Jesus Christ, to send down his blessing and his spirit on all you who are now assembled together, and hear this read. Peace be unto you, even the peace that passeth all understanding. Look for it every moment! receive it this—and go in peace to that heavenly country, whither we are hastening to meet you!"

Intending to visit Mr *Gwynne's* family at *Garth* in *Wales*, he took horse the next morning, and by three in the afternoon came to *Baldon-Ferry*. Here he observes, " We overfilled the small old boat, so that,

Gemuit

Gemuit fub pondere Cymba futilis, et fud' a a accepit
limofa paludem * " The wind being ſtrong, and the
waves high, in the middle of the channel his young
Ioiſe took fright, and they had a very narrow eſcape
from being overſet But a gracious Providence attended him, he came ſafe to land, and on the 25th,
in the evening reached *Garth*, but great fatigue,
bad weather, and continual pain, had ſo weakened
him, that when he came into the houſe, he fell down
totally exhauſted

Mr. *Weſley* had already conceived a great regard
for Mr *Gwynne's* family, and particularly for Miſs
Sarah Gwynne A kind of embryo-intention of
making propoſals of marriage, had dwelt in his mind
for ſome time. He had mentioned it to his brother in *Dublin*, who neither oppoſed nor encouraged
him in the matter. During his preſent ſtay at *Garth*,
his embryo-intention ripened into more fixed reſolution, but ſtill he thought it neceſſary to take the
advice of his friends. After he had been a ſhort
time in *London*, he went to *Shoreham*, and opened all
his heart to Mr. *Perronet*, who adviſed him to wait.
Much prayer was made, and every prudential ſtep
was taken which his friends could ſuggeſt, and here
the buſineſs reſted for the preſent.

August 13, Mr. *Weſley* arrived again in *Dublin*,
and on the 17th ſet out on horſeback for *Cork*, which
he reached on the 20th, notwithſtanding the inceſſant
rains, the badneſs of the roads, and wretched accommodations at the inns The next day, being
Sunday, he went out to the *Marſh* at five in the
morning, and found a congregation of ſome thouſand perſons He preached from, *Thus it is written,*
and thus it behoved Chriſt to ſuffer, &c. They de-
voured every word with an eagerneſs beyond deſcrip-

* The frail patched veſſel groaned under the weight, and being leaky,
was in plenty of water.

tion.

tion "Much good, he says, has already been done in this place outward wickedness has disappeared, and outward religion succeeded it. Swearing is seldom heard in the streets, and Churches and Altars are crowded, to the astonishment of our adversaries Yet *some* of our Clergy, and all the Catholic Priests, take wretched pains to hinder their people from hearing us.

"At five in the evening, I took the field again, and such a sight I have rarely seen. Thousands and thousands had been waiting some hours, Protestants and Papists, high and low The Lord endued my soul, and body also, with much strength to enforce the faithful saying, ' That Jesus Christ came into the world to save sinners ' I cried after them for an hour, to the utmost extent of my voice, yet without hoarseness or weariness The Lord, I believe, hath much people in this city. Two hundred are already joined in a Society At present we pass through honour and good report The chief persons of the town favour us no wonder, then, that the common people are quiet We pass and repass the streets, pursued only by their blessings. The same favourable inclination is all round the country wherever we go, they receive us as Angels of God Were this to last, I would escape for my life to *America* "

" I designed to have met about two hundred persons who have given me their names for the Society, but such multitudes thronged into the house, as occasioned great confusion I perceived it was impracticable, as yet, to have a regular Society. Here is, indeed, an open door, such as was never set before me till now even at *Newcastle* the awakening was not so general The congregation last Sunday was computed to be ten thousand As yet there is no *open* opposition The people have had the word two months, and it is not impossible but their love may

may laſt two months longer, before any number
of them riſe to tear us in pieces

" I met a neighbouring Juſtice *of the Peace*, and
had much ſerious converſation with him   He ſeems
to have a great kindneſs for religion, and determined
to uſe all his intereſt to promote it —For an hour
and an half I continued to call the poor blind beg-
gars to *Jeſus* They begin to cry after him on every
ſide, and we muſt expect to be rebuked for it.—
Waited on the Biſhop at *Rivers-Town*, and was received with great affability by himſelf and family.
After dinner rode back to *Cork*, and drank tea with
ſome well diſpoſed Quakers, and borrowed a volume
of their dying ſayings. A ſtanding teſtimony that
the life and power of God was with them at the beginning, as it might be again, were they humble
enough to confeſs their want of it "—How amiable
is the candour of Mr. *Weſley*, when contraſted with
the bigotry of others, who, in their great zeal for
ceremonies, have contended that the *Friends* ought
not to be acknowledged as *Chriſtians*, becauſe they
neglect the uſe of Baptiſm and the Lord's Supper.
They do not condemn thoſe who uſe theſe ordinances,
but they deny the neceſſity of uſing them, in order
to ſalvation; and they were evidently led, or rather
driven into this opinion at firſt, by the extravagant
manner in which Baptiſm and the Lord's Supper
were at that time ſpoken of, the people being generally taught that thoſe who had been baptiſed and afterwards received the Sacrament, were true Chriſtians
and had a ſure title to eternal life. The Friends
thought themſelvs called upon to bear a public teſtimony againſt an error of ſuch dangerous conſe-
quence, which had a tendency to perſuade perſons
that ſomething merely external could make them
Chriſtians, and prepare them for heaven and they
ſeemed to think, that the moſt effectual way of

P 3   bearing

bearing this teftimony, fo as to attract the notice of
the public, would be by uniting practice to theory,
and totally laying afide the ufe of thele ordinances.
Without pretending to give any opinion on their
conduct in this refpect, we may venture to fay, that
o e extreme has a natural tendency to produce another, in oppofition to it —Mr *Wefley* goes on

"Auguft 27, I had much converfation with Mr.
C— a fenfible pious Clergyman, one after my own
heart, in his love to our defolate Mother He is
clear in the doctrine of Faith, and gave a delightful
account of the Bifhop.—Sometimes waiting on great
men, may do good, or prevent evil. But how dangerous the experiment! how apt to weaken our
hands, and betray us into an undue deference, and
refpectof perfons! The Lord fend to them by whom
he will fend but hide me ftill in difgrace or ob-
fcurity '

Auguft 28   He went out about five miles from
Cork, where, fays he, " Juftice P— received us,
and ufed all his authority with others to do the fame
He fent word to the Romifh Prieft, that if he forbid
his people from hearing us, he would fhut up his
Mafs-houfe —Several of the poor *Roman Catholics*
ventured to come, after the Juftice had affured them,
he would himfelf take off the curfe their Prieft had
laid upon them.   I exhorted all alike to repentance
towards God, and faith in Jefus Chrift —I haftened
back to the Marfh, on feeing the multitudes, I
thought on thofe words of *Prior*, ' Then, of all
thefe whom my dilated eye with labour fees, how
few will own the meffenger of God when the ftream
turns.' Now they all received me with inexpreffible eagernefs —I took occafion to vindicate the Methodifts from the fouleft flanders that they rail
againft the Clergy   I enlarged on the refpect due
to them, prayed particularly for the Bifhop, and
                                                        laid

laid it on their confciences to make mention of them
(the Clergy) in all their prayers.—Auguft 29, I
paffed an ufeful hour with Mr C   He rejoiced that
I had preached in his parifh laft Sunday. If our
Brethren (the Clergy) were like minded, how might
their hands be ftrengthened by us¹ But we muft have
patience, as he obferved, till the thing fpeak for itfelf, and the mift of prejudice being removed, they
fee clearly that all our defire is the falvation of fouls,
and the eftablifhment of the Church of *England*

"Sept. 1. I met the Infant Society for the
firft time, in an old Playhoufe —Our Lord's prefence confecrated the place. I explained the nature
of Chriftian fellowfhip, and God knit our hearts together in the defire of knowing him. I fpake with
fome, who told me they had wronged their neighbours in time paft, and now their confcience will
not let them reft till they have made reftitution. I
bid them tell the perfons injured, it was this preaching had compelled them to do juftice —One poor
wretch told me before his wife, that he had lived in
drunkennefs, adultery, and all the works of the
Devil for twenty-one years that he had beat her
almoft every day of that time, and never had any
remorfe till he heard us, but now he goes conftantly
to Church, behaves lovingly to his wife, abhors the
thing that is evil, efpecially his old fins   This is
one inftance out of many."

Sept 5   He obferves that the work now increafed rapidly, one and another being frequently
juftified under the word. Two, fays he, at the Sacrament yefterday two at the Society   One overtook me going to the Cathedral, and faid, "I have
found fomething in the preaching, and cannot but
think it is forgivenefs   All the burden of my fin
funk away from off me, in a moment   I can do no
thing but pray and cry Glory be to God. I have

fuch

fuch a confidence in his love, as I never knew I
trample all fin and forrow under my feet." I bid
him watch and pray, and expect greater things than
thefe.—Our old mafter the world, begins to take it
ill, that fo many defert and clean efcape its pollutions.
Innumerable ftories are invented to ftop the work,
or rather are repeated, for they are the fame we
have heard a thoufand times, as well as the primitive
Chriftians

Sept 6   He rode to *Kinfale*, and at noon walked to the market-place   The windows were filled
with fpectators rather than hearers   Many wild
looking people ftood with their hats on, in the ftreet,
and the boys were rude and noify   Some well
dreffed women ftood behind him and liftened   His
text was, *Go out quickly into the ftreets and lanes of
the City, and bring in hither the poor and the maimed,
and the halt and the blind.* " I did, fays he, moft
earneftly invite them all to the great Supper   It was
fallow ground, yet the word was not all loft.   Several fettled into ferious attention, others expreffed
their approbation, a few wept —In the evening the
multitude fo trod on one another, that it was fome
time before they could fettle to hear   I received a
blow with a ftone on the fide of my head, and called
on the perfon to ftand fo th, and if I had done him
any wrong, to ftrike me again.   This little circumftance increafed their attention   I lifted up my
voice like a trumpet, and fhewed the people their
tranfgreffions, and the way to be faved from them
They received my faying, and fpake well of the
truth.   A fudden change was vifible in their behaviour afterwards, for God had touched their hearts
Even the *Roman Catholics* owned, ' None could
find fault with what the man faid '   A lady of the
Romifh Church, would have me to her houfe.   She
affured me, the Governor of the town, as foon as he
            heard

heard of my coming, had iffued orders that none
fhould difturb me that a gentleman who offered
to infult me, would have been torn in pieces by the
Roman Catholics, had he not fled for it and that
the Catholics in general are my firm friends '—It is
worth obferving, that every denomination of Chriftians in *Kinfale*, claimed him as their own He tells
us, " The Prefbyterians fay, I am a Prefbyterian;
the people who go to Church, that I am a Minifter
of theirs, and the Catholics are fure, I am a good
Catholic in my heart " This is good evidence, that
he confined himfelf, in his public difcourfes, to the
moft effential doctrines of the Chriftian religion ;
which undoubtedly ought to be the practice of every
itinerant Preacher

Mr *Wefley*, in his excurfions from *Cork*, had already vifited *Bandon* once or twice, where the words
he fpake had confiderable effect On his return at
this time from *Kinfale*, a poor man and his wife from
Bandon met him, and preffed him fo earneftly to give
them another vifit, that he could not refift their importunity He went thither again, September the
12th, and the poor man and his wife foon found him
out, and took him to their houfe in triumph The
neighbours flocked in, and " We had indeed, fays
Mr. *Wefley*, a feaft of love A Prodigal came,
who had been a monfter of wickednefs for many
years, but is now returned to his Father fo are
many of the town, who were wicked to a proverb.
In the evening, I invited about four thoufand finners to the great Supper God hath given them the
hearing car I went to Mrs *Jones's*, a widow gentle-
woman, who is determined to promote the work of
God to the utmoft of her power . all in the place
feem like-minded, except the Clergy ! O why fhould
they be the laft to bring home their King ! It grieved
me to hear the poor encouragement given laft Sunday

day to the crowds that flocked to Church; which place some of them had not troubled for years before. We send them to Church to hear ourselves railed at, and, what is far worse, the truth of God "

Tuesday, September 13. " We parted with many tears, and mutual blessings I rode on to *Kinsale* Here also the Minister, Mr. *P* instead of rejoicing to see so many publicans in the temple, entertained them with a railing accusation against me, as an impostor, an incendiary, and messenger of Satan. Strange justice! that Mr *P.* should be voted a friend of the Church, and I an enemy, who send hundreds into the Church for him to drive them out again.— September 16, the power of the Lord was present in the Society at *Cork,* I marvel not that Satan hates it we never meet but some or other is plucked out of his teeth After a restless night of pain, I rose to confer with those who desired it A woman insisted that the Lord had spoken peace to her trembling soul at the Sacrament *Thomas Warburton* asserted, that faith came to him by hearing, and that now he hates all sin with a perfect hatred, and could spend his whole life in prayer *Stephen Williams* witnessed, ' Last night I found my heart burdened in your prayer, but I repeated after you till my speech was swallowed up Then I felt myself, as it were, fainting, falling back, and sinking into destruction, when, on a sudden, I was lifted up, my heart lightened, my burden gone, and I saw all my sins at once so black, so many—but all taken away I am now afraid of neither death, devil, nor hell I am happier than I can tell you I know God has, for Christ's sake, forgiven me ' Two others, in whom I found a real work of grace begun, were Papists, till they heard the Gospel, but are now reconciled to the Church, even to the invisible Church, or communion of Saints. A few of these lost sheep we

3

we pick up, but feldom fpeak of it, left our good
Proteftants fhould ftir up the Papifts to tear us in
pieces At Mr *Rolf's*, a pious Diffenter, I heard
of the extreme bitterneſs of his two Minifters, who
make it their bufineſs to go from houfe to houfe, to
fet their people againft the truth, threatening all who
hear us with excommunication. So far beyond the
Papifts are thefe *moderate* men advanced in perfecution.'—Mr *Wefley* now quitted this part of the
kingdom, and, vifiting feveral towns in his way back,
he came fafe to *Dublin* on the 27th of September

    October 8, he took his paffage for *England*, and
the next night landed at *Holyhead*. He wrote to a
friend the following account of the dangers he had
efcaped " On Saturday evening, at half paft eight,
I entered that fmall boat, and were two hours in
getting to the veffel There was not then water to
crofs the bar, fo we took our reft till eleven on
Sunday morning Then God fent us a fair wind,
and we failed fmoothly before it five hours and a half.
Towards evening the wind frefhened upon us, and
we had full enough of it I was called to account
for a bit of cake I had eat in the morning, and
thrown into violent exercife. Up or down, in the
cabin or on deck, made no difference yet in the
midft of it, I perceived a diftinct heavy concern, for
I knew not what. It was now pitch dark, and no
fmall tempeft lay upon us The Captain had ordered in all the fails I kept moftly upon deck till
half paft eight, when, upon inquiry, he told me, he
expected to be in the harbour by nine I anfwered,
we would compound for ten. While we were talking, the mainfail, as I take it, got loofe, at the fame
time the fmall boat, for want of faftening, fell out
of its place The Mafter called all hands on deck,
and thruft me down into the cabin, when, in a mi-
nute, I heard a cry above, ' We have loft the maft !
                                        A paffenger

A paffenger ran up, and brought us worfe news, that it was not the maft, but the poor Mafter himfelf, whom I had fcarcely left, when the boat, as they fuppofed, ftruck him and knocked him overboard. From that moment he was feen and heard no more. My foul was bowed before the Lord   I kneeled down, and commended the departing fpirit to his mercy in Chrift Jefus   I adored his diftinguifhing goodnefs. *The one fhall be taken, and the other left.* I thought of thofe lines of *Young*   'No warning given' unceremonious death! a fudden rufh from life's meridian joys, a plunge opaque beyond conjecture' The failors were fo confounded they knew not what they did   The decks were ftrewed with fails, the wind fhifting about the compafs, we juft on the fhore, and the veffel driving, where or how they knew not.   One of our cabin paffengers ran to the helm, and gave orders as Captain, till they had righted the fhip   But I afcribe it to our invifible Pilot, that we got fafe to fhore foon after ten   The ftorm was fo high, that we doubted whether any boat would venture to fetch us.   At laft one anfwered and came   I thought it fafer to lie in the veffel, but one calling, Mr *Wefley*, you muft come, I followed, and by eleven o'clock found out my old lodgings at *Robert Griffiths*   October 10, I bleffed God that I did not ftay in the veffel laft night   a more tempeftuous one, I do not remember "—He now wrote the following thankfgiving hymn

All praife to the LORD,
Who rules with a word
The untractable fea,
And limits its rage by his ftedfaft decree
Whofe providence binds,
Or releafes the winds,
And compels them again
At his beck to put on the invifible chain.

Even

Even now he hath heard
Our cry, and appear'd
On the face of the deep,
And commanded the tempest its distance to keep
His piloting hand
Hath brought us to land,
And no longer distress'd,
We are joyful again in the haven to rest.

O that all men would raise
His tribute of praise,
His goodness declare,
And thankfully sing of his fatherly care!
With rapture approve
His dealings of love,
And the wonders proclaim
Perform'd by the virtue of Jesus's name

Through Jesus alone
He delivers his own,
And a token doth send
That His love shall direct us, and save to the end.
With joy we embrace
The pledge of his grace,
In a moment outfly
These storms of affliction, and land in the sky.

" At half past nine o'clock, I took horse in a perfect hurricane, and was wet through in less than ten
minutes, but I rode on, thankful that I was not at
sea Near five in the afternoon, I entered the boat
at *Baldon-Ferry*, with a Clergyman and others, who
crowded our small crazy vessel. The water was exceedingly rough, our horses frightened, and we looking to be overset every moment. The Minister acknowledged he never was in the like danger. We
were half drowned in the boat. I sat at the bottom,
with him and a woman, who stuck very close to me,
so that my being able to swim would not have helped
me. But the Lord was my support. I cried out to
my brother Clergyman, fear not Christian—the hairs
of our head are all numbered, Our trial lasted near
half

half an hour, when we landed wet and weary in the dark night The Minister was my guide to *Carnar-von*; and by the way entertained me with the praises of a Lay-Preacher, he had lately heard and talked with He could say nothing against his preaching, but heartily wished him ordained. His name, he told me, was *Howel Harris.* He took me to his own inn, and at last found out who I was, which increased our intimacy."—Mr *Wesley* pursued his journey to *Garth*, which place he reached October 13 Here he staid about a week, and, on the 21st, arrived safe in *Bristol.*

He now confined his labours in the Gospel, for some months, to *London*, *Bristol*, and the neighbouring places, making an occasional excursion to *Garth* in *Wales* April 9, 1749, he was married by his brother, at *Garth*, to Miss *Sarah Gwynne*, a young lady of good sense, piety, and agreeable accomplishments. Mr *John Wesley* observes, " It was a solemn day, such as became the dignity of a christian marriage "

CHAPTER VI.

Stating some further Particulars concerning Mr. CHARLES WESLEY, *with an Account of his Death in* 1788

Mr *Wesley's* Journal now begins to fail us There is no account of his proceedings, sometimes for months, sometimes for years together. There are, however,

however, a few particulars recorded till the year
1756, which may be useful and entertaining to the
reader, and throw some light on the History of Me-
thodism It does not appear that his marriage either
interrupted his labours, or lessened his usefulness.
April 29, about three weeks after he was married,
he wrote thus to his brother " I hope this will find
you prospering in *Ireland*. I left *Garth* yesterday
sennight. Mr. *Gwynne*, with *Sally* and *Betty*, accompanied me to *Abergavenny*. There I left them on
Saturday morning, and got hither *(Bristol)* by one
o clock Over-riding occasioned a fever—I was *too
eager* for the work, and therefore believe, God
checked me by that short sickness Till Wednesday
evening at Weaver's Hall, my strength and understanding did not return, but from that time the Lord
has been with us of a truth. More zeal, more life,
more power, I have not felt for some years (I wish
my mentioning this may not lessen it), so that
hitherto marriage has been no hinderance You
will hardly believe it sits so light upon me Some
further proof I had of my heart on Saturday last,
when the fever threatened most. I did not find, so
far I can say, any unwillingness to die, on account
of any I should leave behind neither did death appear less desirable than formerly—which I own gave
me great pleasure, and made me shed tears of joy.
I almost believe, nothing shall hurt me that the
world, the flesh, and the devil, shall keep their distance, or, by assaulting, leave me more than con-
queror. On Thursday, I propose setting out for
London, by *Oxford*, with *T. Maxfield*. If they will
give me a year of grace, I shall wonder and thank
you I hope you came time enough to save *J.
County*, &c. Set your time for returning, *when
abouts* at least. Will you meet me at Ludlow? It

13

is a thousand pities * you should not be here, when
the library makes its first appearance   The Lord
cut short your work and his, and make a few weeks
go as far as many months! What say you to *T. May-
field* and me taking a journey, when you return,
through all the Societies, Northern and Western,
and settling correspondencies with the Stewards, *alias*
Bookfellers   My kindeft love to Mr. *Lunell*, Mr.
Lloyd, Mr. *Fowks*, Mr *Gilbons*, and all friends at
Cork and *Dublin*   We make mention of you in all
our prayers, be not unmindful of us.   The Lord
preferve us all to his Day."

February 8, 1750.   He obferves there was an
earthquake in *London*   This place he reached on
the 1ft of March, and on the 8th wrote thus to his
brother   " This morning, a quarter after five, we
had another fhock of an earthquake, far more violent than that of February 8   I was juft repeating
my text, when it fhook the *Foundery* fo violently,
that we all expected it to fall on our heads.   A great
cry followed from the women and children.   I immediately cried out, *Therefore we will not fear,*
though the earth be moved and the hills be carried into
the midft of the fea   for the Lord of Hofts is with us,
the God of Jacob is our refuge   He filled my heart
with faith, and my mouth with words, fhaking their
fouls as well as their bodies   The earth moved
Weftward, then Eaft, then Weftward again, through
all *London* and *Weftminfter*   It was a ftrong and jar-
ring motion, attended with a rumbling noife like that
of thunder.   Many houfes were much fhaken, and
fome chimnies thrown down, but without any further hurt."

* The phrafeology here is rather low, and I am perfuaded would not
have been ufed by Mr *Wefley*, but in this familiar and carelefs way of
writing to his Brother.

March

March 10. He expounded the 24th chapter of
Isaiah, a chapter, he tells us, which he had not taken much notice of, till this awful providence explained it. April 4, he says, " Fear filled our Chapel, occasioned by a prophecy of the return of the
earthquake this night I preached my written sermon on the subject, with great effect, and gave out
several suitable hymns. It was a glorious night for
the disciples of Jesus April 5, I rose at four
o'clock, after a night of sound sleep, while my neighbours watched. I sent an account to *M. G.* as follows —The late earthquake has found me work.
Yesterday I saw the *Westminster* end of the town full
of coaches, and crowds flying out of the reach of
Divine Justice, with astonishing precipitation. Their
panic was caused by a poor madman's prophecy Last
night they were all to be swallowed up. The vulgar
were in almost as great consternation as their betters.
Most of them watched all night, multitudes in the
fields and open places, several in their coaches:
many removed their goods London looked like a
sacked city. A Lady just stepping into her coach to
escape, dropped down dead Many came all night
knocking at the *Foundery* door, and begging admit-
tance for God's sake "—These, however, were not
Methodists, but others, who, under the general ap-
prehension of danger, thought there was more safety
under the roof of religious persons than elsewhere.
A plain proof that those who neglect religion, and
perhaps despise the professors of it, while in health,
and free from apparent danger, yet when great and
public calamities approach them, even in apprehen-
sion, they plainly discover that they think the state of
religious persons better than their own Mr *Wesley's* account of the great confusion in *London*, on
the 4th of April, is confirmed by a letter of Mr.
W. Briggs, to M*r*. *John Wesley*, dated on the 5th
of

of the same month, in which he says, "This great
city has been, for some days past, under terrible apprehensions of another earthquake   Yesterday thousands fled out of town, it having been confidently
asserted by a dragoon, that he had a revelation, that
great part of *London*, and *Westminster*, especially, would
be destroyed by an earthquake the 4th instant, between twelve and one at night   The whole city was
under dreadful apprehensions   Places of worship were
crowded with frightened sinners, especially our two
chapels, and the Tabernacle, where Mr *Whitefield*
preached   Several of the Classes came to their Leaders, and desired, that they would spend the night with
them in prayer, which was done, and God gave them
a blessing.   Indeed all around was awful! Being not
at all convinced of the prophet's mission, and having
no call from any of my brethren, I went to bed at
my usual time, believing I was safe in the hands of
Christ, and likewise, that by doing so, I should be
the more ready to rise to the preaching in the morning—which we both did, praised be our kind pro-
tector "—In a postscript he adds, " Though crowds
left the town on Wednesday night, yet crowds were
left behind, multitudes of whom, for fear of being
suddenly overwhelmed, left their houses, and re-
paired to the fields, and open places in the city.
Tower-Hill, *Moorfields*, but above all, *Hyde-Park*,
were filled best part of the night, with men, women,
and children, lamenting.   Some, with stronger ima-
ginations than others, mostly women, ran crying in
the streets an earthquake! an earthquake! Such a
distress, perhaps, is not recorded to have happened
before in this careless city.   Mr *Whitefield* preached
at midnight in *Hyde-Park*   Surely God will visit this
city   'it will be a time of mercy to some.   O may I
be found watching! '

                                        Mr.

Mr *Wesley* proceeds with his Journal.—April 15,
" I met with Mr *Salmon's* Foreigner's Companion
through the Universities of *Cambridge* and *Oxford*,
printed in 1748, and made the following extract
from page 25 ' The times of the day the University go to this Church, are ten in the morning, and
two in the afternoon, on Sundays and holidays, the
sermon usually lasting about half an hour But when
I happened to be at *Oxford*, in 1712, Mr. *W.* the
Methodist, at *Christ-Church*, entertained his audience
two hours, and having insulted and abused all degrees, from the highest to the lowest, was in a manner hissed out of the pulpit by the lads.' And high
time for them to do so, if the Historian said true:
but, unfortunately for him, I measured the time by
my watch, and it was within the hour. I abused
neither high nor low, as my Sermon, in print, will
prove neither was I hissed out of the pulpit, or
treated with the least incivility, either by young or
old. What then shall I say to my old High-Church
friend, whom I once so much admired? I must rank
him among the apocryphal writers, such as the ju-
dicious Dr. *Mather*, the wary Bishop *Burnet*, and
the most modest Mr *Oldmixton*."

The censure here passed on *Oldmixton* I think is
just He appears to me to be a bold, dashing, im-
pertinent writer His prejudice is so great, that his
assertions, as an historian, deserve no credit, unless
supported by authentic documents. I think far
otherwise of Dr. *Mather*, and Bishop *Burnet* It is
indeed true, that *Burnet's* History of his own Time,
is written with great caution, but this surely does.
not deserve censure, but commendation. The truth
seems to be, that *Burnet* was a man of great moderation, on which account the zealots, both of the
High and Low Church party, became his inveterate
enemies. For the satisfaction of the reader, I shall

Q 2   give

give a fhort account, both of Dr. *Mather* * and of
Bifhop *Burnet* †.

                                                  June

* Dr *Cotton Mather*, an eminent *American* Divine, was born at *Bofton*
in *New-England*, in 1663. He became Minifter of *Bofton* in 1684, and
fpent his life in the difcharge of his office, and in promoting feveral excellent focieties for the public good, particularly one for fuppreffing dif-
orders, one for reforming manner, and a fociety of peace-makers, whofe
profeffed bufinefs it was to compofe differences, and prevent law-fuits.
His reputation was not confined to his own country, for, in 1710, the
Univerfity of *Glafgow* fent a diploma for the degree of doctor in divinity,
and, in 1714, the Royal Society of *London* chofe him one of their Fellows. He died in 1728. His chief work was, *Magnalia Chrifti Ameri-
cana*, or an Ecclefiaftical Hiftory of *New-England*, from its firft planting,
in 1620, to 1698, in folio.

† *Gilbert Burnet*, was born at *Edinburgh* in 1643, of an ancient family
in the fhire of *Aberdeen*. His father being bred to the ftudy of the law,
was, at the Reftoration, appointed one of the Lords of Seffion, with the
title of Lord *Crimond*. Our author, the youngeft fon of his father, was
fent to continue his ftudies at *Aberdeen*, at ten years of age, and was admitted M A before he was fourteen. His own inclination led him to
the ftudy of the civil and federal law, and he ufed to fay, that it was from
this ftudy he had received more juft notions of civil fociety and government, than thofe which divines maintain. About a year after, he began
to apply himfelf to the ftudy of divinity, and was admitted preacher before he was eighteen. Sir *Alex Burnet*, his coufin german, offered him
a benefice, but he refufed to accept of it. In 1663, he came to *England*,
and fpent a fhort time at *Oxford* and *Cambridge*. In 1664, he made a tour
through *Holland* and *France*. At *Amfterdam*, by the help of a *Jewifh*
Rabbi, he perfected himfelf in the *Hebrew* language, and likewife became
acquainted with the leading men of the different perfuafions tolerated in
that country, as *Calvinifts*, *Arminians*, *Lutherans*, *Anabaptifts*, *Brownifts*,
Papifts, and *Lutherans*, amongft each of which he ufed frequently to declare, he met with men of fuch unfeigned piety and virtue, that he became fixed in a ftrong principle of univerfal charity, and an invincible abhorrence of all feverities on account of religious diffentions.

Upon his return from his travels, he was admitted Minifter of *Saltor*,
in which ftation he ferved five years in the moft exemplary manner. He
drew up a memorial, in which he took notice of the principal errors in
the Scots Bifhops, and fent a copy of it to feveral of them, which ex-
pofed him to their refentments. Being engaged in drawing up the "Me-
moirs of the Dukes of *Hamilton*," Duke *Lauderdale* invited him to *London*, and introduced him to King *Charles* II. After his return to *Scotland*, he married Lady *Margaret Kennedy*, daughter of the Earl of *Caffilis*,
a Lady of piety and good underftanding, and ftrongly inclined to the Prefbyterians. The day before their marriage, he delivered the Lady a deed,
renouncing all pretenfions to her fortune, which was confiderable, and
which muft have fallen into his hands, fhe having no intention to fecure
it.

Burnet's intimacy with the Dukes of *Hamilton* and *Lauderdale*, occafioned him to be frequently fent for by the King and the Duke of *York*,

June 22 "I met, says he, a daughter of my worthy old friend Mr *Erskin*, at the *Foundery* she was deeply wounded by the sword of the spirit . confessed she had turned many to Deism, and feared there could be no mercy for her.—July 28, I had the satisfaction of bringing back to Mr. *Erskine* his formerly disobedient daughter She fell at his feet it was a moving interview—all wept—our Heavenly Father heard our prayers"—December 2 Being in *Wales*, he observes, "I encouraged a poor girl to seek a cure from him who hath wounded her. She has the outward mark, too, being daily threatened to be turned out of doors by her master, a great swearer

who had conversations with him in private But *Lauderdale*, being offended at the freedom with which *Burnet* spoke to him, took pains to prejudice the King against him In 1673, Sir *Harbottle Grimstone*, Master of the Rolls, appointed him preacher of the chapel there, notwithstanding the opposition of the Court In 1679 and 81, he published his History of the Reformation, for which he had the thanks of both Houses of Parliament About this time he became acquainted with the Earl of *Rochester*, and spent one evening in a week with him, for a whole winter, discoursing on those topics on which Sceptics, and men of loose morals, object to the Christian religion The happy effect of their conferences, occasioned his publication of the account of the life and death of that Earl When the inquiry concerning the Popish plot was on foot, the King consulted him often, and offered him the Bishopric of *Chichester* if he would engage in his interests, but he refused to accept it on these terms

On the accession of King James to the Throne, he obtained leave to go out of the kingdom He lived in great retirement for some time at *Paris*, then travelled to *Italy* and *Rome*, where he was favourably received by the Pope He afterwards pursued his travels through *Switzerland* and *Germany*, and, in 1688, came to *Utrecht*, with an intention to settle in some of the *Seven Provinces* Here he received an invitation from the Prince and Princess of *Orange*, to come to the *Hague*, which he accepted He was immediately acquainted with all their designs, and entered heartily into them When the Prince of *Orange* came over to *England*, *Burnet* attended him in quality of Chaplain, and was soon advanced to the See of *Salisbury* He declared for moderate measures with regard to the Clergy who scrupled to take the oaths, and many were displeased with him, for declaring for the toleration of Nonconformists In 1699, he published his Exposition of the 39 Articles, which occasioned a representation against him in the Lower House of Convocation, in 1701, but he was vindicated by the Upper House He died in 1715, and was interred in the Church of St *James*, *Clerkenwell*, where he has a monument erected to him See *Encyclopædia Britannica.*

Q 3

and

and ſtrict chuichman, a conſtant communicant and habitual drunkard "

1751. _James Wheatley_ was at this time a Preachei among the Methodiſts, and a dabbler in phyſic. Some very heavy complaints were brought againſt him, foi impropei conduct to ſeveral women, of which Mr. _John Wiſley_ has given a pietty full ſtatement in his printed Jouinal foi the yeai 1751, which account is fully confiimed by Mi _Chailes Wefley_ s piivate Journal, now before me　They biought _Wheatley_ and his accuſeis face to face, and the charges weie ſo clearly proved, that he was obliged to confeſs the truth　To ſcieen himſelf as fai as poſſible, he accuſed others, and ſaid the ieſt of the Pieachcis weie like himſelf　This was a feiious chaige　Ten of them were called togethei to meet _Wheatley_, and _T Maxfield_ firſt, then each of the otheis, aſked him —What ſin can you chaige me with ?—_Wheatley_ was ſilent, which convinced them that he was guilty of wilful lying　They weie now obliged to ſilence him, and Mi. _John Wefley_ has been cenſuied foi uſing too much ſeverity towards him　but as the facts weie cleaily proved, he and his Brothei, for they acted jointly in the matter, could do no leſs than put him away fiom the connexion.

Mr _Wefley_ goes on with his Journal, and obſerves, that _Wheatley_'s charge put his biothei and him upon a ieſolution of ſtrictly examining into the life and moral behaviour of every Pieachei in the connexion with them ; "and the office, layshe, fell upon me.' —It ceitainly could not have fallen into fittei hands. Mi _John Wefley_'s great weakneſs was, a pioneneſs to believe eveiy one ſinceie in his piofeſſions of ieligion, till he had the moſt poſitive, and, peihaps, repeated proofs of inſinceiity, and to believe theii teſtimonies of things as true, without making piopei allowance foi their ignorance. This expoſed him

to

to frequent imposition and miftake. The cafe was far otherwife with Mr *Charles* he quickly penetrated into a man's character, and it was not eafy to impofe upon him. He totally differed from his brother concerning the qualifications neceffary for an Itinerant Preacher, and fometimes filenced a man whom his Brother had admitted The one looked at the poffible harm an unqualified Preacher might do to many perfons, the other, at the poffible good he might do to fome. This was the real principle which governed the two Brothers in their very different conduct towards the Lay-Preachers, which made fome of them reprefent Mr *Charles* as an enemy to them all But this certainly was far from being the cafe Mr. *Charles Wefley* being clothed with his new office, fet out the next morning, June 29, to vifit the Societies in the midland and northern counties, as far as *Newcaftle,* in which journey Mrs. *Wefley* accompanied him I do not find, however, in the whole of his Journal, the leaft accufation, of a nature fimilar to that of *Wheatley*, againft any Preacher in the connexion. In this journey he was a great bleffing to the people where ever he came; many were added to the Societies, and the old members were quickened in their zeal and diligence, to work out their own falvation with fear and trembling —July 21, he obferves, " I rode to *Briftal* (near *Leeds*) where *John Nelfon* comforted our hearts with his account of the fuccefs of the Gofpel in every place where he has been preaching, except in *Scotland* There he has been beating the air for three weeks, and fpending his ftrength in vain Twice a-day he preached at *Muffelborough* to fome thoufands of mere hearers, without one foul being converted I preached at one, to a different kind of people Such a fight have I not feen for many months. They filled the valley and fide of the hill as grafshoppers

for

for multitude, yet my voice reached the moſt diſ-
tant—God ſent the word home to many hearts."—
July 25, he was taken ill of a fever, and on the 28th,
his fever increaſing, he ſays, " I judged it incumbent
on me, to leave my thoughts concerning the work
and the inſtruments, and began dictating the following letter."—Unfortunately the letter was not tran-
ſcribed into the Journal, a blank ſpace being left for
it I apprehend it is not now to be found any
where.

He goes on. Auguſt 3, "I was enabled to ride
out, and to confer with the Preachers and others.
Auguſt 5, I went to the Room, that I might hear
with my own ears, one (of the Preachers) of whom
many ſtrange things had been told me. But ſuch a
Preacher never have I heard before, and hope I never ſhall again It was beyond deſcription. I cannot ſay he preached falſe doctrine, or true, or any
doctrine at all, but pure unmixed nonſenſe Not
one ſentence did he utter that could do the leaſt
good. Now and then a text of Scripture was dragged
in by head and ſhoulders I could ſcarcely refrain
from ſtopping him He ſet my blood a galloping,
and threw me into ſuch a ſweat, that I expected the
fever to follow Some begged me to ſtep into the
deſk and ſpeak a few words to the diſſatiſfied hearers.
I did ſo, taking no notice of M I—k, late ſuper-
intendant of all Ireland ! I talked cloſely with him,
utterly averſe to working, and told him plainly he
ſhould either work with his hands, or preach no
more He complained of my brother, I anſwered
I would repair the ſuppoſed injury by ſetting him up
again. At laſt he yielded to work "—The ſame day
he ſilenced another Preacher

Auguſt 12, being at *Newcaſtle*, he deſired *W Sheut*,
who was with him, to go to *Muſſelborough*. Before he
ſet out, he gave Mr. *Weſley* the following account of
a re-

a remarkable trial they had lately had at *Leeds*.——
" At *Whitecoat-Hill*, three miles from *Leeds*, a few
weeks fince, as our Brother *Maſkew* was preaching,
a Mob aroſe, broke the windows and doors, and
ftruck the Conftable *Jacob Hawley*, one of the Society   On this we indicted them for an aſſault, and
the Ringleader of the Mob, *John Hellingworth*, indicted our Brother the Conftable, and got perſons to
ſwear the Conftable ftruck him.   The Grand Jury
threw out our indictment, and found theirs againft
us, ſo we ftood trial with them, on Monday July 15,
1751   The Recorder, *Richard Wilſon*, Efq. gave
it in our favour, with the reft of the Court.   But
the Foreman of the Jury, *Matthew Prieſtley*, with
two others, *Richard Cloudſly*, and *Jabez Brunel*, would
not agree with the reft, being our avowed enemies.
The Foreman was Mr. *Murgatroyd*'s great friend and
champion againft the Methodifts.   However the Recorder gave ftrict orders to a guard of Conftables, to
watch the Jury, that they ſhould have neither meat,
drink, candles, or tobacco, till they were agreed in
their verdict   They were kept priſoners all that
night and the next day till five in the afternoon, when
one of the Jury ſaid, he would die before he would
give it againft us.   Then he ſpake cloſely to the
Foreman concerning his prejudice againft the Methodifts, till at laft he condeſcended to refer it to
one man   Him the other charged to ſpeak as he
would anſwer it to God in the day of judgment.
The man turned pale, and trembled, and deſired that
another might decide it.   Another, *John Hardwick*,
being called upon, immediately decided it in favour
of the Methodifts   After the trial, Sir *Henry Bryſon*,
one of the Juſtices, called a Brother, and ſaid, You
ſee God never forſakes a righteous man, take care
you never forſake him."

Beſides

Befides *Richard Wilfon*, Efq. Recorder of *Leeds*, the following Juftices were prefent, *J. Frith*, Mayor, Alderman *Micklethwait*, Alderman *Denifon*, Alderman *Sawyer*, Alderman *Smith*, and *Alderman* Brooks. Sir *Henry Ibifon* was mentioned above —Mr *Wefley* left *Newcaftle*, Auguft 24, and on the 26th, reached Thurfk in Yorkfhire, where his Journal for the prefent year ends

It is evident from the nature of the thing, that he muft have met with great difficulties in executing the defign of his journey, and have made himfelf many enemies. But he feldom regarded confequences, when he was convinced that he was doing his duty. His mind, however, was fometimes much burdened. On one occafion, he obferves, " Preaching, I perceive, is not my principal bufinefs God knoweth my heart, and all its burdens O that he would take the matter into his own hand, though he lay me afide as a broken veffel !"—But he was frequently comforted and ftrengthened in preaching and praying with the Societies After one of thefe opportunities he fays, " My faith was greatly ftrengthened for the work. The manner, and the inftruments of carrying it on, I leave entirely to God "

July 8, 1754 Mr *Charles Wefley*, with his Brother, who was indifpofed [*], Mr *Charles Perronet*, and another friend, fet out for *Norwich* On the 10th, in the evening, they reached *Lakenham*, where they were informed the whole city was in an uproar about *James Wheatley*, " whofe works of darknefs, fays Mr *Wefley*, are now brought to light, whereby the people are fo fcandalized and exafperated, that they are ready to rife and tear him in pieces. We do not therefore wonder that the Clergy are not forward to fhew their friendly inclination to us, yet one

* See alfo Mr *J Wefley's* printed Journal in his Works, vol xxix. page 99

has

has fent us a civil meffage, excufing his not vifiting
us till the tumult is over.'—The next day the
Gentleman with whom they lodged at Lakenham
dined with the Mayor of Norwich, a wife refolute
man, who laboured for peace.   He was employed
all day in taking the affidavits of the women whom
Wheatley had tried to corrupt, their accounts were
printed and cried about the ftreets, which occafioned
great confufion   " What could Satan, or his
apoftles, fays Mr Wefley, do more, to fhut the door
againft the Gofpel in this place for ever ? Yet feveral
came to us, entreating us to preach.   The adver-
tifement we had printed here laft year, difclaiming
Mr Wheatley, did much good, and, with the bleffing of God, helped the people to diftinguifh.   Our
hoft alfo, has affured the Mayor, that Mr. Wheatley
is no Methodift, or affociate of ours   A letter of
Charles Perronet's to Wheatley they have printed
there, contrary to our exprefs orders   It is not fit
that our hand fhould be upon him   Frefh difcove-
ries are daily made of his lewdnefs, enough to make
the ears of all who hear to tingle   yet he is quite infenfible !"   Thefe things are now mentioned, becaufe
the notoriety of them at the time appears a fufficient
juftification of Mr. John Wefley's conduct towards
Wheatley.

Sunday, July 14   They walked to Mr Edward's
in Norwich, and at feven o'clock in the morning
Mr Charles Wefley took the field.   He preached on
Hog-Hill to about 2000 hearers, his brother ftanding
by him   A drunkard or two were troublefome, but
more out of mirth than malice.   They afterwards
went to Church, and the people, both in the ftreets
and at the Cathedral, were remarkably civil   He
adds, " The Leffons, Pfalms, Epiftles, and Gofpel,
were very encouraging   The Anthem made our
hearts rejoice.   *O pray for the peace of Jerufalem,*
th y

they shall prosper that love thee. Peace be within thy walls, and prosperity within thy palaces. For my brethren and companions' sake will I now say, peace be within thee. Because of the house of the LORD *our* GOD, *will I seek thy good.*—We received the Sacrament at the hands of the Bishop. In the afternoon I went to St. *Peter's*, and at five o'clock to *Hog-Hill*, where it was computed that ten thousand persons were present. Again I preached repentance towards God, and faith in our Lord Jesus Christ. They listened with great seriousness—their hearts were plainly touched, as some shewed by their tears. Who could have thought the people of *Norwich* would ever more have borne a Field-Preacher? It is the Lord's doing, and it is marvellous in our eyes. To him be all the glory, who saith, *I will work, and who shall hinder?*

July 19. Mr. *John Wesley* left them, and Mr. *Charles* continued his labours. " At night, he says, I had multitudes of the great vulgar and the small to hear me, with three Justices, and nine Clergymen: many, I am persuaded, felt the sharp two-edged sword.—Sunday, July 21. My audience at seven in the morning was greatly increased. I dwelt chiefly on those words, *He hath sent me to preach glad-tidings to the meek*, or poor, and laboured, as all last week, to bring them to a sense of their wants, and for this end I have preached the law, which is extremely wanted here. The poor sinners have been surfeited with smooth words and flattering invitations. The greater cause have we for wonder and thankgiving, that they can now endure sound and severe doctrine. I received the Sacrament again from his Lordship, among a score of communicants. If the Gospel prevail in this place, they will by and by find the difference.—July 22, God is providing us a place, an old large brewhouse, which the own-

er

er, a Juſtice of Peace, has reſerved for us. He has
refuſed ſeveral, always declaring he would let it to
none but Mr. *John Weſley*. Laſt Saturday Mr. *Edwards* agreed, in my Brother's name, to take a leaſe
for ſeven years, and this morning Mr. *S.* has ſent
his workmen to begin to put it into repair. The
people are much pleaſed at our having it · ſo are not
Satan and his Antinomian Apoſtles."

July 27. He was informed of the death of a per-
ſon whom he conſidered and loved as a ſon in the
Goſpel, but whoſe unſteadineſs had given him great
pain. His obſervations on the occaſion ſhew, that
he had a mind ſuſceptible of the fineſt ſentiments of
friendſhip. " Juſt now, ſays he, I hear from *Leeds,*
that my poor rebellious ſon has taken his flight But
God healed his backſlidings firſt, and he is at reſt!
My poor *J H—n* is at reſt in the boſom of his heavenly Father. O what a turn has it given my heart!
what a mixture of paſſions do I feel here! But joy
and thankfulneſs are uppermoſt I opened the book
of conſolation, and caſt my eye upon a word which
ſhall wipe away all tears *I will ranſom them from
the power of the grave, I will redeem them from
death* —Sunday, July 28, I met our little Society,
or rather candidates for a Society, at five in the
morning At ſeven, I preached Chriſt Jeſus, the Saviour of all men, to a numerous quiet congregation,
and afterwards heard the Biſhop preach, and received
the Sacrament from him. At five in the evening,
after prayer for an open door, I went forth to ſuch
a multitude as we have not ſeen before in *Norwich.*
During the hymn, a pale trembling oppoſer laboured
to interrupt the work of God, and draw off the
people's attention but as ſoon as I began to read the
hiſtory of the Prodigal Son, his commiſſion ended,
and he left me to a quiet audience Now the door
was opened indeed. For an hour and a half I ſhewed
                                                    them

their fins and wanderings from God, and invited them back to their Father's houſe And ſurely he had compaſſion on them, inclining many hearts to return. God, I plainly found, had delivered them into my hard He filled my mouth with perſuaſive words, and my heart with ſtrong deſires for their ſalvation I concluded, and began again, teſtifying my good will towards them, which was the ſole end of my coming But if I henceforth ſee them no more, yet is my labour with my God They have heard words whereby they may be ſaved, and many of them, I cannot doubt, will be our crown of rejoicing in the great day. Several ſerious perſons followed me to Mr Edwards's, deſiring to be admitted into our So-ciety I told them, as others before, to come among us firſt, for ſome time, and ſee how they liked it. We ſpent ſome time together in conference, praiſe, and prayer I am in no haſte for a Society firſt let us ſee how the candidates live '—Had this cautious and prudent conduct been obſerved, through every part of the Methodiſt diſcipline, the Preachers, and members of the Societies, would not indeed have been ſo numerous as at preſent, but they would have had a degree of excellence, they have not yet at-tained.

Mr. Weſley goes on. July 30, " I preached at five, and found the people's hearts opened for the word The more Satan rages, the more our Lord will own and bleſs us A poor rebel at the concluſion lifted up his voice, for whom I firſt prayed, and then turning full upon him, preached repentance and Chriſt to his heart I deſired him to turn his face towards me, but he could not However he felt the inviſible chain, which held him to hear the offers of grace and ſalvation I have great hope that Satan has loſt his ſlave, ſome aſſured me they ſaw him de-part in tears.—July 31, I expounded Iſaiah xxxii. 1

to

to my conftant heareis, who feem moie and moie to know their wants. At night, I laid the axe to the root, and fhewed their actual and original corruption, from Rev. iii. 17. *Thou fayeft, I am rich, and knoweft not that thou art wretched, and miferable, and poor, and blind, and naked.* The ftrong man was difturbed in his palace, and roaied on every fide. My ftrength increafed with the oppofition. A Gentleman on horfeback, with others, was ready to gnafh upon me with his teeth, but my voice prevailed, and they retreated to their ftrong hold, the alehoufe. There, with difficulty, they procuied fome butchers to appear in their quaiiel; but they had no commiffion to approach till I had done Then, in the laft hymn, they made up to the table with great fury. The foremoft often lifted up his ftick to ftike me, being within his reach, but he was not permitted. I ftaid to pray for them, and walked quietly to my lodgings. Poor *Rabfhakeh* muttered fomething about the Bifhop of *Exeter*, but did not accept of my invitation to Mr *Edwards's*. The concein and love of the people were much increafed, by my fuppofed danger We joined together in prayer and thankfgiving as ufual, and I flept in peace "

Mr *Wefley's* Journal gives us no further information of his labours, or of any of his proceedings, till the latter end of the year 1756. The number of Lay-Preachers was now greatly increafed, and though very few of them had enjoyed the benefits of a learned, or even a good education in the common branches of knowledge, yet there were among them men of ftrong fenfe, and great powers of mind, who foon became ufeful and able preachers of the Gofpel We may naturally fuppofe, that thefe, confcious of their abilities and ufefulnefs, would begin to feel fome uneafinefs under the very humble character of a Methodift Preacher, which the public at that

that time held in great contempt. This seems to
have been actually the case, for they wished to promote a plan, which no doubt they hoped might both
be useful to the people, and give them a greater degree of respectability in the public opinion. To ac-
complish this purpose, they were desirous that the
Preachers, or some of them at least, should have
some kind of ordination, and be allowed to administer the ordinances to the people, through all the Societies. Both Mr. *John* and *Charles Wesley* opposed
this attempt, as a total dereliction of the avowed
principles on which the Societies were first united together When they became Itinerant Preachers, and
began to form Societies, they utterly disclaimed any
intention of making a separate party in the nation:
they never intended that the Societies should be se
parate churches the members were constantly exhorted to attend their respective places of worship, whether the Established Church, or a Dif-
senting Meeting, and the times of preaching on the
Lord s Day were purposely fixed, to give them liberty so to do. They had no intention to separate
any from their former church-membership, but to
awaken persons of all denominations to a serious
sense of religion, to call them back to their first
principles, to be helpers of their faith, and to stir
them up to work out their salvation with fear and
trembling! Their leading object was, to bring persons of all persuasions to an experimental and practical knowledge of the fundamental truths of the
Christian religion; to unite them together in brotherly love, while each retained his former religious
connection, and his peculiar opinions on church government and modes of worship. It is evident that
the Methodist Societies were formed on these broad
and disinterested principles, however narrow-minded
and interested men may have misconstrued them, or

2   endeavoured

endeavoured to pervert them. It was, indeed, a
new thing in the world, but the two Brothers were
fully perfuaded that this was the peculiar calling of
the Methodifts.   They had been gradually led
into this plan, under a concurrence of circumftances which appeared to them providential, and
many years experience of its extenfive ufefulnefs,
had confirmed them in this opinion   To feparate
the people, therefore, from their former connexions,
and unite them into an independent body, they
thought was departing from their proper calling,
and quitting the ftation which God had appointed
them for the benefit of the nation.   This fubject
has often been difcuffed, but the queftion has never
been fairly ftated.   It is not merely, whether the
Methodifts fhall feparate from the Church of
England? but whether they fhall feparate from the
Church, and from every denomination of Diffenters
hitherto known in the kingdom, and become a
body, diftinct and independent of both.   Thus far,
they have been a kind of middle link, uniting
the Diffenters, and members of the Church, in the
interefts of experimental religion, and in chriftian
love and charity to one another   A feparation
therefore, will make the breach wider than ever
it will overturn the original conftitution of Methodifm, and totally fubvert the very fpirit of it
This in my opinion will be of ferious confequence, not only to the Methodifts themfelves,
but to the nation at large*.

The contagion, however, had gone forth   the
plague was begun   a divifion in the Society of *Leeds,*
had already taken place, and the minds of many in

* This fubject is here incidentally mentioned, as it gave rife to
Mr *Charles Wefley's* journey through many of the Societies this year
It will be confidered more at length, in the latter part of the life of
Mr *John Wefley.*

R   different

different Societies were greatly unfettled, by a few of the Preachers. Mr. *Charles Wefley* was much affected with thefe proceedings. He confidered the prefent attempts to feparate thofe of the people from the Church, who had belonged to her, and the Dif- fenters among them from their former connexions, as a partial evil only; but he looked forward to the confequences, which would probably follow, when none were left to oppofe them. While under thefe painful exercifes of mind, the words of the Lord by the prophet, often gave him comfort. *I will bring the third part through the fire.* He often preached from thefe words in the journey we are going to defcribe, and would often mention them to his friends in converfation, even to the clofe of his life. He feemed to expect, that when he and his Brother were removed hence, troubles would arife in the Societies; but that, after various ftruggles, a third part would be found to adhere to their ORIGINAL CALLING, and to the original fimplicity of the Methodifts.

September 17. He left *Briftol*, and vifited the So- cieties in *Gloucefterfhire* and *Staffordfhire*, every where confirming the brethren in the truths of the Gofpel, and in their peculiar calling as Methodifts. On the 22d, he came to *Nottingham*, and fpent the afternoon in taking down the names of thofe in the Society, and converfing with them. He adds, " We rejoiced to meet once more, after fo long a feparation. My fubject both at night and in the morning, was, *I will bring the third part through the fire*. It was a time of folemn rejoicing. There had been, twelve months ago, a great revival and increafe of the Society; but Satan was beginning again to fow his tares. My coming at this feafon, I truft, will be the means of preventing a divifion."— The next day he came to *Shffield.* " Here alfo,
2   he

he fays, I delivered my own foul, and the people feemed awakened and alarmed. I fpake plainly and lovingly to the Society, of continuing in the Church and though many of them were Diffenters and Predeftinarians, none were offended."—It is probable they underftood his meaning, and then there was no juft caufe of offence. By advifing thofe who belonged to the Church, to continue in it, he advifed the Diffenters to continue in their refpective Meetings, or Churches His object was, to diffuade the members of the Methodift Societies from leaving their former connexions, and uniting into a feparate body. In doing this he fometimes mentioned the Diffenters, as well as the members of the Church of *England*, but not always, as in moft places thefe formed the bulk of the Methodift Societies.

Paffing through *Huntflet*, the Rev Mr *Crook*, Minifter of the place, ftopped him and took him to his houfe Here he met with Dr. *Cockburn*, his old fchool-fellow and friend, who had waited for him near a week, to take him to *York*. Mr *Wefley* fpent a delightful hour in converfation with them, full of life and zeal, and fimplicity, and then went on to *Leeds*. Sunday, September 26, he preached at feven in the morning, they walked to *Huntflet*, and preached twice for Mr. *Crook*, in the evening he returned to *Leeds*, and preached a fourth time to a very crowded audience In the Society, he obferves, "I could fpeak of nothing but love, for I felt nothing elfe Great was our rejoicing over each other Satan, I believe, has done his worft, and will get no further advantage by exafperating their fpirits againft their departed brethren They were unanimous to ftay in the Church, becaufe the Lord ftays in it, and multiplies his witneffes therein. Monday the 27th, I breakfafted with Mifs *N.* who

was

was not fo evil-affected towards her forfaken brethren as I expected Nothing can ever bring fuch as her back, but the charity which hopeth all things, beareth all things, endureth all things —I went to the Church-prayers, with feveral who have been long dealt with to forfake them utterly. They will ftand the firmer, I hope, for their fhaking."

September 28. " I fet out with Dr. *Cockburn*, for *York*, and preached from Hab iii. 2. *O Lord, re- vive thy work* The crowd made our room ex- ceffively hot. but that did not hinder their at- tention.—Our Preacher ftationed here, had quite left off preaching in the morning. Many told me, I could not get a congregation at five o'clock but I found it otherwife The room was almoft full, while I explained, *Being made free from fin, and become the fervants of God, ye have your fruit unto holinefs, and the end everlafting life* I infifted largely on—the neceffity of labouring after holinefs The hearers appeared much ftirred up —I fpent the day (September 29) in conferring with all comers. The Doctor's houfe was open to all, and his heart alfo his whole defire being to fpread the Gofpel"

October 1. He met with a Mifs *T.* earneftly feeking falvation, who had been awakened by reading *Theron* and *Afpafio*, written by Mr *Hervey*. —While at *York*, Mr. *Wefley*'s time was fully oc- cupied not merely with preaching night and morning, and converfing with the members of the Society but in attending perfons of learning and character, who were defirous of his company, to ftate their objections to the doctrines and economy of the Methodifts, and to hear his anfwers. This day he fpent an hour with Mr. *D* and anfwered his candid objections He had alfo an opportunity of defending his old friend Mr. *Ingham*, " It is hard, fays says he, that a man should be hanged for his looks; for the appearance of M——nism Their spirit and practices, he has as utterly renounced as we have their manner and phrase cannot so soon be shaken off '—Simplicity and goodness constantly met with his approbation under whatever dress or form he saw them, they attracted his notice and ensured his friendship He found *Merry Bell* here, and these amiable qualities shone so bright through the little singularities of her profession, that he had sweet fellowship with her. He adds, " I marvel not that the friends, so fallen from their first simplicity, cannot receive her testimony."—Thus speaks Mr *Wesley* of a *woman*, who was a public teacher among the friends. Many similar instances occur in his life, which plainly shew that his love of truth and goodness, always broke through his high Church prejudices, and united his heart, in Christian fellowship, to the wise and good of every communion

October 2. The whole day was spent in singing, conference, and prayer. " I attended, says he, the Quire Service The people there were marvellously civil, and obliged me with the anthem I desired, Hab. iii a feast for a king, as Queen *Anne* called it. The Rev Mr. *Williamson* walked with me to his house, in the face of the sun. I would have spared him, but he was quite above fear. A pious sensible Dissenter cleaved to us all day, and accompanied us to the preaching I discoursed on my favourite subj ct, *I will bring the third part through the fire* We glorified God in the fire, and rejoiced in hope of coming forth as gold —
Sunday, October 3 From five till near eight in the morning I talked closely with each of the Society. then, at Mr. *Williamson's* request, I preached on the Ordinances from Isaiah lxiv. 5 *In this is continuance*

tinuance and we shall be saved I dwelt longest on what had been most neglected, family prayer, public prayer, and the sacrament. The Lord set to his seal, and confirmed the word with a double blessing —I received the sacrament at the Minster. They were obliged to confecrate twice, the congregation being doubled and trebled through my exhortation and example   Glory be to God alone —I went to Mr. *Williamson's* Church, who read prayers as one who felt them, and then beckoned me. I stepped up into the pulpit, when no one expected it, and cried to a full audience, *The kingdom of God is at hand, repent ye, and believe the Gospel* They were all attention   The word did not return void, but accomplished that for which it was sent.   Neither is he that planted, any thing, neither is he that watereth."

October 5. Being returned to *Leeds*, he conversed with one of the Preachers who seemed desirous of making a separation, and adds, " I threw away some words on one, who is wiser in his own eyes than seven men who can render a reason "—The next day, he again conversed with the same Preacher, who frankly confessed, if any of the Societies should desire him to take charge of them as a distinct Body, he should not refuse them   Mr. *W——ß y* told him plainly, that the ground of all such designs was pride   but his words were spoken into the air —He now set out for *Seacroft*, and rode on to *Aberford*, to see his old friend Mr. *Ingham*, who was absent, labouring in his Lord's vineyard   " I had the happiness, says he, of finding Lady *Margaret* at home, and their son *Ignatius*   She informed me that Mr *Ingham's* circuit takes in about four hundred miles, that he has six fellow-labourers, and a thousand persons in his Societies, most of them converted. I rejoiced in his success.

cefs *Ignatius* would haidly be fatisfied at my not preaching We paffed an hour and a half pio-fitably, and got fafe back to *Scacroft* before night. Soon after, our deareft Brother *Grimfhaw* found us, and biought a bleffing with him I pieached from Luke xxi 34 *Take heed to youifelves, &c.* and further enforced our Loid's waining on the So-ciety —Our hearts were comforted and knit to-gether —October 8, we had another bleffed hour with them, before we left this lively people. I continued till one o'clock, in conference with my worthy friend and fellow-labourer, Mr *Grimfhaw* ; a man after my own heart, whofe love of the chuich, flows from his love of Chrift. With fuch, may my lot be caft in both worlds

" I iode with my faithful Brother *Grimfhaw* to *Bramley*, and pieached to a multitude of ferious fouls, who eagerly received our Lord's faying, *Look up, and lift up your heads, &c.* They feemed bioad awake when I called again in the moining, October 9, *Watch ye theiefore, and pray always, &c.* Their fpirit quickened mine We had fweet fel-lowfhip together I have no doubt but they will oe counted woithy to efcape, and to ftand befoie the Son of Man —Returning to *Leeds*, I met my Brother *Whitefield*, and was much iefiefhed by the account of his abundant labours. I waited on him to oui Room, and gladly fat under his woid —October 10 From Ifaiah liv 5 I eaineftly pieffed the duties of conftant communicating, of heaiing, reading, pieaching the word, of fafting, of piivate, family, and public piayer. The fpirit of love and union was in the midft of us —I came to *Birftal* befoie noon My congregation was a thoufand or two lefs, through *George Whitefield's* pieaching to-day at *Haworth* Between four and five thou-fand weie left, to receive my warning from Luke

xxi. 34 After Church fervice, we met again.
every foul feemed to hang on the word Two
fuch precious opportunities, I have not enjoyed
this many a day. It was the old time revived.
a weighty fpirit refted on the congregation, and
they ftood like men prepared to meet the Lord "

October 11. Mr. *Whitefield*, and Mr *Grimfhaw*,
were prefent at a Watch-night at *Leeds* Mr.
Wefley preached firft, and Mr *Whitefield* after
him. It was a time of great folemnity, and of
great rejoicing in hope of the glorious appearing
of the great God.—He now left *Leeds*, but continued preaching in the neighbouring places a few
days. At *Briftal*, he makes the following obfervation "The word was clothed with power, both
to awaken and to confirm. My principal concern
is for the difciples, that their houfes may be built
on the rock, before the rains defcend I hear in
moft places, the effect of the word, but I hearken
after it, lefs than formerly, and take little notice
of thofe, who fay they receive comfort, or faith,
or forgivenefs Let their fruits fhew it "

October 17 He came to Mr *Grimfhaw's*, at
Haworth, and was greatly refrefhed with the fimplicity and zeal of the people Here a young
Preacher in Mr. *Ingham's* connexion came to fpend
the evening with him. "I found great love for him,
fays Mr *Wefley*, and wifhed all our fons in the
Gofpel, were equally modeft and difcreet."—He
was now more fully informed of the ftate of the
people in feveral Societies that, having been prejudiced againft the Church of *England*, by fome
of the Preachers, their minds had been unfettled,
and rendered diffatisfied with the Methodift econo
my. Thefe were eafily induced to leave the Society, and unite themfelves to fome independent
body. feldom with advantage, but often with lofs.
                                                    He

He talked largely with Mr. *Grimshaw*, how to remedy the evil. " We agreed, says he, 1 That nothing can save the Methodists from falling a prey to every seducer, but close walking with God, in all the commandments and ordinances, especially reading the word, and prayer, private, family, and public 2 That the Preachers should be allowed more time in every place, to visit from house to house, after Mr *Baxter*'s manner 3. That a small treatise should be written, to ground *them in their calling*, and preserve them against seducers, and be lodged in every family."

He now set out for *Lancashire*, accompanied by his zealous friend Mr. *Grimshaw* They reached *Manchester* on the 20th. They found the Society in a low divided state, and reduced nearly one half. " I make more allowance, says Mr *Wesley*, for this poor shattered Society, because they have been neglected, if not abused, by our Preachers. The Leaders desired me not to let *J T.* come among them again, for he did them more harm than good, by talking in his witty way against the Church and Clergy As for poor *J H* he could not advise them to go to Church, because he never went himself. But some informed me, that he advised them not to go I talked with the Leaders, and earnestly pressed them to set an example to the flock, by walking in all the commandments and ordinances. I wrote my thoughts to my Brother, as follows " Mr *Walker*'s letter * deserves to be seriously considered One only thing occurs to me now, which might prevent in great measure the mischiefs which will probably ensue after our death and that is, *greater, much greater deliberation and care in admitting Preachers*

---

* Several letters passed between Mr *John Wesley* and the Rev Mr *Walker*, of *Truro*, about this time They are published in the Arminian Magazine

Confider ferioufly, if we have not been too eafy and
too hafty in this matter   Let us pray God to fhew
us, if this has not been the principal caufe, why fo
many of our Preachers have lamentably mifcarried.
Ought any new Preacher to be received before we
know that he is grounded, not only in the doctrines
we teach, but in the difcipline alfo, and particularly
in the communion of the Church of *England* ? If we
we do not infift on that ϛοϱγη * for our defolate Mother, as a prerequifite, yet fhould we not be well affured that the candidate is no enemy to the Church ?
—I met the Society in calm love, and exhorted them
to ftand faft in one mind and one fpirit, in the old
paths, or ways of God's appointing. Henceforth
they will not believe every fpirit. The Lord ftablifh
their hearts with grace "

October 23   He breakfafted with Mr *Richard
Barlow*, whofe uniform conduct, for a great many
years, has done honour to the Methodift Society,
and to religion in general. " I rejoiced, fays Mr
Wefley, in the remembrance of his bleffed fifter, now
in glory. For feven years, fhe adorned the Gofpel
in all things "—He afterwards took horfe with Mr
Philips, for *Hasfield*   The next day, Sunday the 24th,
he preached in the church, which was better filled
than had ever been known in a morning, and in the
evening was exceedingly crowded   He makes a
fhort obfervation here, that fhews his attachment to
the Church of *England*, in a much ftronger light than
any thing which another perfon could fay of him
" I tafted the good word, fays he, while reading it.
Indeed the Scripture comes with double weight to
me *in a Church*   If any pity me for my bigotry, I
pity them for their blind prejudice, which robs them
of fo many bleffings "

* Natural affection, fuch as parents have for their children, or children for their parents

October

October 24 He returned to *Manchester*, and makes the following obfervations on Mr *Whitefield's* candour and liberality " Here I rejoiced to hear of the great good Mr *Whitefield* has done in our Societies He preached as *univerfally* as my Brother He warned them every where againft apoftacy, and infifted on the neceffity of holinefs after juftification He beat down the feparating fpirit, highly commending the prayers and fervices of our Church: charged our people to meet their bands and claffes conftantly, and never to leave the Methodifts, or God would leave them In a word, he did his utmoft to ftrengthen our hands, and he deferves the thanks of all the Churches for his abundant labour of love '

October 29, he wrote to Mr *Grimfhaw* as follows " I could not leave this fhattered Society fo foon as I propofed They have not had fair play from our treacherous fons in the Gofpel, but have been fcattered by them as fheep upon the mountains. I have once more perfuaded them to go to Church and Sacrament, and ftay to carry them thither the next Lord's Day —Nothing but Grace can keep our children, after our departure, from running into a thoufand fects, a thoufand errors Grace, exercifed, kept up and increafed in the ufe of all the means; efpecially family and public prayer and the Sacrament, will keep them fteady Let us labour, while we continue here, to ground and build them up in the Scriptures, and in all the ordinances Teach them to handle well the fword of the fpirit, and the fhield of faith Should I live to fee you again, I truft you will affure me, there is not a member of all your Societies but reads the Scripture daily, ufes private prayer, joins in family and public worfhip, and communicates conftantly. *In thofe is continuance; and we fhall be faved.*

" To

" To my beloved Brethren at *Leeds*, &c

" Grace and peace be multiplied! I thank my
God on your behalf, for the grace which is given
unto you, by which ye stand fast in one mind and in
one spirit. My Master, I am persuaded, sent me to
you at this time to confirm your souls in the present
truth—in your calling, in the old paths of Gospel ordinances O that ye may be a pattern to the
flock for your unanimity and love O that ye may
continue stedfast in the word, and in fellowship, and
in breaking of bread, and in prayers (private, family, and public) till we all meet around the great
white throne!—I knew beforehand, that the *Sanbal-
lats*, and *Tobiahs*, would be grieved when they
heard, there was a man come to seek the good of
the Church of *England*. I expected they would
pervert my words, as if I should say, *The Church
could save you* So indeed you and they thought,
till I and my Brethren taught you better, and sent
you in and through all the means to JESUS CHRIST
But let not their slanders move you. Continue in
the Old Ship JESUS hath a favour for our Church,
and is wonderfully visiting and reviving his work in
her. It shall be shortly said, *Rejoice ye with Jerusalem, and be glad with her, all ye that love her · rejoice for joy with her, all ye that mourn for her.*
Blessed be God you see your calling. Let nothing hinder you from going constantly to Church
and Sacrament. Read the Scriptures daily in your
families, and let there be a church in every house.
The word is able to build you up, and if ye watch
and pray always, ye shall be counted worthy to stand
before the Son of Man.—Watch ye therefore, stand
fast in the faith, quit yourselves like men, be strong.
let all your things be done in love I rejoice in
1   hope

hope of prefenting you all in that day. Look up, for your eternal falvation draweth near.

" I examined more of the Society. Moft of them have known the grace of our Lord Jefus Chrift — October 30, I dined with my candid friend and cenfor, Dr. *Byrom.* I ftood clofe to Mr. *Clayton* in Church, as all the week paft, but not a look would he caft towards me,

" So ftiff was his Parochial pride,"

and fo faithfully did he keep his covenant with his eyes, not to look upon an old friend, when called a Methodift.—October 31, I fpake with the reft of the Claffes. I refufed tickets to *J* and *E R* all the reft were willing to follow my advice, and go to Church and Sacrament. *The Diffenters I fent to their refpective Meeting.*"—Thefe extracts from Mr. *Charles Wefley's* Journal for the prefent year, fhew, in the cleareft light, that he had a juft view of the peculiar Calling of the Methodifts, and that he was exceedingly anxious they fhould abide in it He was fully convinced, that all attempts to form the people into an independent Body, originated in the pride and felfifhnefs of fome of the Preachers, and would be injurious to the progrefs of the work He faw, however, that, under various pretences, the Preachers would firally prevail, and obtain their purpofe, though not during the life of his Brother. He was ftill comforted with the hope, that whenever fuch an event fhould take place, there would be found, perhaps, a third part of the people in the Societies who would have judgment and virtue enough left to withftand it, and continue a connexion on the original plan How far his expectations will be realized, time muft difcover.

November

November 1, Mr *Wesley* left *Manchester*, and
on the 6th came safe to his friends at *Bristol* This,
I believe, was the last journey he ever took through
any confiderable part of the kingdom   He afterwards divided his labours chiefly between *London* and
Bristol, and continued to preach till within a short
time of his death.   Many conjectures have been
made concerning the reasons which induced him to
desist from travelling, and from taking the same active part in the government of the Societies which
before he had done   Not a few have attributed his
conduct, in this respect, to a loss of zeal, and true
vital religion, and I confess that I was once of that
opinion, but I have since been more perfectly informed, and better acquainted with the nature of
his situation   The following circumstances will
throw some light on this matter   1 His determined
oppofition against all attempts to unite the members
of the Methodift Societies into an independent Body,
made the leading Preachers, who wished it, his enemies   2 His avowed opinion, that many Preachers
were admitted into the connexion, as Itinerants,
who were not qualified for that station, united all of
this description with the former, and both together
endeavoured to persuade the people, that Mr *Charles
Wesley* was an enemy to *all* the Lay-Preachers, and
no friend to Methodilm itself   nor were persons
wanting, who whispered these things into the ears of
Mr *John Wesley*, to prejudice his mind against his
Brother.   Mr *Charles*, being fully aware of all this,
and wishing to avoid a low and illiberal oppofition,
and especially occafions of frequent difference with
his Brother, thought it beft to retire from a situation
in which all his words and actions were artfully mis-
conftrued and mifreprefented, and from having any
fhare in the government of the Societies, which he
faw, or thought he faw, was approaching towards a
                              fyftem

fyftem of human policy, that in the end could not be
carried on without fometimes having recourfe to the
arts of mifreprefentation and deception Thefe he
abhorred in all perfons, but when practifed under the
mafk of religion, they always appeared to him more
deteftable

He ftill continued, however, firmly attached to
the Methodifts, and laboured by every means which
his fituation would permit, to avert the evils he
feared, and to promote the good of the Societies.
He never loft fight of any attempts to detach the
people from their former connexions, and unite them
into an independent Body, and uniformly oppofed
them with all the influence he had In 1758, he
publifhed his teftimony on this fubject in the following words " I think myfelf bound in duty, to add
my teftimony to my Brother s *His tender reafons
against our ever feparating from the Church of England*, are mine alfo I fubfcribe to them with all
my heart Only, with regard to the firft, I am quite
clear, that it is neither expedient nor lawful for
me to feparate. And I never had the leaft inclination or temptation fo to do My affection for the
Church is as ftrong as ever and I clearly fee my
CALLING, which is to live and to die in her communion. This therefore I am determined to do, the
Lord being my helper."

In 1786, after Mr *John Wefley* had been prevailed upon to ordain fome of the Preachers, he re-
publifhed the fame Teftimony, and in other ways
fhewed the moft marked difapprobation of his Brother's conduct Yet he ftill continued to preach in
the Societies as ufual, and to correfpond with his
Brother, not only on matters relating to the new
ordination among the Methodifts, but on other fubjects In a letter to his Brother, dated April 9,
1787, he obferves, " I ferved *Wef-Street Chapel* in
Friday

Friday and yesterday. Next Saturday I propose to sleep in your bed S B and I shall not disagree.

"Stand to your own proposal 'Let us agree to differ' I leave *America* and *Scotland* to your latest thoughts and recognitions only observing now, that you are exactly right 'He did nothing before he asked me Truc, he asked your leave to ordain two more Preachers, *before* he ordained them but while your answer was coming to prohibit him, he took care to ordain them both. Therefore, his asking you was a mere compliment This I should not mention, but out of concern for your authority. Keep it while you live, and, after your death, *detur digniori*—or rather, *dignioribus* * —You cannot settle the succession you cannot divine how God will settle it. Have the people of —— given you leave to die E. A P J¹ †

In this letter, speaking of genius, he observes, "I never knew a genius that came to good What can be the reason? Are they as premature in evil as in good, or do their superior talents overset them? Must every man of a superior understanding lean to, and trust and pride himself in it?—I never envied a man of great parts I never wished a friend of mine possessed of them.

"Poor *f H* ! What has genius done for him? ruined his fortune, and ruined his body Last night I heard he was dying of a putrid fever. We prayed for him at the table but I know not whether he is alive or dead His sickness was sent to prepare him either for Paradise, or for Orders Such a messen-

---

* *Let it be given to one more worthy* , or rather, in the plural, *to those who are more worthy, of it* He speaks ironically of these *worthies*, who aimed at the supreme power in the Societies, over the head of his Brother

† *Ecclesiæ Anglicana Presbyter Johannes*, *John*, Presbyter of the Church of *England* This signature I believe Mr *John Wesley* sometimes used in the early part of life, when writing to his Brother

ger may perhaps take *Sam* or *Charles*, from the evil. I never fought great things for them, or greater for myfelf, than that I may efcape to land—on a broken piece of the fhip   It is my daily and hourly prayer, that I may efcape fafe to land—and that an entrance may be miniftered to you abundantly, into the everlafting kingdom of *Jefus Chrift* "

Mr *Charles Wefley* had a weak body, and a poor ftate of health, during the greateft part of his life I believe he laid the foundation of both, at *Oxford*, by too clofe application to ftudy, and abftinence from food   He rode much on horfeback, which probably contributed to lengthen out life to a good old age. I vifited him feveral times in his laft ficknefs, and his body was indeed reduced to the moft extreme ftate of weaknefs   He poffeffed that ftate of mind which he had been always pleafed to fee in others—unaffected humility, and holy refignation to the will of God   He had no tranfports of joy, but folid hope and unfhaken confidence in Chrift, which kept his mind in perfect peace   A few days before his death he compofed the following lines   Having been filent and quiet for fome time, he called Mrs *Wefley* to him, and bid her write as he dictated,

> " In age and feeblenefs extreme,
> Who fhall a finful worm redeem?
> Jefus, my only hope thou art,
> Strength of my failing flefh and heart,
> O! could I catch a fmile from thee,
> And drop into Eternity !"

He died March 29, 1788, aged feventy-nine years and three months, and was buried, April 5, in *Marybone* church-yard, at his own defire   The pall was fupported by eight Clergymen of the Church of *England*.   On his tomb-ftone are the following lines, written by himfelf on the death of one of his friends:

they

they could not be more aptly applied to any person,
than to Mr *Charles Wesley.*

> With poverty of spirit blefs'd,
> Reft, happy Saint, in Jefus reft
> A Sinner fav'd through grace forgiv'n
> Redeem'd from earth to reign in heav'n!
> Thy labours of unwearied love,
> By thee forgot, are crown'd above,
> Crown'd, through the mercy of thy Lord,
> With a free, full, immenfe reward!

Mr *Wesley* was of a warm and lively difpofition,
of great franknefs and integrity, and generous and
fteady in his friendfhips His love of fimplicity,
and utter abhorrence of hypoerify, and even of af-
fectation in the profeffors of religion, made him
fometimes appear fevere on thofe who affumed a confequence, on account of their experience, or, were
pert and forward in talking of themfelves and others.
Thefe perfons were fure of meeting with a reproof
from him, which fome, perhaps, might call precipitate and imprudent, though it was evidently founded
on a knowledge of the human heart In converfation he was pleafing, inftructive, and cheerful, and
his obfervations were often feafoned with wit and
humour His religion was genuine and unaffected.
As a Minifter, he was familiarly acquainted with
every part of divinity, and his mind was furnifhed
with an uncommon knowledge of the Scriptures
His difcourfes from the pulpit were not dry and fyf-
tematic, but flowed from the prefent views and feelings of his own mind He had a remarkable talent
of expreffing the moft important truths with fimplicity and energy, and his difcourfes were fometimes
truly apoftolic, forcing conviction on the hearers in
fpite of the moft determined oppofition As a hufband, a father, and a friend, his character was amiable. Mrs. *Wesley* brought him five children, of

3   whom

whom two fons and a daughter are ftill living The fons difcovered a tafte for mufic, and a fine mufical ear, at an early period of infancy, which excited general amazement, and are now juftly admired by the beft judges for their talents in that pleafing art

From a review of the life of Mr. *Charles Wefley*, as delineated in the preceding fheets, it will appear evident, that the Methodifts are greatly indebted to him for his unwearied labours and great ufefulnefs at the firft formation of the Societies, when every ftep was attended with difficulty and danger *. And being dead he yet fpeaketh, by his numerous and excellent hymns, written for the ufe of the Societies, which ftill continue to be the means of daily edification and comfort to thoufands. It has been propofed to publifh a volume of Sermons, felected from his manufcripts, for the benefit of his widow if this fhould be done, it is hoped the Methodifts will fhew their gratitude to his memory, and that they are not unworthy of the benefits they have received from him.

His lively turn of thought did not leave him in his old age, as the following lines will teftify.

THE MAN OF FASHION.

Written in 1784.

What is a modern Man of Fafhion?
A man of tafte and diffipation
A bufy man, without employment,
A happy man, without enjoyment
Who fquanders all his time and treafures,
On empty joys, and taftlefs pleafures,
Vifits, attendance, and attention,
And courtly arts, too low to mention

* The labours of the Methodift Preachers at prefent, are mere amufement, compared with his laborious and fatiguing as

In fleep, and drefs, and fport and play,
He throws his worthlefs life away,
Has no opinion of his own,
But takes from leading Beaux the ton;
With a difdainful fmile or frown,
He on the rif raf crowd looks down
The world polite, his friends and he,
And all the reft are——Nobody!

Taught by the Great his fmiles to fell,
And how to write, and how to fpell,
The Great his oracles he makes,
Copies their vices and miftakes,
Cuftom purfues, his only rule,
And lives an ape, and dies a fool!

Had Mr. *Charles Wfley* engaged in the higher
walks of verfe, there is no doubt but he would have
been efteemed a confiderable poet, even by thofe
who now defpife his hymns. He chofe the moft
excellent way—the writing of hymns for the inftruction and edification of the many, rather than devote
all his life in attempts to pleafe the fancy of the few.
Some of his hymns are certainly among the beft
pieces in that fpecies of compofition. The following hymn has, through miftake, been attributed to
his Brother.

Written after a Riot.

" Ye fimple fouls that ftray
   Far from the path of peace,
(That unfrequented way
   To life and happinefs,)
How long will ye your folly love,
And throng the downward road,
And hate the wifdom from above,
And mock the fons of God?" &c.

9 781379 774099